Hollow Justice

The Henry Roe Cloud Series on American Indians and Modernity

SERIES MISSION STATEMENT

Named in honor of the pioneering Winnebago educational reformer and first known American Indian graduate of Yale College, Henry Roe Cloud (Class of 1910), this series showcases emergent and leading scholarship in the field of American Indian Studies. The series draws upon multiple disciplinary perspectives and organizes them around the place of Native Americans within the development of American and European modernity, emphasizing the shared, relational ties between indigenous and Euro-American societies. It seeks to broaden current historic, literary, and cultural approaches to American Studies by foregrounding the fraught but generative sites of inquiry provided by the study of indigenous communities.

Hollow Justice

A History of Indigenous Claims in the United States

DAVID E. WILKINS

Yale UNIVERSITY PRESS
New Haven and London

Published with assistance from the foundation established in memory of James Wesley Cooper of the Class of 1865, Yale College.

Yale University Press books may be purchased in quantity for educational, business, or promotional use. For information, please e-mail sales.press@yale.edu (U.S. office) or sales@yaleup.co.uk (U.K. office).

Set in Electra type by IDS Infotech Ltd., Chandigarh, India.
Printed in the United States of America.

Library of Congress Cataloging-in-Publication Data

Wilkins, David E. (David Eugene), 1954–
Hollow justice : a history of Indigenous claims in the United States / David E. Wilkins.
pages cm. – (The Henry Roe Cloud series on American Indians and modernity)
Includes bibliographical references and index.
ISBN 978-0-300-11926-8 (hardback)
1. Indians of North America—Claims. I. Title.
KF8205.W528 2013
346.7304'32—dc23

2013013904

A catalogue record for this book is available from the British Library.

This paper meets the requirements of ANSI/NISO Z39.48–1992 (Permanence of Paper).

10 9 8 7 6 5 4 3 2 1

I RESPECTFULLY DEDICATE this book to my dear friend Daniel (Danny) Bell, Jr., a citizen of the Coharie people of eastern North Carolina. Danny has worked tirelessly for more than four decades to improve the lot of his people and of each of the Native nations in North Carolina. Early in his career he devoted his energy to the North Carolina Commission of Indian Affairs, a public service agency charged with facilitating the rights of indigenous peoples in the state. For the last twenty years or so, he has put in countless hours as the hardest-working staff member at the University of North Carolina, Chapel Hill, where he fought to develop a bona fide Native Studies Program, saw to the hiring of additional Native faculty, and where he has tirelessly worked on behalf of Native students, guiding them through their college years to reach their full potential.

In a quiet and dignified manner he has challenged the university to fulfill its legal and moral mandate to serve the distinctive educational and cultural needs of Native students and also the small nations to which these students are intimately connected. Danny has long believed in the power of education and the role of government to right the wrongs that both these institutional arrangements have inflicted on indigenous peoples throughout history; wrongs that in order to be corrected require a deep understanding of historical forces, political dynamics, economics, law, and particularly culture.

Danny, thank you for all the years you have unselfishly labored in the trenches and in the shadows in your principled quest to secure justice and fairness for Native peoples and to educate non-natives about indigenous affairs. A humble man, you have always selflessly conceded the spotlight to others, even though you were generally the one who had put the most effort into whatever the assignment was. For all you have done and continue to do, I dedicate this book to you.

Contents

Preface

In the fall of 1980 I arrived in Tucson, Arizona, excited to be embarking on a master's degree in federal Indian policy, under the auspices of the Political Science Department at the University of Arizona. The program, the first of its kind in the nation, had been developed by that singular indigenous figure Vine Deloria, Jr. I quickly discovered that Deloria and his political science colleagues had designed a curriculum that was equal parts politics, policy, law, and history. In each class he taught, Deloria emphasized that students needed a deep, unvarnished, and unrelenting immersion in each of these broad and interrelated areas in order to understand the contemporary status of indigenous nations.

He stressed that a new kind of academic was being groomed by this unique program: the policy specialist. This person, after taking a bevy of seminars and regular courses offered by Deloria, Clifford M. Lytle, Thomas Holm, Robert K. Thomas, and others—including, for example, Development of Federal Indian Policy (a two-part course spread over two semesters), Congress and the American Indian, American Indians and the Supreme Court, Tribal Government, Indian Water Rights, Indian Treaties—would be capable of conducting research, analyzing data, and preparing reports or testimony on Native land disputes, boundary problems, hunting and fishing rights cases, treaty rights, intergovernmental conflicts and would be effective in the classroom as well.

Deloria had several degrees, including a law degree. Early in his career he opted not to become a full-time lawyer. Instead, he liberally critiqued the discipline's practitioners and doctrines and wrote searching reviews of leading casebooks, while teaching a number of law-related courses at several of the universities with which he was affiliated over the years. Well aware of the powerful position of law in American society, and in the way it has been used to contour the status of Native nations, their citizens, and indigenous relations with the federal and state governments, Deloria teamed up with Clifford Lytle, a constitutional law expert in the Political Science Department at Arizona in the early 1980s; together they wrote two major and well-received books.

The first, *American Indians, American Justice* (1983), was a detailed treatment of the distinctive legal and political rights of indigenous peoples, with an emphasis on the role that the courts—Native, state, and federal—played in either clarifying or muddying aboriginal status. Their follow-up book, *The Nations Within: The Past and Future of American Indian Sovereignty* (1984), was a splendid policy analysis of the efforts of John Collier, commissioner of Indian Affairs in the 1930s, to generate a new deal for Native governments that would restore to them a measure of political, legal, and economic autonomy.

The two men planned, but never completed, a third book that was to focus on one of the more persistent problem areas for Native peoples, both individually and in their relations with the federal and state governments—the field of claims.[1] For example, in 2010 and 2012 the federal government reached settlements in two major claims cases. In 2010 in *Keepseagle v. Vilsack* Native farmers and ranchers reached a $760-million class action settlement with the Department of Agriculture (DOA); in the case they had alleged discriminatory treatment by DOA officials in denying them equal access to credit in the Farm Loan Program.[2] And in 2012, forty-one Native nations (in a companion suit to the *Cobell* suit) filed a suit against the federal government for mismanagement of tribal money and trust lands received a settlement of more than $1 billion, to be divided among those nations.[3] Other claims cases that have been resolved in the last quarter century are listed in table 1.

Deloria's and Lytle's projected claims study would have been a logical follow up to their first two books. Justice and equity have only sometimes been accorded to indigenous peoples, a fact well known to

Table 1 Selected Native Land and Other Claims, 1970–2008

Act	Nation(s)	Subject Matter
Taos Blue Lake Act (1970)	Taos Pueblo	Land return
Alaska Native Claims Settlement Act (1971)	Various Alaskan Native communities	Extinguish aboriginal title, land claim
Rhode Island Claims Settlement Act (1978)	Narragansett	Extinguish aboriginal title, land claim
Maine Indian Claims Settlement Act (1980)	Passamaquoddy, Penobscot, and Maliseet	Extinguish aboriginal title, land claim, recognition
Florida Indian (Miccosukee) Land Claims Settlement Act (1982)	Miccosukee	Land claims, water rights
Connecticut Indian Land Claims Settlement Act (1983)	Mashantucket Pequot tribe	Extinguish aboriginal title, land claim
Houlton Band of Maliseet Indians Supplementary Claims Settlement Act (1986)	Maliseet	land claim
Massachusetts Indian Land Claims Settlement Act (1987)	Wampanoag	Extinguish aboriginal title, land claim
Florida Indian (Seminole) Land Claims Settlement Act (1987)	Seminole	Water rights
Washington Indian (Puyallup) Land Claims Settlement Act (1989)	Puyallup	Extinguish aboriginal title, fisheries resources
Seneca Nation (New York) Land Claims Settlement Act (1990)	Seneca	Renewal of leases and land acquisition

continued

Catawba Indian Tribe of South Carolina Land Claim Settlement Act (1993)	Catawba	Extinguish aboriginal title, recognition, and repeal of termination
Mohegan Nation (Connecticut) Land Claims Settlement Act (1994)	Mohegan	Extinguish aboriginal title, land claim
Crow Land Claims Settlement Act (1994)	Crow	Reservation boundary surveying error
Michigan Indian Land Claims Settlement Act (1997)	Ottawa and Chippewa	Judgment funds
Santo Domingo Pueblo Land Claims Settlement Act (2000)	Santo Domingo Pueblo	Extinguish aboriginal title, Spanish land grant title
Torres-Martinez Desert Cahuilla Indian Claims Settlement Act (2000)	Torres-Martinez Desert Cahuilla	Reservation flooding
Cheyenne River Sioux Tribe Equitable Compensation Act (2000)	Cheyenne River Sioux	Compensation for prior land acquisition
Cherokee, Choctaw, and Chickasaw Nations Claims Settlement Act (2002)	Cherokee, Choctaw, and Chickasaw	Mismanagement of resources
Pueblo de San Ildefonso Claims Settlement Act (2006)	Pueblo de San Ildefonso	Extinguish aboriginal title, land claim
Soboba Band of Luiseno Indians Settlement Act (2008)	Soboba band of Luiseno Indians	Water rights

Source: Updated from U.S. Code, Title 25, Chapter 19, Indian Land Claims.

both scholars. Traditionally, claims have been made in a number of areas: land cessions (the largest and most well known type), treaty provisions, injury to persons, loss of property, unfair and dishonorable dealings, and inadequate or fraudulent accounting procedures. These injustices usually arose from violations of explicit treaties or agreements, failure to adhere to congressional statutes, and an inability or unwillingness to follow the edicts of judicial rulings. A number of these examples will be addressed in the pages that ensue.

Efforts to address certain aspects of Native claims have intensified in recent years, but Native claims remain an underexplored area of the law. This is so, in part, because federal Indian law remains a quagmire, and federal officials continue to struggle to understand precisely where indigenous peoples fit in the political, economic, constitutional, and cultural frameworks of American culture and U.S. politics. Many of those who study federal Indian law insist that it is a bona fide "field" of law. But the facts and history speak otherwise. How can it be called a field when there are no central or consistently enforced doctrines other than the judicially concocted and constitutionally problematic notion of congressional "plenary power," defined here as virtually unlimited authority,[4] which is almost always used against indigenous rights? As noted in the Supreme Court ruling in *South Dakota v. Yankton* (1998), "Congress possesses plenary power over Indian affairs, including the power to modify or eliminate tribal rights."[5]

There are now numerous legal texts devoted to the subject of federal Indian law, most of which hark back to the first such study, Felix S. Cohen's *Handbook of Federal Indian Law,* published by the federal government in 1942. As important as Cohen's book was, for it was the first and remains the most comprehensive attempt to gather together much of the raw data—treaties, cases, statutes, executive orders, commissioner of Indian Affairs reports generated by the federal government's three branches and myriad federal agencies—it was only a handbook, not a treatise, and it failed to identify a common set of verifiable doctrines that are required to constitute a genuine field of law.

As Deloria observed in a stirring critique of Cohen's book and the so-called field of Indian law theory, "with this publication, and in large measure because of this publication, federal treatment of Indians became a 'field' of law with its own structure and, unfortunately, with a set of doctrines," most of which, Deloria said, were "cruel fictions" designed more to improve the image of the federal government than to actually protect the remaining rights of indigenous peoples.[6] What was missing, Deloria insisted, in the way law was understood and practiced in relation to Native peoples, was a recognition of the roles that history, morality, justice, and humanity should be contributing but were not.

One way to possibly instill some of these missing dimensions in the organized chaos that is federal Indian law would be to take one specific sub-area and critically examine the vocabulary, doctrines, dogma, history, and institutions that might contribute to deepening our understanding of what actually transpired between Native peoples and the U.S. The subject of claims, the focus of this book, is an excellent topic to use to perform this task. It does not have the urgency that jurisdiction has; it does not quite have the vested federal and state interests that taxation has; and it often does not have the same degree of immediacy or contestation that water rights or hunting and fishing rights has. Claims, if more fully understood, might be used as the primary vehicle to resolve, or at least bring greater clarity to, the other issues because they all involve the fundamentally important question of what one nation *owes* another nation, or what one nation owes to the individual citizens of another nation in the case of the individual trust allotments.

According to Felix Cohen, writing in 1945, Indian claims were "by and large, the backwash of a great national experiment in dictatorship and racial extermination. This episode in our national history reached its fluorescence in the period from the close of the Civil War to the First World War. It is the wrongs committed or at least initiated by our public servants in that period that give rise to most of the claims that we are trying to redress today."[7] And importantly, the fact that indigenous claims continue to pose a substantial issue today not only points to the fact that many profound injuries were and continue to be committed against Native peoples, but also acknowledges the equally important fact that indigenous peoples, as the original sovereigns of this land, frequently had their rights acknowledged in diplomatic accords, in policy pronouncements, in congressional statutes, and in Supreme Court opinions. Thus, until and unless Native claims are fully resolved, intercultural, interracial, and intergovernmental relations will not be fundamentally reconciled and the U.S. will not have fulfilled its constitutional, treaty, or moral obligations to Native nations.

Although, as noted earlier, there is no actual "field" of federal Indian law, that does not mean that there are not powerful, competing paradigms or paths that make this such a volatile area of study. Vine Deloria noted in 1992 that the subject of federal Indian law and policy had taken three distinct courses: (1) treaty relations, (2) trust relations, and (3) property ownership of the public domain.[8] While emphasizing that legal practitioners and policymakers frequently treat these three aspects as interchangeable or complimentary in an effort to support the false belief that Native peoples exist at the sufferance of the federal government, Deloria argued that this was not the case. He said they were, in fact, exclusive of one another and needed to be understood as such.

Treaties were the principal diplomatic tool used to cement relations between Native peoples and various foreign powers and later the U.S. government. Treaties recognized inherent tribal sovereignty, acknowledged Native title to lands, and gave structure to the growing field of international law. It is important to note that tribal nations reserve all rights not explicitly ceded in a treaty arrangement.

The trust relationship, by contrast, evolved during the so-called Discovery Era of European exploration of the Americas and came to serve as the "operative principle to describe the internal location of Indian nations within the area claimed by the U.S. and [as] a practical guideline for the administration of services promised to the Indians in treaties and agreements."[9] In effect, the trust doctrine stands outside the constitutional framework largely as a moral force, to ostensibly guide federal relations with Native nations. Interestingly, the doctrine of discovery—the idea that European powers and later the U.S., as successor to Great Britain's alleged "discoveries" in North America, gained superior title to North America—is intimately connected to the trust doctrine, with the idea being that the "discovery" power secured for the so-called discoverer the legal right to be the first purchaser of the natives' territory, with the discoverer also becoming responsible for assisting Native peoples to become more enlightened because of their presumed culturally inferiority.[10]

Finally, the path of property ownership dates to the 1880s when the federal government ramped up its efforts to coercively assimilate Native peoples. In *United States v. Kagama* (1886) the Supreme Court was called upon to determine the constitutionality of the Major Crimes Act of 1885, in which Congress had assumed jurisdiction over seven major crimes—including murder—in Indian Country. In *Kagama* the justices rejected the explicit constitutional clauses that mention Indians or tribe—the tax and representation clauses of Article I and the Fourteenth Amendment, and the Commerce Clause—as bases for the federal government extending its criminal jurisdiction reach into Indian Country. Instead, the court relied on geography as the basis for this power: "Indians are within the geographical limits of the United States," wrote Justice Miller. "The soil and the people within these limits are under the political control of the Government of the United States, or of the States of the Union." In other words, "ownership of the country" vested in the federal, not state, government, the virtually unreviewable plenary power of the Congress to do whatever it deemed essential to civilize and control Native peoples. But as Deloria pointed out, "The U.S. holds public domain lands on behalf of its citizens, and this ownership is not held against the citizens as if the U.S. were a competing private landowner."[11]

Despite the distinctive origins of each of these three paths, federal lawmakers frequently treat them as if they are synonymous or, in some cases, as if one is subject to the other. For example, in 2011 the Supreme Court in *United States v. Jicarilla Apache Nation* held, with Justice Antonin Scalia speaking for the court, that "the organization and management of the trust [relationship] is a sovereign function subject to the plenary authority of Congress." Strangely, Scalia went on to say, "The Government has often structured the trust relationship to pursue its own policy goals." When trustees have such power, the beneficiaries of that trust have little hope that their own rights will be respected.

In short, Native peoples have been reminded time and again that even when they succeed in pursuing a claim against the U.S., the federal government often attempts to extract some of the very resources that the tribal nation has filed for, leaving the Native community or individual member wondering about the justice of the "resolved" claim.[12]

In order to understand indigenous claims in the U.S., then, we will have to explore a broad range of historical incidents and personalities, institutional arrangements, treaty accords, judicial pronouncements, statutes, and administrative rules and regulations established to address such matters.

Native nations have nearly always faced a weltering array of legal, political, economic, and perceptual inconsistencies, ambiguities, and dilemmas in law and policy that make their quest for claims justice difficult to secure. For instance, why have Native peoples, unlike certain other racial and ethnic groups, only sometimes received compensation for many of their property and human rights losses? Why has the federal government, despite the existence of the trust doctrine, never arrived at a consistent and enforceable definition of what its legal and moral obligations are to indigenous communities? Why did the federal government, from 1863 to 1946, prohibit Native nations from even entering the Court of Claims to seek redress for treaty violations? Why are indigenous claims—filed under the Indian Claims Commission Act—the only claims that have *offsets* (a deduction by which a given claim may be lessened or even cancelled) that can be raised against them? When private non-Indian citizens and corporations successfully bring lawsuits against the federal government, nothing is deducted for the subsidies they have previously received.

Finally, and most problematically, in virtually all claims cases the federal government, as the self-defined dominant power, is often "both playing the game and making the rules."[13] In other words, when Native nations make claims, particularly to lands, they frequently learn that the state is in turn making "unexpected claims on their land and livelihoods." Often it is the complex interaction of state and market demands that "results in the reshaping of claimants' original demands."[14] We will see evidence of this especially in the situation of the small nations of Maine in their historic land claims case and also in the chapter on the *Cobell* litigation and settlement.

In this book I generally adhere to a chronological format, beginning with an analysis of the Court of Claims in the 1850s (chapter 1) and moving on to discuss the Indian Depredations Acts of the late nineteenth and early twentieth centuries (chapter 2), the life of the Indian Claims Commission in the 1940s to 1970s (chapters 3, 4, and 5), and the history of the Maine Indian Land Claims Settlement Act (1960s to 1980) within the broader context of eastern Indian land claims (chapter 6). An exploration of the *Cobell* litigation and settlement (1990s–2012+) follows in chapter 7, and the final chapter concludes by charting a possible research agenda for indigenous claims.

My greatest debt in writing this book is to Clifford M. Lytle, who graciously shared with me the well-written chapters he had prepared many years ago for the proposed third installment in his productive scholarly relationship with Vine Deloria, Jr. The final chapter, outlining a comprehensive research agenda for claims, owes its structure and some of its content to Deloria. In fact, the broader contours of the entire manuscript were heavily influenced by both Deloria and Lytle. Both men strongly encouraged me several years ago to forge ahead on this important subject. Deloria emphasized in many of his voluminous works that until and unless a moral dimension based on justice and the principle of consent was infused in federal Indian policy and law and in the indigenous-state relationship, affairs between Native nations, the states, and the federal government would remain tense and combative, thus precluding the clear thinking that is required to address the continuing problems that still bedevil indigenous-state affairs.

My thanks to my colleagues in the Department of American Indian Studies at the University of Minnesota for their friendship and good counsel, especially Patricia Albers, Carter Meland, and Carol Miller, each of whom read parts of the manuscript and offered constructive criticism. And to Edna Day, Sasha Bordeau, and Rodrigo Sanchez-Chavarria, who keep American Indian Studies and Chicano Studies humming along. I am also grateful to the friendship and support offered by June Lowery, Tsianina Lomawaima, David Gibbs, Lini D. Wilkins, Sam Scinta, Steve Pavlik, and Shelly McDonald.

I am especially grateful for the support and confidence that Christopher Rogers had for this project and for the reviewers who offered constructive ideas on how to improve the manuscript. Eliza Childs did a wonderful job copyediting the manuscript. Her expertise led to an improved work.

As always, the reference librarians at the University of Minnesota Law School, especially Mary Rumsey, provided me with thorough and expeditious research assistance. Mary, where would I be without your meticulous and expeditious research assistance and your friendship?

Finally, I reserve my deepest appreciation for my mother, Thedis R. Wilkins, and for my children: Sion, Niltooli, and Nazhone.

1. NATIVE NATIONS AND THE COURT OF CLAIMS

A Study in Frustration and Despair

IN THE BEGINNING the land now known as North America belonged to the indigenous peoples. Indeed, the lyrics of folksinger Woody Guthrie defined the boundaries well: from California to the New York Island; from the redwood forests to the Gulf Stream waters. Native peoples indisputably were the possessors and owners of all this rich territory. Unfortunately, the title of Guthrie's folksong, "This Land Is Your Land," does not quite hit the mark. From a Native perspective, the title should have been "This Land Was Our Land." Whereas once the entire North American landmass belonged to Native nations, by 1900 they had cumulatively lost title and control to more than 2 billion acres, with most of the loss occurring between the 1850s and 1900. The United States had purchased about half that amount via treaties or agreements, while another 32.5 million acres, according to Russel Barsh, had been "confiscated unilaterally by Act of Congress or executive order without compensation."[1] Finally, another 725 million acres in the lower forty-eight states and Alaska were taken by the federal government "without agreement or the pretense of a unilateral action extinguishing native title."[2] In fact, by 1934 Native holdings had dwindled even further, to a meager 47 million acres. The non-Indian's quest for land was being satisfied but at the expense of indigenous peoples.

How did this come about? Contrary to popular belief, the land was not simply stolen and confiscated by non-Indians, though such theft did sometimes occur. Instead, the federal government's dispossession of Native territory was done largely via several hundred negotiated treaties and agreements.[3] But as Nell Jessup Newton points out, although some of the early treaties were mutually beneficial, many others "were procured by fraud or simply by the threat of force so great that tribes had no choice but to cede more land, further blurring the line between consent and coercion in American Indian policy."[4] The vaunted legal realist Felix Cohen went so far as to remark that "the purchase of the land of the United States from the Indian was, I suppose, the largest real estate deal recorded in the history of the world."[5] While U.S presidents appointed treaty commissioners and the Congress ratified the treaties and provided the funding for fulfilling treaty commitments, the courts also played an important role in this legitimizing process. In an early nineteenth-century Supreme Court decision, *Johnson v. McIntosh*,[6] Chief Justice John Marshall concluded that *conquest* elevated whites and the federal government to a superior territorial position vis-à-vis land title in the U.S. Although the U.S. claimed a superior land title, it was subject to the continued right of Native use and occupancy. Indigenous interest in their lands had not been completely extinguished, but it was altered significantly in that the federal government, under the problematic doctrine of discovery,[7] claimed a superior title to the soil. Native peoples were effectively thrust into a landlord-tenant relationship with the tenancy lasting only so long as the federal government allowed.

Although having been reduced to a position of territorial subordinance, Native nations did not lose their political independence or sovereignty. In the so-called *Cherokee Nation* cases—*Cherokee Nation v. Georgia* (1831) and *Worcester v. Georgia* (1832)—Chief Justice Marshall, in establishing a foundation for the negotiated acquisition of Native land, acknowledged that indigenous peoples possessed a fund of sovereignty that permitted the federal government to deal with them as recognized legal entities. He coined the awkward and novel phrase "domestic dependent nations" to describe Native peoples in the first case, but in the second ruling he more accurately referred to them as "distinct and independent political communities" possessing their own institutions and capable of self-government.

While refusing to recognize Native nations as being on an equal sovereign footing with the United States, Marshall made sure that he recognized them as having sufficient sovereignty so that the government could legally and politically bargain with them. At the same time, however, the Chief Justice sought to enshrine federal superiority over the rest of their affairs. This was really nothing more than a continuation of the policy the United States had embarked upon in 1778 when it entered into its first formal treaty with the Delaware Indians. Treaty making thus became the device for defining the political and legal relationships between Native nations and the federal and state governments. In fact, it became the primary legal mechanism by which the federal government dispossessed natives of most of their land holdings.

In its early treaties with Native nations, the federal government was interested in achieving two basic goals. First, it needed to establish peace with the Native peoples; second, and of equal importance, it desired to obtain additional land so as to satisfy the ever-increasing demands of white settlers, corporate interests, state and territorial governments, and many federal policymakers. Thus, immediately following the adoption of the U.S. Constitution in 1789, Congress began to exercise its power in Indian affairs by enacting the Trade and Intercourse Act of 1790.[8] This act vested in the federal government the right of preemption—that is, the power to deny others, notably the states and white settlers, the right to directly acquire Native land. More specifically, the act stipulated that Indian lands could not be sold or disposed of except through a treaty negotiated between the federal government and a Native nation. This was but the first of a series of several similar acts that extended federal control over the field of aboriginal affairs.

One of the major objectives of this legislation was to protect Native peoples from unscrupulous white traders and entrepreneurs seeking to obtain land from the Indians, often under conditions of duress, fraud, or outright theft. But more important, it provided the federal government with a monopoly. There could be no Native land transactions without first securing the express approval of federal officials: federal preemption in regards to aboriginal land sales became "an enduring feature of federal Indian policy reenacted in a series of subsequent statutes. It is still in force today."[9]

But even as the national government sought to fulfill its role as the alleged *guardian* of Native lands, federal policies facilitated an ever-increasing erosion of Indian territory. Hundreds of treaties were negotiated with Native nations, and in many of these accords tribal land holdings dwindled further; the dispossession of indigenous peoples was carried out under the color of law. Stuart Banner points out that the manner in which natives surrendered the vast majority of their territory can be placed on a spectrum bounded by poles of *conquest* and *control.* As he notes, "At most times, and in most places, the Indians were not exactly conquered, but they did not exactly choose to sell their land either. The truth was somewhere in the middle."[10] Every land deal, he continued, involved elements of power and law. And as whites became more powerful in comparison to natives, the "more they were able to mold the legal system to produce outcomes in their favor—more sales, of larger tracts, at lower prices than would have existed had power relationships been more equal."[11]

In most cases the U.S. president's treaty commissioners would negotiate the treaty accords, the Senate would be called upon to ratify the arrangement, and aboriginal land, sometimes in small tracts but sometimes in great swaths, slowly but inexorably left indigenous control and came to be owned by non-Indians. The federal courts, not surprisingly, provided Native nations with little protection in these land transactions. They generally deferred to the wishes of Congress and the president, and they crafted a number of legal rationales, such as the doctrines of discovery and conquest, the doctrine of congressional plenary power, and the notion of wardship, to justify federal superiority in relation to tribal nations.

Initially, Native peoples may not have fully comprehended the profundity of the territorial or cultural threat posed by non-Indians. Furthermore, tribal nations generally believed that their lands would never be taken from them without their express consent—as laid out in numerous treaties and congressional policies like the Northwest Ordinance of 1787—and there is substantial political and legal discourse that substantiates this understanding. Thomas Jefferson, for instance, when he was president reasoned that the federal government had a right to preemptively claim aboriginal land only if natives wanted to sell the same.

Despite the policy and legal protections put in place to protect aboriginal landholdings, within the span of three hundred years, through treaties, congressional acts, and policy directives, title to nearly the entire North American continent was transferred from Native nations to the federal government. This has been referred to by the Indian Claims Commission (ICC) as "the largest real estate transaction in history."[12] For many Native peoples, however, these were not "real estate transactions" so much as they were the establishment of shared and reciprocal relations on lands that no human being or nation truly owned and therefore had no right to sell.[13] During these early years of negotiation and exploitation, Native nations were faced with a number of difficulties. In many instances, few Indians spoke English and fewer still understood the political and economic systems employed by white traders. As a result, Native Americans frequently received an astonishingly low price for their lands. As Harvey Rosenthal noted in his study of the ICC, "Despoliation of the land and its former possessors was inherent in this mad, largely undisciplined, rush to the Pacific. The U.S. acquired about 443 million acres from 1789 to 1840 for some 31.3 million in cash and 53.8 million acres for Indian settlement further west. This cost to the government of about ten cents per acre compared favorably to the value of 1.25 per acre that was the minimum purchase price for lands of the public domain."[14]

It was not too difficult to defraud or use duress to overcome the reluctance of Native leaders who initially may not have wanted to sell. As Banner noted in his study, "The best that can be said is that many of the purchases were made deceitfully."[15] Margaret Hunter

Pierce, a former member of the Indian Claims Commission, noted that natives were frequently compensated by amounts that were ridiculously low. The "disparity between the price paid and the value of the land was so great as to shock almost anyone's conscience."[16] Robert W. Barker, an attorney who represented a number of tribal nations, noted that the federal government was never hesitant to persuade Indians to cede their lands for "only token consideration."[17]

Exploitation of Indians constituted a major problem in these historic land transactions, but perhaps a more serious concern for Native peoples involved the failure of the government to consistently fulfill its treaty obligations. "Treaties guaranteeing tracts of land 'in perpetuity' to displaced Indian groups were broken as soon as the government discovered some need for the awarded area," wrote Sandra Danforth. "Other treaty provisions for food, medicine, tools, annuities, and other supplies to assist destitute and disintegrated Indian societies to rebuild were ignored as often as not."[18]

As described by Vine Deloria, Jr., in *Behind the Trail of Broken Treaties*, "The ink was hardly dry on the treaties before white settlers began their trek overland into Indian country, breaching the solemn promises of the United States."[19] And as Banner put it, "In the end, the acquisition of land in North America is a story of power, of the displacement of the weak by the strong; but it was a more subtle and complex kind of power than would have been necessary to seize land by force. It was the power to supplant Indian legal systems with the English [and later the U.S.] legal system, the power to have land disputes decided by English officials using English law rather than Indian officials using Indian law."[20]

When the natives turned to the government for protection, too frequently the federal government refused to use the army against the settlers. In far too many instances the U.S. simply opted not to fulfill its legal and moral commitments to Native peoples. Occasionally tribal nations, or their non-Indian allies, turned to the federal courts in an attempt to force the national government to honor its treaty obligations. In a few instances, such as *Worcester v. Georgia* (1832), the

Indians legally prevailed. In this case the High Court concluded that the U.S. had a legal obligation both to recognize and to enforce treaty covenants. This decision, unfortunately, proved to be a hollow victory for the Cherokee nation as the Cherokee and thousands of other tribal citizens were ultimately forcibly evicted from the Southeast and relocated to what would become Oklahoma.

As the first half of the nineteenth century came to a close, the situation confronting Native peoples was bleak. Most of their land had been stolen, swindled, or negotiated away, and there appeared to be little relief on the horizon. But then federal lawmakers, in a fleeting moment of wisdom, created the U.S. Court of Claims and this, at first glance, appeared to provide Native nations with a potential promise of hope.

The Court of Claims

Some truths are self-evident. For instance, if someone steals your property, or defrauds you of your land, or contracts to buy goods but ultimately fails to pay you, you can go to a court of law and sue for damages. But what if the culprit happens to be a government? Does one still have the right to remedy by going to a court of law and suing? The answer is usually no. Under the doctrine of sovereign immunity, a person does not have the right to sue the government unless the government expressly consents to being sued. This protective shield that governments have cloaked their institutional arrangements in is as old as the law itself. And the United States, like individual states and Native nations as well, as sovereign powers, are no exception to this rule. The doctrine of sovereign immunity is indelibly lodged in the American system of law.

Governments, of course, are not always the villains that individuals, interest groups, and corporations make them out to be. They have the capacity, when properly led and inspired by clear goals and with sufficient revenue, to rise to the occasion and address burdensome issues. An opportunity for just such an action arose in 1855 for the United States. For years the only way that an injured party could bring a suit for damages against the federal government had been to petition Congress for relief. This put an inordinately large burden on the legislative branch. The volume of private bills introduced seeking redress was exceptionally heavy. Inequities abounded in that the political clout possessed by some claimants resulted in their succeeding while the complaints of many others were not addressed. From the standpoint of the lawmakers, too much of their time and energy was consumed in dealing with these "peripheral" private problems.

In an attempt to rectify this administrative morass, Congress in 1855 moved to create the U.S. Court of Claims.[21] This remedial piece of legislation established a federal court composed of three judges. The court sat in Washington, D.C., yet its jurisdiction extended to claims arising throughout the nation. Initially the powers of the court were somewhat limited. The 1855 act empowered the court only to hear claims based on statutes, federal regulations, or contracts and then forward its findings to Congress, along with the draft of a private bill for its consideration. Congress, not the Court of Claims, ultimately decided whether a claim would be satisfied.[22]

This new procedure reduced some of the burden that Congress had previously been carrying, but the lawmakers were still saddled with the laborious necessity of examining the merits of numerous private bills. In 1861 President Abraham Lincoln recommended that the court be authorized to issue final judgments. Lincoln reasoned that it was "as much the duty of the Government to render prompt justice against itself, in favor of citizens, as it is to administer the same between private individuals."[23] Congress, heeding the wisdom of Lincoln's remarks, responded to the president's suggestion and passed an act on March 3, 1863, that made the court's judgments final.[24] This law also permitted a party who lost in the Court of Claims to appeal to the Supreme Court under certain circumstances.

The establishment of the Court of Claims eliminated an important barrier that heretofore had precluded injured individuals from seeking redress from the federal government. The doctrine of sovereign immunity no longer served as an absolute bar to suits against the United States. Native peoples were still actively involved in treaty making at this time, and in some cases claims were dealt with by treaty provision. For example, the Choctaw and Chickasaw signed a treaty in 1855 that stipulated that the two nations, concerned "with the whole subject-matter of their unsettled claims" against the U.S., were willing to submit to the U.S. Senate "for final adjudication and adjustment" claims for proceeds ceded to them in their 1830 treaty with the U.S.[25]

But a number of Indian nations decided to take advantage of the process established by the Court of Claims and began to file complaints against the federal government for treaty violations. Before long, it was apparent that this was not what Congress had in mind in creating the court. It was one thing for the lawmakers to recognize and attempt to compensate bona fide claims that individual whites had against the federal government. It was quite another, however, to extend this same right to Native peoples. Fearing the danger in permitting Indians to bring suits against the government, and before any claims had actually been settled, Congress in 1863 passed legislation that expressly excluded Indians from the jurisdiction of the Court of Claims. Section 9 of the act of 1863 stipulated that the jurisdiction of the court "shall not extend to include any claim against the Government. . . growing out of or dependent on any treaty stipulation entered into with foreign nations *or with Indian tribes*" (emphasis added).[26]

What Congress gives, Congress can take away. And so it did. There was little opposition to this exclusionary provision. After all, it was reasoned, Indians were not even American citizens. In fact, they were not even recognized as "persons" from a constitutional perspective and would not be so recognized until 1879.[27] The facts that some Native individuals had held African Americans as slaves and some 10,000 Indians had fought on the side of the Confederacy during the Civil War were also used to rationalize this discriminatory decision.[28] It is interesting to note that once the Civil War ended, non-Indian members of the former Confederacy were permitted to go before the Court of Claims, but this gesture of benevolence was not extended to the Indians. Little was said about the fraud and duress that occasionally had been used to divest Indians of their land. Nor was there any mention of the fact that the federal government had failed to honor many of its treaty obligations. An attempt was made to provide tribal plaintiffs with access to the Court of Claims in 1878, but this never reached fruition.[29] Rosenthal points out that the rationales used to preclude natives from access to the Court of Claims had baser motives: "It is certain that Congress recognized the danger of allowing Indian claimant's access to the Court. The claims had become numerous and many officials were aware of their value and validity."[30] Having been effectively denied the access that whites enjoyed in taking grievances to the Court of Claims, natives found themselves where they were before the 1855 Court of Claims Act. Faced with the obstacle of governmental immunity, which barred them from filing suits without first obtaining Congressional approval, indigenous people once again had to resort to petitioning federal lawmakers for permission to sue. This was a time of frustration and disillusionment for Indians. Decades of contact with non-Indians had left Native peoples with vastly reduced land holdings and with even less political and legal dignity. Foreclosed from virtually all political outlets and denied treaty-making authority in 1871, a number of Native nations felt compelled to resort to violence and war to defend their remaining lands and dwindling rights. These conflicts would later profoundly complicate the lives of Native citizens. Many of the treaties that aboriginal nations had negotiated with the federal government contained provisions declaring that if an Indian tribe committed "depredations" against citizens of the United States, the tribal nation would be held liable for the damages incurred. As the sporadic Indian rebellions arose, so did the potential claims against the tribes.

An important incident occurred in 1879 that provided natives with the hope that they might again renew their efforts to settle their claims through the legal process. A federal district court in Nebraska handed down an important decision, *Standing Bear v. Crook*, which for the first time recognized that Indians were "persons" under the Fourteenth Amendment.[31] As such, they qualified for some of the basic rights guaranteed to all other individuals, whether citizens or not, under the Constitution. Because of this decision, a presidential commission of investigation was conducted into certain claims raised by the Ponca Indians, and Congress responded favorably to this inquiry by recognizing the justness of the Indians claims.[32] In addition, the investigation also concluded that it was of the "utmost importance to white and red men alike that all Indians should have the opportunity of appealing to the courts for the protection and vindication of their rights of person and property."[33] This activity set the door ajar, and in 1881, Congress was finally moved to pass the first special statute bestowing jurisdiction on the Court of Claims to hear the fifty-year-old treaty grievances of the Choctaw nation and individual tribal members.[34]

The Choctaws' success in obtaining congressional approval to take their case to the Court of Claims institutionalized a procedure that Native peoples would be required to follow for the next sixty-five years. It mattered little to federal officials that Indians had to wage a long, expensive, and more often than not futile battle in Congress just to get permission to go to court while an aggrieved white claimant could avoid all of this. Whites were permitted direct and immediate access to the Court of Claims. Compounding native frustrations was the fact that most of the struggles that tribal nations waged in attempting to get congressional approval were unsuccessful. Even when they succeeded in securing consent to sue, their rate of success in the Court of Claims was discouragingly low. Between 1886, the year of the first final judgment in an Indian claims case, until the passage of the Indian Claims Commission Act in 1946, the courts decided 134 dockets involving Indian claims. Native groups prevailed in only 28 of these cases, and after 1920 they lost nearly every case.[35]

The number of cases decided—134—represent a fairly substantial figure, but as Glen Wilkinson, a prominent Washington attorney who represented several Indian nations noted, "It pales in comparison with the number [of cases] filed during the five-year period between August 1946 when the Indian Claims Commission Act became effective, and August, 1951, the cutoff date within which claims could be filed. During that [brief] five-year period, 370 petitions involving approximately 850 claims were filed."[36]

There were, of course, a few spotty efforts by Congress to introduce comprehensive legislation authorizing lawsuits before the ICC's enactment. In 1907 Senator Moses Clapp noted as much when he said: "There are a great many old [Indian] claims pending in Congress, and the idea was simply to give the Indians an opportunity to go to a court. They would get no judgment, but they would get a finding of fact which would present their matters in concrete form before the committee and before the two Houses of Congress."[37] These would be claims based upon treaties or acts of Congress that diminished the size of reservations. Similarly, in 1915 a bill, S. 7524, was introduced in the Senate that would have authorized any nation, tribe, or band of Indians to submit claims to the Court of Claims "with the right of either party to appeal to the Supreme Court of the United States."[38] In that same session, Senator Thomas Sterling submitted an amendment to the appropriations bill authorizing the Committee of Indian Affairs to "investigate claims and negotiate agreements with any tribe or bands of Indians for the final adjudication and settlement of claims and payments" to those groups.[39]

Finally, in 1920 there was some discussion in the House about a bill that would have authorized Native nations in Washington State to file in the Court of Claims suits arising out of the treaties of 1854 and 1855 that had the support of the Northwestern Federation of American Indians, led by T. G. Bishop. As part of the debate, Representative James C. McLaughlin of Michigan pointedly said: "Is it necessary that there be a large number of separate bills substantially for the same purposes? Would it not be advisable to have some general law applying to all alike? It seems to me it is a waste of the time of the House and would result in some confusion to have separate bills considered by the House and submitted to take care of claims of each separate tribe of Indians."[40] But Representative Melville Clyde Kelly of Pennsylvania retorted, noting "that the policy of the Committee of Indian Affairs is exactly the opposite, because each case arises on a separate treaty and has entirely different conditions."[41] It was also pointed out during the debate that bills allowing Indians to go to the Court of Claims were required because in most cases these claims were barred by the statute of limitations, which generally specify a time period during which suits could be filed.

When World War I ended, a rather dramatic change emerged with regard to the attitude of both the public and the federal government toward Indians. This is an interesting phenomenon that seems to have occurred at the end of every international war in which the U.S. has been involved. Native individuals played an important and visible role during the war effort—even though many were not American citizens—and this did not go unnoticed in Washington. A new, more sympathetic view toward Native peoples thus evolved, culminating first in the bestowing of U.S. citizenship on Native soldiers who were honorably discharged, and then, in 1924, in granting citizenship to all remaining Native individuals.[42] It also resulted in a groundswell of congressionally authorized aboriginal claims before the Court of Claims. In the three years following the passage of the Indian Citizenship Act of 1924, almost as many claims were filed with the Court of Claims—thirty-seven—as were filed in the forty-two years prior to the act's passage.

The Court of Claims and Native Frustrations

The policy requiring Native peoples to seek a special jurisdiction act from Congress before taking a grievance to the Court of Claims proved troublesome for all concerned. The entire process was fraught with problems. Tribal groups frequently had to go to Washington many times before they could even get their claims' legislation introduced. Then they had to make several more trips in the hope of insuring passage of their bill. In the rare cases when they succeeded in getting Congress to act, the jurisdictional statute often failed to support their claims, making the process fruitless and extremely costly.[43] At this time, Native peoples possessed virtually no political clout in Washington. "Political considerations, such as the standing in Congress of the bill's sponsor, the make-up of Indian committees and the attitude of the current administration, were often more important than the merits of the cases in determining whether or not the enabling legislation would be passed."[44]

Before a petition could be heard by a congressional committee, it had to be approved by the Department of Interior. Investigations and reports also had to be obtained from the Department of Justice and the General Accounting Office (GAO). The GAO was required to make an analysis of massive amounts of historic accounts, and such an endeavor took an enormous amount of time. These steps were required just to determine if a special jurisdiction act should be granted by Congress. A more detailed investigation by the General Accounting Office was required once the case was brought before the Court of Claims. The Department of Interior was placed in a particularly delicate position. On one hand, the department was charged with promoting the welfare and well-being of its Native constituency; on the other hand, Interior was often the target of tribal complaints. It was precisely because of the alleged wrongdoing in Interior that natives frequently felt the need to go to the Court of Claims for relief. Yet the Department of Interior had the authority to prevent Native nations from securing a hearing before Congress.

These institutional, political, and perceptual barriers constituted major obstacles that tribal nations had to surmount. Not surprisingly, they frequently failed in their attempts. The time lag between the point at which an attempt was first made to secure permission from Congress to sue and the ultimate conclusion of a case was oftentimes inordinately long. In what was called the *California Indians* case, from 1922 to 1928 the natives' claims bill received conflicting reports from the secretary of the Interior. Finally, in 1928 Congress authorized the

State of California to sue on behalf of the Indians for claims on eighteen treaties California natives had negotiated in good faith in 1851 and 1852 but that the U.S. Senate had refused to ratify on the grounds that the reservations that were to have been created by the treaties contained lands deemed too valuable to California. The natives remained virtually landless as a result. Although the Senate concluded in the 1920s that the Indians had been "deprived of their property in a manner shockingly in disregard of every consideration of justice and humanity,"[45] sixteen years would elapse before the California Indians finally received their award.[46]

In another example, the Winnebago Indians initiated a suit in 1928 seeking restitution for having been removed from their reservation in Minnesota to one in South Dakota without their consent. The Winnebago never cared for South Dakota and eventually settled among the Omaha Indians. Many tribal elders died in the removal, and the social and cultural life of the Winnebago had been profoundly disrupted by the transition to reservation life.[47] When the case finally reached the Court of Claims, it was dismissed. The court found that the value of the new reservation in South Dakota was comparable in land value to the one the Winnebago's had left in Minnesota. Compounding the tragedy of the loss was the fact that the Court of Claims did not render its decision until 1942, *fourteen* years after it had been initiated.

The time span that plagued the natives of California and the Winnebago people, however, are nothing compared to the difficulties experienced by the Turtle Mountain band of Chippewa Indians who signed a land cession agreement with the U.S. October 2, 1892.[48] In 1892, the two parties negotiated a land agreement for a transfer to the U.S. of 10 million acres for $1 million. Natives opposed to the agreement contemptuously referred to it as the "ten cent treaty." They fought to prevent its ratification by Congress but succeeded only in delaying ratification until 1904. Band members then began to petition Congress to either revise the agreement's terms or provide for an adjudication by the Court of Claims. Although they persisted in their efforts, it was not until 1928 that anything was accomplished. At that time a favorable Senate committee report on a bill to vest jurisdiction in the Court of Claims was adopted, and by 1933 the band had convinced congressional committees that its claims should be heard. As Glen Wilkinson points out, Congress passed a bill in 1934, but it was vetoed by President Franklin Roosevelt. Another bill was introduced, but it, too, was vetoed. Other measures were introduced through the Seventy-Sixth Congress, though none were successful. The claim was eventually filed in 1951 under the Indian Claims Commission Act, although it was not until 1964 that final action on the matter was taken.[49] The case had been carried over a period of *seventy-two* years.

The time lag burden that Native nations had to overcome was not the only barrier that frustrated Indians in their attempts to pursue claims against the government. Money, or the lack thereof, constituted a formidable problem. Native peoples lacked the financial resources to pursue a long and costly campaign before Congress and the Court of Claims. Attorney fees were extremely high, and the cost of gathering data to support tribal claims could be staggering. Much of the evidence required to prove a case went back decades, back to an era when account books were not only suspect and inaccurate but often nonexistent. Faced with these roadblocks, many Native communities were unable to press their claims.

If justice were truly the goal, it would seem that once Native nations were able to meet the rigorous challenge of securing a special jurisdiction act from Congress, success, or some semblance thereof, would be forthcoming. Clearly Congress would not have granted a special jurisdictional statute if the tribal cause was not well founded. It would seem that all that remained was for the court to formally hear the complaint and determine an appropriate award—but this was seldom the case. The Court of Claims, with alarming frequency, found against the Indians. One technique often employed by the court to dismiss a case was to narrowly interpret Congress's special jurisdictional acts. Given that many of the jurisdictional statutes were inexpertly drafted, this was not difficult to do. The Meriam Report in 1928 focused on this salient problem as one of the key difficulties in preventing Native nations from securing proper redress before the Court of Claims.[50]

Examples of the court's use of this narrow construction technique to frustrate indigenous claims are plentiful. In a 1942 case, *Northwestern Bands of Shoshone Indians v. United States*,[51] for instance, the Shoshone sought compensation for the unlawful taking of their lands in violation of the Treaty of Box Elder.[52] The Court of Claims conceded that the Shoshone had proved exclusive use and occupancy of the lands in dispute and that these lands had been taken by the federal government. However, the court dismissed the claim on the grounds that the jurisdictional act passed by Congress authorized recovery only on claims growing *out of a treaty*, and the land involved in this case was determined to be held by the Indians not pursuant to a treaty but rather under original title. Congressional ineptitude played a partial role in defeating the Shoshone cause of action, but the Court of Claims itself was equally guilty because of its restrictive interpretation of the jurisdictional act that Congress had passed.

In *Sisseton & Wahpeton Bands of Sioux Indians v. United States*,[53] the Court of Claims again demonstrated its semantical dexterity in depriving tribal members of their rights. The jurisdictional act in this 1923 case gave the court the authority to hear "all claims of whatsoever nature . . . under any treaties or laws of Congress [and to] . . . settle the rights, both legal and equitable, of said bands of Indians and the United States."[54] This is exceptionally broad language. Yet the Court of Claims found this language too narrow to justify considering whether by mutual mistake of fact the federal government had obtained 11 million acres of Dakota land while bargaining for a tract thought to contain only 8 million acres. This astonishing rigidity in interpreting jurisdiction acts was not an isolated occurrence.

In *Creek Nation v. United States*,[55] the court reasoned that a jurisdictional act permitting the Court of Claims to review Creek grievances, both of an equitable and legal nature, arising from or growing out of any treaty or agreement did not permit the court to "set aside a treaty alleged to have been made under duress or procured by threat." The court concluded that the claim could not be asserted "both as a claim under the treaty and as a claim against the treaty" simultaneously.[56]

The license that the Court of Claims took in narrowly construing the jurisdictional act in the *Creek Nation* case is also revealed in *Western (Old Settlers) Cherokee Indians v. United States.*[57] Congress had impliedly provided the court with a great deal of interpretive leeway in its consideration of the Old Settlers' claims against the federal government. The 1889 statute permitted the Court of Claims "unrestricted latitude in adjusting and determining the said claim, so that the rights, legal and equitable, both of the United States and of said Indians, may be fully considered and determined."[58] In significantly restricting its own power to decide this case, contrary to what Congress had instructed it to do, the Court of Claims held that the jurisdictional statute was insufficient to allow an inquiry into allegations of fraud and duress perpetrated by the government in negotiating the treaty.

The technique of dismissing aboriginal claims through a narrow and restrictive interpretation of jurisdictional acts was not the only device used to deny tribal justice in the court. The court was generally so hostile to Native claims during this era that it frequently found ways of denying redress even where the liability of the federal government was virtually beyond dispute. Take, for example, the case of the Cheyenne and Arapaho, a number of whom had been massacred at Sand Creek in Colorado in 1864 by a contingent of Colorado militia under a Methodist preacher, John Chivington. Chivington's men destroyed the Cheyennes and Arapahos, committing numerous atrocities on the peaceful Indians, including scalping infants and mutilating the sexual organs of Indian women. After the massacre the exultant militia returned to Denver with its trophies and paraded them at the Opera House.

When word of the atrocity spread, natives were furious, and the Lakota, under Crazy Horse, promptly burned Julesburg, Colorado.

Conflicts ensued for several years as the tribes of the northern plains sought to exact revenge for the slain Indians. One of the provisions of the 1867 Treaty of Medicine Lodge between the United States and the Cheyenne and Arapaho was the admission of guilt by the United States and the promise to pay a substantial sum of money to those tribal members who had lost relatives or property in the massacre. But as Deloria pointed out, although the United States had signed the treaty, it never fulfilled the payment provision because political pressures in Washington by the army high command called into question whether the massacre was a battle, as the army maintained, or a bloody massacre, as a House of Representatives investigating committee classified it. The Cheyenne and Arapaho tribes sought compensation, but the courts refused to consider the claim.[59]

It was not too difficult for the federal government to counter the complaints brought by aggrieved Indians. At times tribal claims were dismissed simply because the government refused to admit facts that were beyond dispute or because it presented its own interpretation of events so as to avoid liability or to save face. An example of this misconstruing of facts is the Lakota of the Pine Ridge Reservation in South Dakota, who for years sought reparations from the federal government for the massacre of their people at Wounded Knee in 1890.[60] The army claimed that the massacre had been a legitimate battle. This, however, was in direct conflict with the testimony of General Nelson Miles who supported the Indians' understanding of events. Attempts to secure compensation from Congress failed despite the testimony of several of the survivors. The Lakota were also unsuccessful in getting a hearing before the Court of Claims. Congress stymied them until the admission of regret in 1990.

Of all the difficulties that confronted Native nations seeking compensation from the Court of Claims, none was more burdensome than the problem of *offsets* (occasionally referred to as "set-offs"). Offsets came into play on those rare occasions when a tribal community was fortunate enough to have prevailed before the Court of Claims. When the court ruled in a tribe's favor and established a dollar figure defining the government's liability, a determination was made as to whether any offsets should be deducted from the liability figure.[61] Offsets generally referred to the costs of goods and services provided free by the federal government to a tribal community over the course of years. Congress had characterized these costs as being "gratuitously" supplied, that is, goods and services that were given to tribes but were not specifically required by treaty. Offsets, however, were so ill defined that they gave the federal government excessive latitude by which to diminish or even negate a financial award due to a tribe.

Offsets were not automatically considered in all cases that came before the Court of Claims. Congress had to authorize their use in the legislation that bestowed jurisdiction on the Court of Claims. Only then could the court use this as a device by which to reduce an award. Before 1920, Congress inserted an offset provision in only one of the sixteen special jurisdictional acts passed. But after that date nearly all special jurisdictional acts provided that the U.S. could offset the sums paid out to the tribe, with a few exceptions against the amount the tribe had been awarded by the court.[62] As a result, between 1926 and 1946 awards to Native peoples totaled $49 million, but once offsets were factored in that amount was reduced by $29 million, a diminution of nearly 60 percent of the total award.[63] Interestingly, the special jurisdictional acts permitting the Five Civilized Tribes to take their complaints before the Court of Claims, never contained such provisions.[64]

The problem of gratuitous offsets generated a great deal of controversy among political actors concerned with Indian affairs. There was concern regarding the discriminatory manner in which offset provisions were applied, but many critics took issue with the right of the government to use offsets at all. John R. White, writing in *Ethnohistory*, put the argument well:

> Over the years various Indian tribes have had to make do with federal gifts because of the position they were left in as a result

> of unconscionable actions by an earlier government intent on reifying "manifest destiny." These "gifts" were sometimes minuscule, often unrequested and unnecessary, and generally always costly to the tribes. Wielded by the federal government in the posture of defendant, they were responsible for eliminating tens of millions of dollars from Indian claims.[65]

Examples of the adverse impact that offsets had on Native awards throughout history are legend. In *Blackfeet et al. Nations v. United States,*[66] for instance, the special jurisdictional act permitted the Court of Claims to consider and determine not only the legal and equitable claims alleged by the tribal members but also "legal or equitable defenses, set-offs, or counterclaims, including gratuities, which the United States may have [had] . . . against the Indians."[67] After a long and detailed hearing, the court concluded that the Blackfeet were entitled to an award in the amount of $6,130,874.88. But it also found that the offsets resulting from gratuitous expenditures by the federal government amounted to $5,508,409.31, leaving the Blackfeet with a nominal judgment of only $622,465.57.

In the same year, the Shoshone tribe successfully brought its complaints to the Court of Claims, where it was determined that the federal government was liable for some $2,483,467.99.[68] But after applying gratuitous offsets that amounted to $1,689, 646.50 against the award, the Shoshones received only $793,821.49.

Of all the Court of Claims cases where offsets significantly eroded Indian awards, one of the most notorious involved the Indians of California. Congress, in the special jurisdictional act permitting the Indians of that state to take their grievances to the Court of Claims, inserted a provision in that 1928 statute stating: "Any payment which may have been made by the United States . . . for the benefit of the Indians of California, made under specific appropriations for the support, education, health, and civilization of Indians in California, including purchases of land . . . may be pleaded by way of set-offs."

The Court of Claims found in favor of the natives[69] and awarded them $17, 053,941.98. The court, however, went on to find that offsets needed to be deducted from the final figure, as follows:

> Disbursements made out of specific appropriations for the support, education, health, and civilization of Indians of California . . . . $5,547,805.87.
>
> Disbursements made out of appropriations for the Indian Service generally, but by the appropriations acts apportioned to the Indian Service in California . . . . $1,573,249.66.
>
> Disbursements made for the support and maintenance of the non-reservation Indian schools at Fort Bidwell, Greenville, and Riverside, California . . . . $4,908,044.11.
>
> *Total Offsets* . . . . *$12,029,099.64*[70]

When the total figure was deducted from the liability award figure of $17,053,941.98, the amount the tribal members were entitled to receive was reduced to $5,024,842.34. Such massive deductions left many Native nations and their individual members feeling betrayed.

The burden that offsets posed to Indian nations did not go unnoticed. Indeed, at one point even the federal government appeared to be somewhat embarrassed by its use. At a congressional hearing in 1935, Assistant Solicitor Rufus G. Poole of the Department of Interior testified that the deduction for money that the government would have spent and had spent for all tribes was not only grossly unfair to the tribes with just claims against the government, but as a result, since 1929 "in every case but two where the jurisdictional act allowed offsets of gratuities and where a recovery has been won in the court the petition has been dismissed because the recovery was exceeded by the set-offs."[71] Poole went on to note that set-off provisions were also discriminatorily applied to certain tribes while others were excluded.

In addressing these issues, Congress, as had been its custom for years, failed to provide the desired relief for Native nations. Instead, the lawmakers responded by attaching a rider to a deficiency appropriations act for the War Department, enunciating its new policy requiring the Court of Claims to "consider and offset against any amount found due the . . . tribe or band all sums expended gratuitously by the United States for [the tribe's] benefit."[72] No longer would certain Native communities be discriminated against. Henceforth, all tribes taking their complaints to the Court of Claims would be subject to gratuitous offsets. This was surely not what the Indians desired when they complained about the offsets problem.

The federal government's position on offsets was almost invariably unyielding. After all, offsets were used only against indigenous complainants, not against any other parties taking a complaint to the Court of Claims. A number of arguments were raised to rationalize the government's position. John White pointed out that there were three widely accepted rationalizations for allowing the government to offset gratuities: (1) the offset expenses would have fallen on the Indians themselves had they been properly recompensed at the time the damages were incurred, (2) the offsets are mitigatory, and (3) the offsets are a built-in protection against the Indian claims becoming too costly.[73]

While federal officials and especially Court of Claims personnel were comfortable with these rationales, Native nations more often than not sarcastically referred to offsets as "Indian giving."[74] Not only were offsets considered unfair, but as Michael Lieder and Jake Page reasoned, they perpetuated the inequities that the Court of Claims presumably had set out to eradicate. "When disbursements were made, they were gratuitous: the tribes were not obliged to repay them. By unilaterally converting gifts to loans after the fact, the government gave new meaning to the term *Indian giver.* Many of the disbursements for the tribes were in fact for the benefit of the government itself or of non-Indians . . . and many disbursements that directly and exclusively benefitted Indian people, like purchases of food and clothing, were necessary because the government had prevented a tribe from supporting itself in its traditional manner."[75] These inequities were compounded by the fact that in no other field of law is a defendant permitted to set-off against a valid judgment a gratuity given to the plaintiff. If a non-Indian student, for instance, sued a local school board for injuries incurred by the school's negligence in failing to keep its stairways safe, the school board (government) could not deduct the amount of money that the school spent to educate the child as a proper gratuitous set-off. Only Indian claimants fell under this discriminatory doctrine.

Yet another argument raised in opposition to applying offsets to aboriginal judgments in the Court of Claims relates to the fact that many of the programs that the U.S. invoked as "set-off expenditures" were forced upon the tribes. Indeed, the thrust of most of these expenditures were designed to make sure that Indians remained on their reservations. Indians had little, if any, voice in determining what expenditures would be made for their benefit. Not infrequently, tribes were required to accept programs and services that they had expressly stated they did not want. Furthermore, if the natives had been able to retain more of their aboriginal property, they most likely would not have become economically dependent on the federal government for goods and services.

One final thought on this issue. Indigenous claims never posed a significant threat to the United States Treasury such that offsets were necessary to make sure that settlements were reasonable. The frivolous assertion that aboriginal claims might amount to $3 billion was a rhetorical tactic to intimidate Congress into inserting offset provisions into jurisdictional acts. Monroe Price rather succinctly placed this issue within its proper perspective when he noted that past experience with Court of Claims decisions where gratuities were offset against Indian claims had not led to a fiscal nightmare for the government. In fact, "from 1926 to 1945, when most jurisdictional bills for the Indians *required* offsets, the Court of Claims reported the following figures: Amount of claims alleged by the Indians, just over $1,133,000,000; amount of awards actually received by the Indians, just over $49,000,000; amount of offsets claimed by the government, just over $144,000,000; amount of offsets allowed the government, just over $29,000,000; net judgments for Indians, just over $20,000,000."[76]

The actual evidence produced by the cases adjudicated in the Court of Claims between 1880 and 1946 indicate that the court decided 134 dockets involving Native claims—many tribal nations divided their claims into several dockets. Native communities recovered in only 28 cases and received a total recovery of $37,753,953 (table 2).[77] Under the jurisdictional acts, during this period Indians received, prior to offsets, just over $29 million, or a mere 4.3 percent of what they initially sought. This is hardly a staggering sum that would jeopardize the economic well-being of the country.

Of the many obstacles that have plagued Native nations in their quest for compensation by the United States, the problem of offsets loomed as one of the largest. But it was only one of many burdens that tribes had to concern themselves with. The very fact that Congress singled out Indians and required them to seek special legislation before they could take their grievances to the Court of Claims, a

Table 2 Recoveries by Decade in Cases Decided under Special Jurisdictional Acts

Decade	Number Decided	Percent with Net Recovery	Number with Net Recovery	Total Recovery	Average Recovery
1880–89	2	2	100	3,098,963	1,549,481
1890–99	6	6	100	2.914,042	485,674
1900–09	7	5	71	6,760,823	965,832
1910–19	7	3	43	4,345,794	620,828
1920–29	13	3	23	878,231	67,556
1930–39	60	7	12	12,963,642	216,060
1940–46	39	2	5	6,792,458	174,166
Totals	134	28	21	37,753,953	281,746

Source: From *Wild Justice: The People of Geronimo vs. The United States* by Jake Page and Michael Lieder, copyright © 1997 by Jake Page and Michael Lieder. Used by permission of Random House, Inc. Any third party use of this material, outside of this publication, is prohibited. Interested parties must apply directly to Random House, Inc. for permission.

burden not imposed upon non-Indians, was not only an affront to indigenous people but a deeply discriminatory policy. On the infrequent occasions when Indians made it to the Court of Claims, they did not fare well.

Narrow interpretations of the jurisdictional acts by both the Court of Claims and the Supreme Court effectively stifled the hopes many natives had of receiving what they believed was their just due. In other words, the courts clearly distinguished between *legal* claims and so-called *moral* claims. Tribal nations sometimes contended that the amount the U.S. paid for a given body of land was too low. Such a figure could have been the result of fraud or duress on the part of the government, or from the natives' unfamiliarity with Western property law. But most of the courts' judges and justices said those types of claims, according to their reading of the jurisdictional acts, were merely of a *moral* claim and could not be considered, or if they were examined they were not subject to compensation.[78] Conversely, a claim that the U.S. had violated the express terms of a treaty provision sometimes gave rise to a *legal* claim that was compensable. As a result, this phase of Native history must be characterized as one filled with bitter frustration and profound disillusionment.

2. THE INDIAN DEPREDATIONS ACTS

MUCH HAS BEEN made of the difficulties that confronted indigenous nations when they sought compensation from the government. Few would argue that the institutional, legal, and perceptual obstacles they faced in this quest were not just high but were, in fact, at times insurmountable. But what about the whites who had been allegedly injured due to some type of Native transgression? Did the white settlers run into the same difficulties as natives when seeking satisfaction? Clearly any attempt to obtain compensation from the federal government can be an onerous task, but compared to the struggles of Native peoples, the difficulties encountered by whites were relatively minor.

The problems posed in this area of concern, while not unique, are complex and differ considerably from the typical cases that ordinarily found their way before the courts. Assume, for instance, that a group of Shoshone Indians strayed from their reservation and stole a number of horses from a white settler living near the reservation. Given the distinctive legal status of Native nations, it would be difficult for the settlers to obtain relief for injuries received at the hand of these Native transgressors. The victimized white man could not go into Indian Country and seek redress through an indigenous legal system, although tribes certainly had customary systems in place that had proven effective for millennia among their own people.[1] And since Native nations were considered to be either *domestic-dependent nations*, *distinct independent political bodies*, or sometimes *alien nations*, depending on which Supreme Court opinion one read, Indians residing on the reservation were not subject to the jurisdiction of the American civil courts. Authors of a 1890 congressional report viewed this problem with alarm: "The injured settler on the frontier, who has perhaps but his faithful yoke of oxen as his reliance in building his American dream home in the wilderness, must fold his arms and quietly submit should some Indian depredator stealthily encroach upon the settler's lines and there take away or destroy his only property. He could pursue the white criminal, could invoke the aid of the law, both to punish for the wrong act and to recover the property if found. But in the case of the Indian depredator, he is restrained by the severe admonition of the law itself."[2]

This troublesome situation was compounded further by the fact that the federal government, serving in its capacity as the principal trust agent of Indian affairs, was charged with the supervision of tribal funds. These funds, held in trust by the United States for the benefit of Indians, were not subject to claims brought against the natives by third parties, save for claims that were specifically authorized by statute or treaty.[3] Absent these conditions, white settlers had no way of securing compensation for any loss.

The difficulties confronting whites regarding the loss of their property were not unlike those facing natives, who were effectively shut out of the U.S. legal system when seeking redress for any injuries they had suffered. But here the similarities come to an end. Whereas the natives struggled unsuccessfully for decades attempting to get the federal government to respond to their needs, the non-native community, not surprisingly, found a much warmer reception in Washington. Like the Indians, the whites had to follow a set of procedures established by Congress in their efforts to resolve continuing legal disputes with the natives. Congress set forth these procedures in several ways. In the beginning, when the government was treating with Indian nations, provisions occasionally would be inserted in a treaty permitting the payment of claims against a tribal nation out of that people's annual annuities to compensate those who had lost property to tribal members. The first such provision was incorporated into a treaty with the Cherokees signed on June 26, 1794.[4] In this treaty the Cherokee agreed to have fifty dollars deducted from their annuity for each horse stolen from the whites by one of their citizens. If a treaty did not contain one of these so-called depredation provisions, Congress had to pass a special statute authorizing payment from tribal funds. This was achieved, for instance, in the Cheyenne and Arapaho Depredations Act passed on March 3, 1883.[5]

This piecemeal approach to resolving indigenous-white civil disputes was acceptable neither to the white community nor to Congress. It was cumbersome, time-consuming, and costly. To overcome these nagging difficulties, as early as 1790 Congress embarked upon a new course of action. It did this through the passage of legislative enactments that assisted whites and made it easier for them to obtain compensation for any alleged offenses and depredations committed by Indians. Congress viewed this problem as one of some magnitude, recognizing that it was not to be a momentary item on the legislative agenda. Indeed, the series of congressional acts dealing with such matters spanned a period of one hundred years, culminating in the Indian Depredations Act of 1891.[6] It is instructive to note the contrast between the manner in which Congress responded to Native demands for resolution to their injuries—nominal progress at best—and the determined and consistent efforts made by the legislature to address and satisfy white settlers' demands for financial compensation.

This initial surge by Congress in dealing with the civil disputes between natives and whites was theoretically designed to protect Indians against the encroachment and crimes committed by white settlers. The legislature, under its constitutional power to regulate commerce with the Indians (Art. I, Sec. 8, U.S. Constitution), enacted the Trade and Intercourse Act in 1790.[7] Section 5 of the act provided that any person who "shall go into any town, settlement, or territory belonging to any nation or tribe of Indians, and shall there commit any crime upon or trespass against the person or property of any peaceful and friendly Indian . . . shall be proceeded against."[8] The thrust of this policy was not simply to protect Indians against potential white offenders, but to also compensate them for any losses they might sustain. As evidence, a formal compensatory statute was enacted by Congress in 1796.[9]

The passage of the Trade and Intercourse Act of 1790 must have been perceived as an encouraging sign by Native nations, or at least those privy to it. Little did they realize that future congressional action would concentrate almost solely on the rights of white settlers. The first Indian depredations measure, which signaled the beginning of a continuing legislative policy to assist the white community, was signed into law in 1796 as a component of the revised Trade and Intercourse Act. The overall thrust of the act was to protect both Indians and whites. One of its key provisions provided compensation as well as protection to natives who had been injured by the tortuous and criminal acts of the whites. Section 14 of the act specifically dealt with Indian depredations, stipulating that "if any Indian or Indians belonging to any tribe in amity with the United States, shall come over or across the boundary line of any State . . . and take, steal, or destroy any horse, horses, or other property belonging to any inhabitant . . . or shall commit any murder, violence, or outrage upon any . . . inhabitant, it shall be the duty of such citizen or inhabitant . . . to make application to [the government]" to redress this grievance.[10] The government, upon being furnished the necessary proof, would then attempt to seek satisfaction of the claim from the Indian nation involved. If for some reason the tribe's leadership refused to honor the claim, the U.S. government guaranteed payment to the injured party out of government funds.

This first depredations provision was not unlike an insurance policy. It guaranteed to indemnify injured parties that were unable to obtain satisfaction from the transgressing Indians. The statute, however, did not apply to all Indians. It was directed only toward those Native peoples who were "in amity" with the United States. The term "amity" refers to friendship and peaceful relations.[11] At first it appeared that this qualifying phrase might pose some problems. The Court of Claims, however, dismissed this in a rather off-handed manner by requiring only that the Indians engaged in the wrongdoing be members of a tribe on friendly terms with the United States. Amity, the court noted, did not require the existence of a treaty relationship, only a condition of peace and friendship with the tribe.[12] The law, therefore, applied to almost all Native nations, not just those that had an existing treaty with the United States. The 1796 Trade and Intercourse Act was set to expire at the end of two years, but it was reenacted by Congress on March 3, 1799.[13]

From a white perspective, this first Indian depredations provision was extremely important. No longer would the reservation border serve as a boundary blocking the white community's access to private redress. Tribal nations whose members occasionally committed criminal or civil acts against white settlers were to be held financially responsible for their actions. And if the tribe for some reason failed to compensate the victim, the federal government guaranteed eventual indemnification. As long as there was documentation to prove the loss and Native responsibility, the white victim would be compensated.

Indeed, there were many occasions when the depredation policy was abused. As Larry Skogen noted, "Ultimately, the indemnity system held unlimited potential for fraud. Indemnity payments were supplemental income to some claimants rather than peace bonds to prevent violence."[14] Not infrequently Indians were held responsible for injuries they had not committed. For instance, a steamboat, valued at $3,000, owned by a white settler, and moored in the Colorado River, accidentally caught fire and burned one evening. Indians were not even in the vicinity of the boat landing when the fire occurred, yet the white settler, possessing a goodly amount of cunning, put in an unsuccessful claim under the Indian depredation statute against the Yuma Indians who lived three miles downriver.[15] The discovery of gold in the Black Hills provided another opportunity for exploitation. Numerous claims were filed against the Lakota people even though whites were forbidden under treaty law to even enter the area.

The Indian depredations law went through a number of minor changes over the years. In 1834, Section 14 of the 1796 act was superseded by the act of June 30.[16] Section 14 now became known as

Section 17, and a few modifications were inserted into the new act. The commissioner of Indian Affairs, who entered the picture at this time, was charged with supervising the process of indemnification whenever a tribe failed to compensate an injured white party. In order to make sure that the government controlled the process, the act went on to stipulate that any injured party who sought to obtain private satisfaction or revenge on the accused Indian tribe would forfeit their chance of seeking indemnification from the federal government. Perhaps the most important aspect of the 1834 act related to the fact that the payment made by the federal government to satisfy white claimants could be deducted from any annuities paid to the tribe. This could have reduced the funds that tribes received from the government for basic reservation services. If a tribe received no annuities, then the funds would come directly from the U.S. Treasury.

Prior to 1859, once a tribe defaulted on its obligation, losses were regularly paid through governmental departments. Congress did not enter the picture at all. Indemnification was made directly from the U.S. Treasury for the property that had been taken or destroyed. Congress at this time, however, became somewhat disenchanted with the entire Indian depredations process. On February 28, 1859, federal lawmakers decided to adopt a new policy. From then on funds designed to compensate whites as a result of Indian depredations could no longer be paid directly from the Treasury.[17] The general procedures as used in the past would continue under the new legislation, but losses would now be paid out of tribal funds and annuities. It was not entirely clear whether this act repealed the government's guarantee of indemnification. Given the confusion surrounding this issue, lawmakers were moved to clarify their position, and on June 25, 1860, Congress passed a joint resolution indicating that the 1859 Indian Depredations Act was not to be interpreted as destroying or impairing any right to indemnity that existed at the date of repeal.[18]

The policy requiring a depredation award to be paid out of the annuities that the government provided Indians caused a good deal of concern among a number of congressional officials. Funds devoted to crucial tribal services were already meager to begin with, and if these funds were diminished further by drawing from them to satisfy claims, it was felt that even more onerous hardships would befall Native peoples. In order to protect tribes from this potential loss, Congress in 1870 passed an act prohibiting the payment of depredations claims out of tribal annuities. Furthermore, no claims were to be paid at all until authorized by Congress pursuant to a special appropriations act.[19] Thus, from 1870 on, claimants had to go through the Congress before they could seek redress. The government, of course, continued to recognize its obligation to compensate victims; it was only the remedy that changed.

Congress never seemed to find lasting comfort in the measures it enacted to deal with the problem of Indian depredations. In May 1872 it again modified the procedures. Under the new set of rules, the secretary of Interior was authorized to prepare and publish regulations prescribing the manner in which claims were to be presented. In addition, the secretary was empowered to "carefully investigate all such claims as may be presented" and recommend a course of action to Congress.[20] For all practical purposes, this gave the secretary significant discretionary power to allow or disallow claims. The final decision, of course, still resided with Congress, which had to legislatively authorize payment of the claim, but the real power now rested with the secretary. The responsibilities of the secretary were extended somewhat further in 1885 when Congress, at the secretary's request, authorized $10,000 and directed Interior to compile a list of all claims filed with the department that had been approved by the secretary but never paid. These were then to be presented to Congress for final approval and disposition.[21] Included among these claims were ones where Native nations by treaty had assumed collective responsibility for the offenses committed by their members. Interior collected the data requested, but Congress never appropriated the money to pay the claims.

In general, while the congressional policy of compensating whites for the depredations inflicted by Indians could be characterized as being sympathetic, even whites suffered from Congress's ineptitude.

The series of Indian depredations acts from 1850 through 1885 resulted in the presentation of 5,710 claims to the department involving about $19 million. Of these, the government had paid out in only 275 claims. Over the next five years, another 1,100 claims were filed involving a sum of $4 million. Of the $4 million claimed in the suits filed between 1885 and 1890, $1.3 million was authorized to be paid by Interior, only 32.5 percent of the money sought.[22] By 1890, Congress had appropriated only $1,654,530. So although the congressional attitude toward white claimants may have been sympathetic at this time, its actions still left much to be desired and it was clear that under existing laws the Office of Indian Affairs "had no hope of ever extinguishing the depredations claims in its files."[23]

By this point in the nineteenth century, it became clear that something had to be done if the issue of Indian depredations were ever to be brought to a conclusion. Congress continued to find itself overwhelmed with private bills for the payment of claims. Although the Department of Interior had been given the power to investigate and process claims, this did not to relieve Congress of the ultimate responsibility to evaluate the Interior's recommendations and pass appropriate legislation to satisfy the valid claims. Federal lawmakers thus found themselves ignoring the reports and recommendations of Interior simply because the business of governing had become overwhelming.

A movement was therefore initiated to establish a separate and independent tribunal as an "indispensable alternative for the speedy and just settlement of claims, arising through Indian depredations."[24] A select committee on Indian Depredation Claims was created to solve this nagging problem, which continued to plague the government for nearly a century. The select committee submitted its report to Congress, stressing the need for immediate action. It noted that the obligation of the government to protect whites was "doubly strong in view of the express guardianship assumed by the Government of the Indian tribes. It undertook to guard, to care for, and to protect the Indians."[25] Given this role, the committee argued that it was imperative that Washington assume a corresponding duty to prevent injury to its citizens from such of these "savage wards as shall escape its surveillance."[26] Committee members stressed that without assistance from the federal government, "no injury can be remedied and no wrong can be punished."[27] If the maxim "for every wrong there is a remedy" had any meaning, the committee's report noted, then the government owed a duty to innocent white victims of Indian depredations.

Congressional sentiment was strong enough at this point to pass an entirely new law. The patchwork approaches taken in the past simply had not worked. Even the commissioner of Indian Affairs, Thomas Morgan, testified in favor of this new proposal.

> Ninety-four years ago, under the sanction of George Washington, . . . Congress solemnly promised eventual indemnity to the citizens and inhabitants of the United States who, through no fault of their own, lose their property at the hands of Indians enjoying treaty relations with the United States. In all this time that promise has been kept in not more than 3 percent of the claims which have been filed. The law forbade these claimants, under a penalty of losing the amount of their claims, from attempting by private efforts to recover their property where such efforts might involve the country in an Indian war-from taking "private satisfaction or revenge"-in the language of the law, and forced the Government upon them as their attorney to collect for them the amounts which might be due. Becoming thus, by its own law, the agent and attorney of these people, and forbidding them any other course of proceeding, it appears to be more than in the ordinary sense bound by honor and good policy to redeem its pledges, and faithfully carry out its promises. I think the jurisdiction conferred, by the inclosed [*sic*] bill, is entirely just and proper, and is sufficiently guarded to protect the Government from the payment of unjust claims to undeserving people.[28]

It is interesting that Commissioner Morgan, the person most responsible for guarding tribal interests, had virtually nothing to say about protecting indigenous interests, such as making sure that compensation payments were not made out of Indian annuities designed to provide Indians with the basic necessities of life. In an emotional appeal, the select committee urged Congress to pass a comprehensive Indian depredations act. The committee members argued at length that the bill would bring "glad tidings to the pioneers in the far West, who conquered the wilderness, reclaimed the desert plains, subdued the savage, and by stubborn occupancy, contended for in many a bloody contest, acquired valuable territory to this nation from Indian as well as foreign foe. . . . Many who were once possessed of large property lost all or nearly all by Indian depredations, and they never recovered from the injury thus inflicted. It is chiefly this class of early settlers of the country who are appealing to the Government, to this Committee, and to Congress for relief before they die."[29]

This emotional and highly partisan appeal by the select committee members evidences the prevailing attitude of most congressional officials toward the relationship of natives to whites in the latter part of the nineteenth century. The full focus of attention was predominantly on the demands of the white community. Natives had been effectively foreclosed from presenting their grievances to the Court of Claims, yet here was Congress ready and able to eliminate the legislative burdens that confronted whites in pursuing their grievances. Moved by the report of the select committee, Congress in 1891 enacted a comprehensive Indian Depredations Act[30] to provide whites with the opportunity to have their claims for property that had been allegedly destroyed by any indigenous band, tribe, or nation in amity with U.S. "without just cause or provocation" paid for.

The institutional mechanism that Congress chose to resolve the depredations problem was the U.S. Court of Claims. The 1891 act conferred jurisdiction on the Court of Claims to inquire into and finally adjudicate all claims "for property of citizens" of the United States taken or destroyed by Native people.[31] This included all cases that the Department of Interior had processed under previous acts prior to March 3, 1885, that had not been fully decided. Setoffs and counterclaims could be considered by the court in resolving controversies as well. The statute of limitations would not apply to the act, but all claims existing at the time of passage had to be presented to the court within a period of three years. Indians were permitted to appear before the court to defend their interests and were allowed to be represented by counsel as long as the attorney was approved by the commissioner of Indian Affairs. Once tribal liability was established, payments to satisfy the awards were to be disbursed within a rigid set of priorities. First, satisfaction was to come from the annuities that were due the defendant tribe. Second, if no annuities were available, then from funds owed the tribe by the United States from the sale of tribal lands. Third, the compensation could be obtained from any funds due the tribe that had been appropriated for their current and necessary support, subsistence, and education. Finally, if no funds were available at all, the award would be paid directly from the federal treasury.[32] These funds would, however, remain an outstanding charge against the Native nation and were subject to deduction from future annuities.

The Indian Depredations Act of 1891 serves as a testament to the apathy and antipathy of the federal government toward Natives peoples during the nineteenth century. It climaxed a series of depredation laws passed by Congress that would have a profoundly adverse impact on indigenous peoples through World War I. When a law did not meet white needs as expected, a new law would be enacted. When the burden became too cumbersome for Congress or the administrative agencies involved, steps were taken to remedy the problem. This focused approach is very different than the one the U.S. took when confronted by the claims issues raised by indigenous peoples.

Natives were barred from direct access to the Court of Claims by the same government that took affirmative steps to make it easier for members of the white community to have their grievances redressed. Not only did Washington frustrate the attempts by Indians to go before the Court of Claims to seek compensation for the land that was taken or defrauded from them, but in 1887 Congress enacted the General Allotment Act,[33] a powerful piece of legislation designed to eventually break up the reservations by bestowing individual parcels of land on tribal members and selling the remainder to non-natives. This act, and its multiple amendments, became the principal instrument by which natives were stripped of millions of additional acres of land. When the act was ratified in 1887, Native peoples held approximately 137 million acres of land. By 1934, when the Indian Reorganization Act[34] came into effect, effectively stopping the allotment of any more land, tribal landholdings had fallen to 47 million acres. Perhaps the callous attitude of the federal government during this period is best personified by the Indian Depredations Act itself. Section 6 of the act permitted the government to deduct money from the funds appropriated for the *necessary* "support, subsistence, and education" of Native communities. This generally meant food, shelter, and schools. Although this, admittedly, was the third priority within the disbursement schedule, it nevertheless indicates the federal government's basic insensitivity toward indigenous peoples.

As Skogen points out in his detailed analysis of depredations claims, "By any measurement of its stated purpose the Indian depredations claims system failed miserably."[35] Interestingly, Native peoples actually played a minor part in the overall system, although there were nearly 11,000 depredations cases filed in the Court of Claims and "thousands more that were administratively resolved by the executive departments between 1796–1920."[36] But "because there were Indians, lawmakers created such a policy." Beyond that, the indemnity system really operated between federal bureaucrats and settlers who claimed that American Indians had deprived them of property. The real beneficiaries of depredations claims were the claims agents and lawyers. This phenomenon would be repeated time and again through the other claims issues.

3. THE STRUGGLE TO CREATE AN INDIAN CLAIMS COMMISSION

THE STAGGERING LOSSES—territorial, political, legal, cultural, psychological—sustained by the indigenous nations of what is now the U.S. during the past half a millennia are incalculable, beyond precise measurement. These losses, and the trauma that accompanied them, were generated by an ever-acquisitive set of European powers and their colonial appendages in North America. The losses continued, indeed were exacerbated, once the U.S. was formally established as a nation in the latter part of the eighteenth century. The fact that the federal government, despite its established treaty and trust relationship with Native peoples, occupied the most critical role in this tragic set of scenarios is a deeply discouraging reality. Senator William H. King captured this concern in an address to the United States Senate on February 8, 1945: "It is remarkable that the National Government, which has been so responsive to the cries of the distress and to humanitarian appeals, should be so deaf and callous to the cries of the Indians and to the moral and legal responsibilities resting upon the National Government as their trustee and guardian." He went on to say:

> From the days of the Pilgrim Fathers to the present time the Indians seem to have been regarded by many as objects of legitimate prey; they have been treated as trespassers and outlaws, and unwelcome and illegal occupants of territory which the white man desired. Treaties have been imposed upon them by chicanery and fraud and often as the result of

> military force; and many treaties that have been made have been shamelessly violated, and measures ostensibly designed for the protection of the Indians have been converted into weapons of destruction. . . . Many investigations have been made by committees and by disinterested groups of persons who desired to learn the facts concerning the Indians. Their findings and conclusions warrant a verdict that the Indians have been robbed, plundered, and despoiled of the greater part of their inheritance and subjected to cruel and inhuman treatment.[1]

The government's failure to live up to its treaty and trust obligations with Native nations constitutes one of the gravest depredations committed against tribes. It is well documented that treaty clauses from 1778 until 1871 that were generally framed to recognize the territorial integrity of the remaining Native lands and provide other benefits—to pay annual annuities to tribes, to provide educational facilities, and to supply Indians with such personal property as horses, cattle, and agricultural equipment—were violated on numerous occasions.[2] Ernest Wilkinson, a Washington attorney who represented a number of tribal nations in the middle part of the twentieth century, testified that for all the treaties the government violated and all of the other wrongs it perpetrated against the Indians, Washington had to pay less than $563,000 per year for all suits brought by Indian tribes. "This amounted," he said, "to only 0.0006 percent of the present (1940) annual budget of the United States."[3]

Over the course of the several decades that aboriginal peoples pressed for a mechanism by which to redress their many grievances, they seldom found the political support necessary to engage such a process, much less to garner any substantial justice. Theodore Roosevelt while president was less than enthusiastic about Indian claims. He argued that "to recognize the Indian ownership of the limitless forest and prairies of this continent, that is, to consider the dozen squalid savages who hunted at long intervals over a territory of a thousand square miles as owning it outright-necessarily implies a similar recognition of every white hunter, squatter, horse thief, or wandering cattleman."[4] Even Franklin D. Roosevelt was reluctant to meet the issue directly. "If Indian claims could be disposed of with finality through the establishment of an Indian Claims Commission my attitude might be somewhat different. The past history, however, of these claims demonstrates the futility that any hope that this purpose would be thus accomplished. Final action by the claims commission would be no bar to the representation of the claim to Congress by the dissatisfied Indians or their attorney."[5]

Despite numerous cautionary warnings such as these, by the third decade of the twentieth century the time to move on this issue had ripened. Although it was clear that a resolution to the Native claims problems was not going to emerge overnight, it was important to lay a foundation upon which a new claims approach for natives could eventually be established. The genesis for this foundation revealed itself in a comprehensive report on the social and economic status of Indians published in 1928. Lewis Meriam had been engaged by the Department of Interior to conduct an exhaustive survey of Native peoples, and parts of the final Meriam Report focused on the issue of Indian claims. The report crystallized the need for Washington to address this continuing problem as the report's authors saw unresolved claims as a major impediment to improving conditions for Native peoples. The author's emphasized that the persistence of claims had a damaging psychological effect on natives; that it caused claimants not to want to work or improve their lives because they expected to receive enough money from claims settlements to be well off without much effort; and that resolving claims was a requirement to accomplishing the ultimate goal of the eventual absorption of natives into the body politic.

The report noted, for example, that the "benevolent desire of the United States Government to educate and civilize the Indian cannot be realized with a tribe which has any considerable unsatisfied bona fide claim against the government. The expectation of large awards making all members of the tribe wealthy, the disturbing influence of outside agitators seeking personal emoluments, and the conviction in the Indian mind that justice is being denied, renders extremely difficult any cooperation between the government and its Indian wards. . . . The simple canons of justice and morality demand that no Indian tribe should be denied an opportunity to present for adjustment before an appropriate tribunal the rights which the tribe claims under recognized principles of law and government."[6] The report went on to recommend the establishment of a special commission to study the unsettled legal claims of natives that had not been approved by Congress for submission to the Court of Claims. Furthermore, it was urged that the commission be empowered to submit recommendations to the secretary of Interior so that the claims found to be meritorious could once and for all be channeled through Congress to the Court of Claims for final settlement.

Partially as a result of the Meriam Report, Congress in 1929 retained the services of Nathan Margold, a New York attorney, to study the Indian claims problem and to draft a bill for legislative consideration. This signaled the beginning of a series of congressional hearings that would span the next sixteen years, ultimately culminating in the creation of the Indian Claims Commission.[7]

The 1930 Hearings

The year 1930 witnessed the first serious attempt by Congress to look into the general problems attendant to Native claims. A subcommittee of the Senate Committee on Indian Affairs conducted a hearing on "Indian Claims against the Government." The first witness to appear before the subcommittee was Charles J. Rhoads, the commissioner of Indian Affairs. Rhoads testified, "Practically every tribe or band of Indians in the U.S. has one or more claims against the U.S. Government. Some of these may be meritorious, others without merit, and still others of such doubtful or close nature that it cannot be determined whether they have merit or not until an exhaustive examination has been made of available data, treaties, agreements, records, and so on."[8] Rhoads went on to note emphatically that the "most pressing need at this time is some sort of machinery to act as a sifter or separator so that the meritorious claims can be separated from those without merit. . . . It is not believed necessary and certainly would prove costly in the end to burden the present Court of Claims with a large number of cases which, after investigation, may prove to be without merit or even those of scant merit only. Some speedier and less costly method of disposing of this class of claims is imminently desirable. Whether the suggested sifter or separator should consist of a committee or commission, with powers only to investigate and report, or should be clothed with greater authority, even to the extent of actually making findings and rendering judgment in accordance with such findings, may be worthy of serious consideration."[9] At this early date, then, the federal government did not have a concrete plan in mind. The proceeding started off as a general exchange of ideas. Later, separate bills were submitted, one urging the creation of a Court of Indian Claims, another simply to establish an Indian Claims Commission.

During the course of Commissioner Rhoads's testimony, he indicated that there were already about fifty Indian claims before the Court of Claims with a face value of about $1,169,000,000. The size of this figure startled the members of the subcommittee, especially Burton K. Wheeler, who feared that the magnitude of such claims might become a costly drain on the U.S. Treasury since, as he put it, "practically every Indian tribe in the U.S. thinks it has a claim against the U.S. for violation of a treaty or on some other ground."[10] This concern continued to reappear periodically over the next sixteen years as the hearings progressed. Rhoads, however, was able to calm Wheeler and the other subcommittee members momentarily by noting that from 1893 to 1928, claims had been awarded only in the amount of $18,515,670 and this, together with attorneys' fees in the amount of $1,805,000, came to only 9.7 percent of what tribes had originally sought.[11]

A fair amount of the subcommittee's time was spent attempting to identify precisely what problems hindered Native peoples in the presentation of their claims under the existing system. As with all skilled bureaucrats who testify before congressional committees, each placed the blame with some other agency. George Stormont, a special assistant to the attorney general, advised the committee that Indian petitions had not caused any congestion in the Court of Claims or in the Department of Justice (DOJ). The delays, according to Stormont, could be attributed to the lax efforts of the Department of Interior (DOI) and the General Accounting Office (GAO), two agencies charged with preparing a number of reports required in claims litigation.[12]

One of the difficulties, Stormont noted, was that Congress had never provided the GAO with sufficient human or material resources to work on the needed reports. Senator Wheeler took sharp exception to this statement and admonished Stormont, declaring that the DOJ was not going to get away with placing the blame on Congress.[13] Wheeler proceeded to list a number of Indian claims cases that had been delayed for years and demanded that Stormont explain this to the subcommittee. Stormont's response was that the GAO was the major stumbling block. Later in the hearings it was brought out that until July 1, 1930, Stormont had been the only attorney in the Justice Department assigned to handle Indian claims against the U.S. Stormont said his agency was so financially strapped that he did not even have his own stenographer. One attorney, with access only to a stenographic pool, was all that was allotted to Indian claims even though there were about eighty-five cases pending before the Court of Claims. Senator Elmer Thomas of Oklahoma noted that in the past eleven years only eleven cases had been disposed of—a rate of one case per year. At that rate and with eighty-five pending cases, Thomas sarcastically suggested that it would take "something like eighty-five years to complete this work," assuming no additional cases would be initiated.[14]

When David Neumann, chief of the Audit Division of the GAO appeared before the subcommittee to testify, an entirely different picture of the delay problems was painted. According to Neumann, the major fault in addressing claims lay with the Justice Department. He admitted that claims work was agonizingly slow but said his agency could not begin to work on a claim until the Department of Justice sent a petition to the GAO requesting a search and analysis. Alluding to a Lakota claim that Senator Wheeler was concerned about, Neumann noted that Congress had passed the jurisdictional act permitting the case to go before the Court of Claims on June 3, 1920. The Department of Justice, however, did not send a petition to the GAO requesting a search of the records until May 7, 1923—three years later. The job confronting the GAO was immense. Sometimes a search required an examination of records that went back half a century. Neumann noted that some of the documents had been in storage so long that they "break up like a piece of charcoal" once they were picked up. He added, "We have a couple of women who pull out these papers and piece them together or copy them on the typewriter."[15]

Returning to the Sioux claim as an example, Neumann advised the subcommittee that this one claim amounted to over $100 million "and that involves the disbursing officer's accounts—and, oh I don't know, hundreds of thousands of claim settlements. Every one of these claim settlements will have to be taken out and analyzed to see whether payments were made on these claims pursuant to a certain section of the treaty, and so on. . . . When we get through with the Sioux case we will have at least 10 volumes of this size, and this is condensed to its absolute irrevocable minimum."[16] Neumann's portrayal of the work involved in researching and analyzing Native claims reveals how difficult and time-consuming the task was for federal officials.

The 1930 Senate hearings were not without Native witnesses or, in their absence, attorneys representing Native nations. E. J. Van Court, an attorney for the Creek nation, had little difficulty in placing blame for the administrative difficulties confronting indigenous nations that were attempting to press their claims. The delays, he argued, clearly could be attributed to the DOJ. Initially, Van Court had thought that these were merely accounting problems. But upon further investigation he discovered that accounting issues were not the major obstruction;[17] instead, the difficulties emanated from rank procrastination by the DOJ and that agency's refusal to assign legal personnel to Indian claims issues. The largest burden, he noted, revolved around the failure of the Justice Department to provide adequate guidelines and reports to the GAO and the Bureau of Indian Affairs (BIA) and its inability to have cases ready for trial in a timely fashion.[18]

In addition, James I. Coffey, a Cass Lake Ojibwe, testified that his people were having problems with the attorney whom they had selected and with a lack of money to move their claim forward. Mr. Coffey noted, "We propose to take it into court, but we can't see our way right now to raise enough money to carry it through." He said they had asked the commissioner of Indian Affairs (CIA) to allow them to use some of their own funds, "but we were turned down on that."[19]

It was imperative that the Justice Department direct the GAO investigators as to what items to focus on for accounting purposes. Under the existing system, the department simply sent over a petition instructing GAO to investigate everything in connection with a tribal government's account. The GAO, therefore, would end up doing a great deal of work that had little or no relevance to the cases involved. "I can say without hesitation," Van Court testified, "that 90 percent of the voluminous reports made have no bearing whatever upon the case, which is a total waste of time and public money, and that is one reason why this docket is so congested."[20] Using past statistics to measure the progress the department had made in the handling of Indian claims, Van Court estimated that it would take at least 59 years to catch up with the current docket and 127 years to address the situation when the anticipated additional cases were brought into the picture.[21] Van Court was convinced that the situation had become utterly hopeless.

Not all of the subcommittee's hearings in 1930 were held in Washington, D.C. Committee members ventured to Oregon, New Mexico, and Oklahoma to receive testimony. At these sessions, Native leaders were permitted to voice their concerns as to why their claims efforts had been frustrated for so many years. One of the more poignant exchanges occurred between John Loco, a Comanche from Lawton, Oklahoma, and the subcommittee members. It merits a verbatim reading:

> MR. LOCO: "You know we have been here at Fort Sill since about 1894, when I came here. Fort Sill was a little bit of an old military reservation, maybe 3 miles square—I do not know how square. The Kiowas, Comanches, and Apaches were here. They give us some land. They told us to put a fence around it and it would be all right. We did. We got a little more cattle. General Scott went to see some of these Indians to give us a little more to be added to the reservation."
>
> SENATOR FRAZIER: "A little more land?"
>
> MR. LOCO: "A little more land so we would have a big reservation around here; and we are sure glad to raise cattle. We were raising crops and we were living almost like a king. That is the way we felt. Everything we raise we sell it right here in Lawton, and our cattle were getting big and we ship them to Oklahoma City and Kansas City. We were living good."
>
> MR. BUNTIN: "This is when he was a captive on the military reservation out here."
>
> MR. LOCO: "We were living good; got everything plenty; we get rations; we get good hay and all we want; we can get all the wood we want; we get plenty of water—everything. I do not see why some day we get bad news. They say they want this military reservation for soldiers' training—we want this land."
>
> SENATOR FRAZIER: "The soldiers want the land?"
>
> MR. LOCO: "The soldiers want the land. I feel bad. I pretty near fainted when I heard that. I was living good. The general

said, 'We will give you 160 acres. We will buy good land, with a good house, good barn, good chicken house, good implements, and everything'—give you a good start. Will you take that?' Why, sure. Anybody would. I am glad to go out; glad to go."

SENATOR FRAZIER: "Who told you that? Who asked you if you would be satisfied with that—General Scott?"

MR. LOCO: "General Scott, and then there is another man, Alcorn. There were three of them. They were meeting together, and we all heard it. All right, we say, we go. So we give up this beautiful home, this beautiful reservation we got here. We turn that over to them. Now, to-day I got only 80 acres, and I have been waiting for this barn for 17 years and it has not come yet."

SENATOR FRAZIER: "Have you got some livestock, implements, teams, and so forth?"

MR. LOCO: "I am waiting for the implements. They have not come yet. I have no chickens yet."

SENATOR FRAZIER: "They have got everything they need out here at the military post, have they?"

MR. LOCO: "Yes, sir, they have got that land. We give it to them. It is there yet. My promises were all good. It is still there yet, but where is their promise? I cannot see it."

SENATOR FRAZIER: "You have lived up to your trade but the Government has not lived up to theirs?"

MR. LOCO: "Yes, sir."

SENATOR FRAZIER: "I am frank to say if the money spent for the military post was spent for Indians you would be a lot better off."

MR. LOCO: "Now, I want that other 80. If they do not want to give me the 80, give me one 40 and give me the money.

I need it. It is dry weather. I am poor. I ain't got nothing to eat. I told you about that."

SENATOR FRAZIER: "I think you are right. I think you should have it, too."

MR. LOCO: "Yes, sir."

SENATOR FRAZIER: "I am sure the Congressmen and the Senators are willing to do what they can to help you out."[22]

As the 1930 Senate hearings came to a close, Nathan Margold, the future solicitor for the Department of the Interior who had been retained by the Institute for Government Research to study the tribes' claims problems, was asked to draft a bill to address Native claims. The Margold bill called for the establishment of an Indian Claims Commission composed of six commissioners, to be appointed by the president. The commission was to continue to use the services of the GAO and the BIA; in addition it was to organize an audit section, a document investigation section, and a field investigation section to help expedite the processing of Native claims. The bill stipulated that once a determination was made that a tribe's claim was justified and a final accounting completed, the decision of the commission would constitute a final judgment against the United States. The commission was to possess wide latitude in the exercise of jurisdictional powers, including the ability to review claims in which tribes alleged damages due to a lack of "fair and honorable" dealings. Though never enacted, the Margold bill offered a preview of coming attractions; much of the substance of the bill was incorporated into the Indian Claims Commission Act (ICCA) of 1946.[23]

A separate legislative effort to craft a claims apparatus was also attempted in 1930. Scott Leavitt, chairman of the House Committee on Indian Affairs, introduced a bill, H.R. 7963, to create a Court of Indian Claims, composed of three judges. It had the support of both the Department of the Interior and the Board of Indian Commissioners. The bill was never reported out of the Judiciary Committee because, as Vine Deloria, Jr., put it, "The climate for reform had not yet reached the point where the U.S. wanted to have its past sins recited in a legal forum."[24]

The 1935 Hearings

Shortly after Franklin Delano Roosevelt became president in 1932, he appointed John Collier as commissioner of Indian Affairs. Collier, a man of brilliant intellect and abounding energy, was deeply committed to bringing about revolutionary changes in federal Indian policy and law and to helping Native nations regain a measure of self-government. His first major effort, with the considerable support of Nathan Margold and Felix S. Cohen, was to draft and then push through Congress the Indian Reorganization Act (IRA) of 1934.[25] This comprehensive piece of legislation brought an end to the devastating allotment program, which had subdivided many Indian reservations and eroded much tribal culture, identity, jurisdictional authority, and territory. The IRA also permitted tribal nations to organize for purposes of self-government and to incorporate with an eye toward economic development. The scope of this regenerating piece of legislation was so broad that Collier felt it would be too much to add to it a provision addressing the problems attendant to Native claims against the federal government, in part because of the high costs likely associated with such an effort. Instead, the decision was made to address the claims issue separately, in the next session of Congress.[26]

The decision not to include a claims provision in the IRA should not be interpreted as an indication that Collier was against adoption of such a measure. Indeed, even before Collier became CIA he evidenced considerable interest and deep concern about this issue. Among other things, a few years earlier he had assisted Charles Rhoads, then commissioner of Indian Affairs, in drafting the letter of December 18, 1929, to the Senate Committee on Indian Affairs, urging it to consider this delicate topic.[27] The letter advocated the creation of an Indian Claims Commission that would be independent of the Department of Interior. "This claims commission might be given power to reach final settlements—essentially judicial power—in specified classes of cases where the Indian claim rested on a legal right assertable as such. But the omission should hear all causes, those that are human and moral as well as those that are legal and equitable."[28] The letter concluded with the admonition that there "can be no liquidation of the Government's guardianship over Indians until this inheritance of treaties and alleged broken treaties and governmental laches of the past is absorbed."[29] "The process," Collier predicted, "even with the most expeditious procedure, will require years. With [the claims] procedure as at present, it might well require 100 years."[30]

Before presenting a bill to Congress one of the first issues that had to be addressed was whether to create a court or commission as the mechanism by which to address Indian claim disputes. The bill envisioned by Margold in 1930 called for the establishment of a commission, and several bills proposed in late 1934 and early 1935 called for the creation of a claims court. Secretary of Interior Harold Ickes, however, opposed the court approach and threw his support behind a bill that contemplated the creation of a claims commission. In a letter to the chairman of the House Committee on Indian Affairs urging passage of the commission bill Ickes discussed many of the nagging problems that had frustrated Native attempts to gain their just due. "After many years spent in preparation the Government and tribe go into combat before the Court of Claims under a jurisdictional act which usually is believed and admitted by all the parties to be inequitable, and which does not and should not have the character of an act for final settlement. Largely because of the unsatisfactory character of the acts, recovery in the Court of Claims by Indian tribes has become very infrequent, with resulting justifiable dissatisfaction by the tribes and their return to Congress for further redress. . . . The total operation is greatly influenced by elements of sheer accident, such as the possession by Indians of the wherewithal to hire attorneys for the initial lobbying of their case."[31]

The bill presented to Congress in 1935 was not nearly as strong as Native nations or their advocates had hoped. For instance, it did not provide for the proposed claims commission to adjudicate claims. Rather, its purpose was simply to expedite the handling of claims and to provide Congress with impartial advice as to the passage of jurisdictional acts and the allowance of appropriations.[32] Additionally, the bill was designed to relieve the Court of Claims of its prolonged burden of making fact determinations. The recommendations of the commission were to be only *advisory* to Congress. Still, some progress was made. The procedures outlined in the House bill would bypass the DOI, which heretofore had assumed the role of clearing cases before they could go to the Court of Claims. The bill permitted the commission to request that the GAO, the Land Office, and the BIA transfer or temporarily assign their employees to the commission so as to assist in the performance of its tasks. The primary functions of the newly proposed Indian Claims Commission, then, were investigatory and advisory in nature, not adjudicatory. In a nutshell, the procedures leading to an award involved several stages. First, the commission would investigate and process information, and on the basis of its findings it would make a recommendation to Congress. Second, Congress could then accept the recommendation and pay the award, or it could modify or reject the commission's recommendation. Under certain circumstances, Congress could request that the Court of Claims hear the case. The final phase of the proceeding involved a formal hearing before the Court of Claims, if it was thought necessary.

While the 1930 congressional hearings had focused primary attention on bureaucratic problems, testimony at the 1935 Senate and House hearings—neither of which included any Native testimony—revolved around a different set of issues. Indeed, Congress itself came under more serious scrutiny for its role in the claims process. Much of the criticism directed toward the legislature dealt with the requirement that a tribal nation had to obtain a jurisdictional act *before* it could take its case before the Court of Claims. Charlotte Westwood, of the Solicitor's Office in Interior, reminded the House committee that very few jurisdictional bills got through Congress.[33] The reason for this was that Native governments were seldom able to secure the necessary political support in Congress. They lacked political clout in Washington and certainly employed no lobbyists at that time. The tragedy of this was that the merits of a claim usually had little to do with whether a Native nation was successful or not. During the course of 1934, only one such bill became law, Westwood testified.

Rufus Poole, an assistant solicitor in Interior, noted that it normally took several years, a great deal of money, and much lobbying to secure passage of a jurisdictional act.[34] And if the act was adopted, on average it was another ten years before the claim ever went to trial. Too many Native nations lacked the political sophistication to be able to navigate DC politics, and they frequently found themselves the objects of self-seeking attorneys. Once a tribal nation arrived at Congress, its demands were frequently thrust into competition with those of other Native governments that were also seeking permission to take their grievances to the Court of Claims. Since all bills had to receive a supportive report from the DOI, the natives were subject to additional administrative delay which oftentimes quashed their fragile hopes for justice. California's natives, for instance, received two favorable and two unfavorable reports from Interior within a six-year period.[35]

Getting Congress to enact any major legislation is a time-consuming and difficult undertaking, unless some national or international crisis is involved. But even when this was accomplished, tribal problems still persisted. The language of most jurisdictional statutes was frequently inadequate to the tasks. In the past, Poole pointed out to the committee, legislative expertise in drafting statutes left much to be desired. The language in the acts was frequently so broad that the act became almost meaningless, permitting the Court of Claims an opportunity to deny tribal awards. On other occasions the wording of a statute was so restrictive that it failed to even permit the court to review the injuries that the natives had presumably incurred. Poole proceeded to cite a large number of cases illustrating the problems that Congress had created for Indian claimants as a result of sloppy drafting. Tribes frequently had to return to Congress for redress of the statutory defects so that they could once again take their complaints to the Court of Claims. Several tribal nations in Oregon, for example, presented their claims to Congress on nine separate occasions, and the Colville and Okanogan Indians did so six times before finally achieving any success.[36]

Too often the money and energy poured into these claim efforts proved fruitless. Rufus Poole testified that in the five years prior to the 1935 hearings, twenty-one of twenty-four cases had been dismissed by the Court of Claims.[37] Adding to this frustration was the fact that the twenty-four cases decided since 1930 had required, on average, eight and one-half years from the time Congress granted a tribe permission to go to the Court of Claims until final decisions were handed down.

The sensitive issue of *gratuity offsets* (a contrary claim or demand by which a given claim may be lessened or even cancelled) was one of the more provocative topics addressed during the 1935 hearings. Several witnesses testified that congressional authorization of offsets was utterly inconsistent and irrational. The claims of the Five Civilized Tribes, for instance, were never burdened with this potential deduction device, whereas many other tribal nations had to contend with sometimes drastic reductions in their settlements because of offsets. Seldom did the DOJ provide the GAO with standards for dealing with the offset issue. Hence, the GAO included among the potential list of offset items just about everything that came to its attention. Whenever the GAO reported a potential gratuity offset so large that it appeared it would negate an award, it was often an early and sometimes fatal blow to a tribe's hope for claims success. While the committee debated the administrative problems that offsets posed to Native claimants, it was really the arbitrary and discriminatory manner in which offsets were applied to different tribal nations that captured the attention of the legislators.[38] And it was not just Congress that contributed to this difficulty; the Court of Claims, as Rufus Poole pointed out, was equally at fault as the following testimony reveals:

> The shocking inconsistency in the various holdings of the Court of Claims as to what may be deducted from the recovery won by the tribe as a gratuity may be illustrated by the following citations. Sometimes the Court of Claims allows the Government to set-off for educating the tribe's children in non-reservation Indian schools (*The Blackfeet, Blood, et cetera, Tribes v. The United States*, E-427, Apr. 8, 1935) and sometimes it does not (*Fort Berthold Indians v. United States*, 71 Ct. Cl. 308). More fatal to recovery is the allowance of a set-off of all the money the Government has spent in the administration of Government agencies, as for superintendents, interpreters, teachers, Indian police, agency buildings, and so forth (*The Duwamish, Lummi, et cetera, Tribes v. The United States*, F-275, June 4, 1934), on the ground that these things are benefits to the Indians. But in another case the Court said it should exclude such items recognizing that the maintenance of a Government agency is simply the performance of a governmental function and an obligation incurred by the United States in developing the reservation policy; and furthermore that such expenditures are common expenditures for all tribes (*The Assiniboine Tribe v. The Uinta*, J-31, Apr. 10, 1933.) Sometimes the court has realized that this argument should exclude set-offs for money expended for education and civilization, but normally the court allows deduction even for this (*The Duwamish, Lummi, et cetera, Tribes v. The United States*, supra: *The Crow Nation v. The United States*).[39]

Is it any wonder that Native peoples were confused and perplexed over the offset issue?

The 1935 congressional hearings on Indian claims produced substantial dialogue crystallizing many of the problems confronting tribes, but like so many issues considered by Congress, no substantive legislative came about. Still, the hearings served an important purpose.

A foundation for action had been laid. Other proposals submitted in 1940 and 1941 kept the dialogue alive, and by 1945 the issue had ripened to a state where determined action was nearly at hand.

The 1945 Hearings

In spring 1945 the battle over aboriginal claims was renewed, and there was a palpable sense that a law might finally be enacted. It seemed that most congressional lawmakers had realized that the time had come to address this issue, which had burdened the federal government for so many years. As Early Welch, associate justice of the Oklahoma Supreme Court noted, "I take it from the joint report of [the] subcommittee and from what has already been said, that practically everyone concedes the advisability of having a special Commission to make final disposition of these various tribal claims."[40] Welch was to offer testimony because two comprehensive bills calling for the establishment of an Indian Claims Commission had been submitted for consideration. The first, H.R. 1198, had been introduced by Congressmen William G. Stigler of Oklahoma. A companion bill, H.R. 1341, was submitted by Congressman Charles R. Robertson of North Dakota. The bills were virtually identical.

The 1945 hearings were different from those held in earlier years in that personalities, not issues, dominated the sessions. Four powerful figures in particular stood out, and each cast impressions upon the bill that finally emerged from the committee. Their names: Thomas Gore, former senator from Oklahoma; Felix Cohen, an associate solicitor from the Department of Interior; Ernest L. Wilkinson, a Washington attorney who represented a number of Indian tribes; and Henry Jackson, chairman of the House Committee on Indian Affairs. Unlike the 1935 hearings, in 1945 a number of Native individuals, leaders of interest groups like the newly formed National Congress of the American Indians (NCAI, established in 1944), and tribal attorneys also offered testimony.

Thomas Gore had long been an Indian affairs advocate, and he testified extensively in support of H.R. 1198 and the creation of a commission. He pointed out to the House committee that in the past five or six years, not one jurisdictional act permitting a tribe to take a case before the Court of Claims had been enacted. The problem was particularly difficult in the House of Representatives since one congressman, who professed to be the guardian of the national treasury, simply refused to permit bills to proceed via the unanimous consent procedure—the customary route that jurisdictional bills had to follow. Gore's statement was substantiated by Charles Robertson of North Dakota: "The thing which has impressed me in Congress so often is the lack of dramatization of claims, at least small claims. They come to the floor on the consent calendar, and someone who has no particular interest or is sick and tired of the long history of Indian claims or whatever the case may be, he can knock it out and at no time does it ever seem to be that Indian claims get a square deal."[41] Paul Niebell, an attorney for the Creek nation, indicated that whenever he went to Congress on behalf of tribes, "some Congressman who might not have any Indians in his district would say: 'Here is another raid upon the Treasury,' and would object; and so [we] just could not get the bill through Congress."[42]

The difficulties that Native nations encountered in Congress were equaled by the lack of success before the Court of Claims, if and when a tribe succeeded in obtaining a jurisdictional bill. Senator Gore noted that of the approximately ninety-eight Indian cases that had gone to the Court of Claims since its establishment, Native communities had been defeated in seventy of those cases. Of the twenty-eight cases in which they prevailed, Native claimants won the exact amount of money they had initially claimed in fifteen of the cases. But in each of these fifteen instances, the gratuity offsets were greater than the awards and the tribes, in fact, received no financial compensation at all. All told, Indians had recovered about $33,000,000 in claim awards. This, Gore noted, was equal to the amount of money that it took to run the United States government for less than four hours. And yet, "lest the Treasury of the U.S. might be exhausted, the Indians are denied a forum in which to assert their constitutional rights." Gore then rhetorically asked the committee, "What price justice in America?"[43]

The problem of gratuity offsets was one of the heaviest burdens that Native peoples had to carry, according to Gore. He cited a case in which the government advanced $1 million from Choctaw funds to another tribe. This money was later used by the Court of Claims as an offset against an award to the Choctaw nation—thus the government used the Choctaw's *own* money as an offset. If offsets had to play a role in Indian claims litigation, argued Gore, then they certainly ought to be limited to monies advanced out of public funds.[44] Henry Jackson, chairman of the House committee, conceded to Gore that some offsets were just and some were unjust. Still he felt that an offset provision needed to be included in the bill. It did not necessarily have to be a mandatory provision. Perhaps, said Jackson, the bill could be drafted so that the proposed Indian Claims Commission could be permitted to use its own discretion.[45]

In concluding his testimony before the House committee, Senator Gore attempted to cast the legislative battle into a bipartisan effort. Gore pointed out that in 1940, Herbert Hyde, a Cherokee Indian from Oklahoma, became chairman of the Resolutions Committee at the Republican National Convention. Hyde was able to insert a plank into the GOP platform calling for the adjudication of Indian claims: "We pledge an immediate and final settlement of all Indian claims between the Government and the Indian citizens of the nation."[46] On the Democratic side, Gore was successful in placing an Indian claims provision in his party's platform as well: "We favor and pledge the enactment of legislation creating an Indian claims commission for the special purpose of entertaining and investigating claims presented by Indian groups, bands, and tribes, in order that our Indian citizens may have their claims against the Government considered, adjusted, and finally settled at the earliest possible date."[47] Casting the Indians claims into a bipartisan setting helped to move the House hearings along expeditiously and with little determined opposition.

Felix Cohen, an attorney in the Solicitor's Office and a well-established figure in federal Indian law and policy, in his testimony on behalf of the Department of Interior presented the House committee with a map of the United States showing to Indian Country as it existed in 1776. Interior had prepared itself well for this hearing. The map was divided into sixty-six areas showing the various Native communities or combinations of nations that had ceded to the United States a staggering amount of land. Cohen made a calculated guess that the government had probably paid the natives somewhere between $500 million and $1 billion for their land over the past two and one-half centuries. Representative William Gallagher of Minnesota asked Cohen if that figure represented "more than the land was worth at the time the deal was made?" Cohen, in defense of the government, stated that he felt "the Indians did not get such a bad deal, considering the value of land at the time the various cessions were made." He optimistically declared, "At least the Indians got more for the Louisiana Purchase than Napoleon did."[48]

The complexities of dealing with historic land claims loomed very large in Cohen's eyes, who for many years had focused on ascertaining and clarifying the rights of Native peoples vis-à-vis the federal government as assistant solicitor.[49] To minimize the difficulties of gathering evidence, he drew the committee's attention to a provision in the bills designed to create an Investigation Division within the proposed commission. Cohen noted that the creation of such a division would be of great assistance in discovering the facts relating to aboriginal claims: the division would perform the vital task of searching the "voluminous records relating to each Indian tribe or group of tribes for the purpose of locating, assembling, digesting, and collating the pertinent materials bearing upon the rights of the respective parties."[50]

One of the reasons for previous litigating delays had been the immense amount of time taken up by these searches. A systematic examination of the records by trained researchers would, it was believed, eliminate duplication and shoddily done work and would be more economically viable. Attorneys for both sides would be entitled to full disclosure of the data collected by the division. Everyone seemed to agree that Native transactions were so complicated that it was essential for the commissioner to have assistants upon whom he could rely for an independent examination of the data. The establishment of the Investigation Division thus became an important ingredient in the proposed solution to the Indian claims problem.

One of the key witnesses who testified before the House Committee on Indian Affairs was Ernest L. Wilkinson, a Washington attorney who had represented a number of Indian tribes in the Court of Claims for about a decade. He had actually won five of the nine cases he had led but as yet had not received any compensation.[51] Wilkinson was held in high esteem, both within the legal profession and the halls of Congress. One of Wilkinson's primary objectives was to dispel the fears that many congressional leaders had concerning the potential costs of Indian claims litigation. An attorney general's memorandum issued on April 5, 1939, had speculated that potential judgments for Native nations regarding their claims could total somewhere between $3 billion and $3.75 billion.[52] This largely speculative figure instilled fiscal fear into the hearts of many lawmakers, and Wilkinson felt the need to address this issue forcefully. He pointed out that although the amount of money initially sought by tribal groups seemed high, up to the present time, 1945, the actual awards to tribal peoples amounted to only about 1 percent of the sums originally sought because the DOJ "has been able to defeat nearly 92 percent of the aggregate amount of tribal claims already determined in the Court of Claims."[53] The $3 billion figure bandied about by the Justice Department, therefore, was simply inaccurate, Wilkinson argued, and was nothing more than a device concocted by the department's personnel to frighten Congress from providing Indians with a fair settlement of their claims. He proceeded to analyze a number of pending cases before the Court of Claims and concluded that $25 million was a much more realistic figure.[54] Wilkinson felt obliged to say to the committee's members, "I am not belittling the fact that

$25,000,000 is of significance, but I am saying that we should not be frightened with the possibility of having to pay such an additional amount to the Native Americans from whom our entire country was obtained."[55]

Wilkinson spent a great deal of time before the House committee speaking on many aspects of the proposed legislation, but two items were of particular concern to him. The first was the fact that under the proposed bills the decisions of the Indian Claims Commission would be final. Earlier bills presented to Congress had not allowed for final decisions. Rather, they required the commission to submit its findings and determinations to Congress, with the legislature empowered with penultimate authority to make the binding decision. This, of course, placed a significant burden upon Congress. Wilkinson forcefully argued that there "is not much purpose for an Indian Claims Commission if it is going to make a report and then we have to come back to Congress and fight it all through again."[56]

The second issue dealt with the so-called unconscionable consideration, which was not included as a basis for recovery in the proposed legislation. To illustrate the need to include a clause listing unconscionable consideration as grounds that would warrant satisfaction, the Washington attorney narrated a grim tale involving the Klamath people of Oregon. The Klamath had a large part of their lands taken by the government. Those lands were then given to a railroad. The Klamath received a mere $125,000 for the land in full settlement. Later the Court of Claims found that the land was actually worth about $5 million, but since the tribe had executed a legal release when it received the $125,000, the Court of Claims held that it could not collect more. When the case was taken to the Supreme Court, the court found that the consideration was "shocking and unconscionable." However, the justices felt that they could not go behind the legal release and therefore were unwilling to award the Klamath what they were rightfully due.[57] Congress at a later date did see fit to compensate the tribe in the amount of $5,015,000, but the point remained that the Klamath could not obtain legal satisfaction. Had the Court of Claims been unable to assume jurisdiction of issues involving "unconscionable consideration," there would have been no need to go back to Congress for a political settlement. The facts presented by Wilkinson had a telling effect on the committee, and it appeared that if the legislature were to enact a law, "unconscionable consideration" would need to be incorporated into the Court of Claims's jurisdiction.

Wilkinson was an impressive witness before the Indian Affairs Committee, and the importance of his testimony and influence should not be underestimated. Along with those of tribal attorneys, other Native voices were heard. Dan Madrano, a Caddo and the secretary of the recently formed National Congress of American Indians (NCAI), spoke in favor of the bill on behalf of the fifty-one tribes represented by his organization, which had voted unanimously in favor of the legislation. The tribes did, however, make one recommendation: that one commissioner be a member of the minority political party for purposes of equal representation and to ensure passage of the bill.

W. W. Short, president of the Choctaw and Chickasaw Confederation testified in favor of the bill for the 13,000 members of both nations. Short also proposed a recommendation, which indicated his people's keen awareness of inherent problems caused by the federal government being both a party in a claim and the arbiter of the decision. He stressed that once the commission had rendered a decision, "the Government should not appeal from these decisions, but only the Indians should be entitled to appeal for the reason that any reasonable judgment in favor of the Indians . . . would not be appealed for the reason that these claims are finally lodged in the Federal courts."[58]

Following his testimony, Wilkinson joined Felix Cohen at an informal conference to draft a modified version of the combined bills that incorporated the various suggestions presented at the committee hearings.[59] This afforded the parties an opportunity to quietly resolve their differences. The conference extended over a two-day period, and on June 14, 1945, Cohen submitted the modified draft to the committee for its consideration.

Wilkinson was particularly pleased with the new bill, for he had been successful in changing the language dealing with the proposed commission's jurisdiction. The authority of the commission to hear "moral" claims was eliminated because the word "moral" was such a loaded concept. In its place, Wilkinson suggested changes that infused the commission with the power to hear cases involving "unconscionable consideration" and in instances when the Indians had been denied "fair and honorable" dealings.[60]

The modified Wilkinson-Cohen version of the proposed Indian Claims Commission Act successfully struck what appeared to be an acceptable compromise on the delicate issue of gratuitous offsets. Cohen advised the committee that no bill had a chance of getting through Congress without some kind of an offset provision. It was therefore necessary to agree on a provision that would be fair both to Native claimants and to the federal government. He went on, saying: "This bill would not achieve its purpose if it were limited to strictly legal claims, and if it is to go beyond that, we do get into situations where it seems fair, where services to Indians should be deducted. We cannot say in advance just where those deductions should be made, but we think that the Commissioner should have the power, as indicated in this amendment, to make deductions where, in good conscience, that should be done."[61]

The key to the Wilkinson-Cohen approach was the idea of permitting only those offsets that the commission "in good conscience" deemed warranted. The commission, in other words, would be permitted to use its discretion as to what constituted "in good conscience." Cohen noted, "If [a] payment has been made on a claim by some act of Congress, that, of course, should be deducted from the payment; or if there is an outstanding debt on the part of the tribe to the United States, that should be deducted. But there should not be deductions based on the appropriations for the benefit of Indians unless the circumstances of the case are such as to make that a fair and just deduction."[62]

Eventually, Cohen concluded, the government would have the opportunity to request an offset of any gratuity as long as it was based on fair and honorable dealings. In an effort to bring the claims legislative battle to a conclusion, Secretary of Interior Harold Ickes on July 11, 1945, sent a letter to Chairman Henry Jackson strongly endorsing the creation of the commission.[63] Ickes pointed out that Congress had more important things to do than spend precious time passing on private Native claims. Too much time, expense, and effort, wrote Ickes, went into indigenous attempts to secure jurisdictional acts from Congress. The time and resources spent, coupled with the duplication of effort by the Justice Department and the GAO, led to only one conclusion: it was time for a change. The creation of an Indian Claims Commission would not only provide relief to Congress, the DOJ, and the GAO, but it would alleviate many of the problems posed by the Court of Claims, which frequently dismissed tribal claims on technical grounds.[64] This, Ickes noted, brought the Native nations right back to Congress to try again for new jurisdictional statements designed to overcome the technical obstacles created by the Court of Claims. It was a vexing and ceaseless cycle.

With pressure coming from the administration through the office of Harold Ickes, and an attitude in the House that it was time to move on this nagging problem, Henry Jackson on October 25, working from the new Wilkinson-Cohen version of the bill, introduced H.R. 4497. It was too late for the bill to pass in 1945, but the expectation was that 1946 would witness the birth of an Indian Claims Commission. Indeed, on May 20, 1946, the House of Representatives passed H.R. 4497 with little difficulty, sending the measure to the Senate where hearings on the proposal were held.[65]

The 1946 Hearings and a Bill Becomes a Law

The 1946 hearings on the bill were not simply pro forma, but the disputes that arose were largely focused on refining the measure that had been passed by the House and on affording critics of the bill a final opportunity to seek modifications. Wilkinson again made his presence known by testifying vigorously in support of the measure, and the representatives of several tribal nations provided input into the hearings. While most of the testimony was a rehash of earlier hearings, several problem areas emerged that warrant comment.

Attorney J. Edward Williams of the DOJ came before the committee and sought to alter certain provisions in the bill in order to make it more palatable to the government. Echoing the testimony of past governmental officials, Williams once again sought to financially unnerve the committee's members by noting that the Court of Claims had already rejected about $3 billion in Indian claims. Since not all of these cases were dismissed on their merits, many would undoubtedly find their way to the ICC, possibly resulting in major decisions in favor of the Indian claimants.[66] Williams went on to argue that the government under the proposed bill was being deprived of all of its defenses. He was particularly concerned about the offset provision fashioned by Wilkinson and Cohen. He proposed a broad amendment that would allow the government the right to claim offsets: "Whenever the Commission shall determine that a claimant is entitled to relief it shall inquire and consider all counterclaims and set-offs and demands that would be allowable in a suit [brought] in the Court of Claims . . . as well as all money or property given to or funds exchanged gratuitously for the benefit of the claimants."[67]

The BIA strongly opposed the Justice Department's amendment, maintaining that public benefits of residence and citizenship should not be considered as gratuities subject to the offset provision. Felix Cohen presented the bureau's stance in a forceful manner. He indicated that if the Justice Department's position meant that

> when an Indian has a valid claim against the United States . . . and the United States [has] failed to live up to that agreement [by making] the payment it promised—if it means that the United States must then, under the decision of the Commission, deduct from what it owes to the Indians all the gratuities which it has spent on educating the Indian children, say, which is something it never does when a white man

> has a claim against the United States, then we would oppose it, because our conception is that this bill is designed to remove a lingering discrimination against the Indians which prevents them from being considered on the same basis as a white man; and if a white man has an agreement with the United States and the United States fails to live up to the agreement, the United States is suable in the Court of Claims, and the white man has a chance to collect what the United States promised to pay, and the United States does not deduct from such a payment sums that it may have given to the white man on relief or for the education of his children in the District of Columbia, or anything else of that sort. That is entirely irrelevant to the claims.[68]

The arguments presented by the DOJ, fell short. While the committee continued to wrestle with the issue, it did so with the understanding that the ICC would use its discretion, limiting the use of offsets to those areas that it, in good conscience, deemed justifiable. In addition to the difficulties confronting the Congress over the offset issue, another nagging problem sat in the periphery of just about every hearing that was held on the Indian claims problems—the role of attorneys. A number of congressional officials and Native leaders believed that attorneys were getting rich off of Indian claims cases.[69] This sensitive issue was reborn during the 1946 hearings when Wilkinson attempted to persuade the committee to make a change in the bill. Wilkinson suggested that where there was a contract with the attorneys that had been approved by the Indian tribe and the secretary of Interior, Congress should consent to the use of its funds to underwrite the litigation.[70] In this way attorney fees and litigation expenses would not have to be taken out of the tribe's awards but rather would be assumed by Congress.

Wade Crawford, a delegate from the Klamath nation, took strong exception to the Wilkinson proposal. He argued that such a proposal was like "closing the gate after the horse is out of the corral, after the money is gone."[71] Noting that Wilkinson already held five or six

Indian contracts, and no doubt aware that Wilkinson had also suggested that attorney fees be raised from 10 to 15 percent, Crawford argued that "to permit him to have a check book on the tribal funds in the Treasury is beyond all common sense and business principles."[72] He urged Congress to check into Wilkinson's activities and those of other attorneys to see if they were gouging their Indian clients. Crawford, who at one time had been a superintendent of the Klamath people, blamed the tribe's attorneys for having had a part in his removal. This had a tempering effect upon Crawford's vigorous attack upon attorneys representing Native peoples. Still, Wilkinson's amendment was not accepted.

Another concern was raised by a number of California natives. F. G. Collett, representing a large number of California Indians, inquired whether non-treaty tribal nations would be able to file claims under the proposed act. This was important since one-half to two-thirds the indigenous population in the state had not signed treaties with U.S. Chairman Joseph C. O'Mahoney, Cohen, and George Stormont, a DOJ attorney, all assured Collett that non-treaty tribes would be allowed to bring suits.[73]

During the the debate on the ICC bill, Congressman Henry Jackson, ordinarily not a great champion of Indian causes, sounded the rallying call in support of the bill: "Let us pay our debts to the Indian tribes that sold us the land that we live on. . . . [L]et us at least pay what we promised to pay . . . and let us see that the Indians have their fair day in court so that they can call the various Government agencies to account on the obligations that the Federal Government has assumed."[74] Congress eventually responded to his earnest plea. President Harry Truman, however, had budget concerns that trumped his views on providing Indians a venue for claims. But Felix Cohen wrote a letter signed by Ickes, secretary of Interior, noting that with the exception of some expense associated with establishing the commission itself, the act would not have much of an impact until 1952–53 since it would take at least that long before any claims were decided in tribes' favor.[75] That letter appeared to ease the president's concern, and he signed the bill into law on August 13, 1946.[76] Truman's signing statement, which happened to have been drafted by Cohen, read in part: "I am glad to sign my name to a measure . . . which removes a lingering discrimination against our First Americans and gives them the same opportunities that our laws extend to all other American citizens to vindicate their property rights and contracts in the courts against violations by the Federal Government itself." He concluded by noting that "with the final settlement of all outstanding claims which this measure ensures, Indians can take their place without special handicap or special advantage in the economic life of our nation and share fully in its progress."[77]

The legislative struggle over the ICCA had been a long and oftentimes bitter battle. Although the seeds were sown in 1930, it took sixteen years before the idea became a reality. Like most laws, the reasons behind its passage varied. The greatest impetus was the relentless effort by many Native governments who were intent on forcing the U.S. to fulfill its treaty and trust obligations to their respective peoples—as sovereign nations and as citizens of the U.S. Additional critical support for the act came from those who had championed the indigenous cause for decades, men like Felix Cohen and John Collier. But a number of conservative congressmen also lent their support to the cause. This is attributable to the fact that many of them believed that passage of the act would help to expedite assimilation. It was thought that unsettled tribal claims served "to hold the Indian to his life on the reservation through fear that separation from the tribe might deprive him of his share of a settlement which he believes the Government may someday make."[78]

William Brophy, BIA commissioner, echoed that sentiment when he told Congress: "My own personal feeling and the official feeling of the Department is that if a bill of this sort is passed it will probably make it possible for large numbers of Indians who now remain on their tribal rolls and retain their membership, to surrender that right. They retain membership now in the expectation that they will get something in the way of a claim. Once the matter is settled finally and judicially, I think we shall find the number of Indians who seek services through a specialized Bureau will be diminished."[79] Testimony like this went a long way in minimizing conservative opposition to the act.

While passage of the ICCA was heralded as a great achievement by most Native peoples, some remained deeply skeptical. For example, Frank Fools Crow, a noted Lakota chief and a leader of the Lakota Treaty Council, did not share the elation of others. "We know," said Fools Crow, "the underlying policy behind the Claims Commission Act and we are not fooled. The government intends to clear title to the land illegally taken, to clear their own conscience before they terminate us. . . . I wonder where the white man ever got the idea that these wrongs had to be settled in his courts by his rules."[80]

And what of those federal officials who prophesied a staggering Native raid on the federal treasury if the bill was enacted? They soon settled down and rationalized their new-found support of the ICCA on the grounds that it would expedite tribal nations on the road to self-sufficiency. The cost of settling Indian claims, in retrospect, did not really concern the government that much; most federal officials quietly believed that most aboriginal claims would be dismissed, as they had been under the Court of Claims. Secretary of Interior Julius A. Krug noted that even "those claims which do ripen into money awards will not represent any long-term cost to the Government [since] appropriations for the welfare of Indians have long been made, first from the Indians own funds, to the extent that they have funds on deposit in the Treasury and then from general treasury funds."[81]

The ICCA was designed to address a variety of concerns, but it is not a coincidence that in the month it was enacted Congress adopted two other laws that signaled a profound diminution to the political status of indigenous peoples and their distinctive issues at the national level: the Legislative Reorganization Act on August 2[82] and the Indian Delegation Act on August 8.[83] The Reorganization Act was meant to create greater efficiency in government by streamlining congressional committees and procedures. Under the law, the two standing committees on Indian Affairs were eliminated, replaced by subcommittees. Under the Indian Delegation Act the secretary of Interior was authorized to delegate power to the commissioner of Indian Affairs, who was also empowered to delegate to lower-ranking officials. As Rosenthal points out, the pairing of these two acts with the ICCA "show[s] the intimate connection between Indian claims reform and the desire of the government to terminate its longstanding relationship with the Indian tribes."[84]

Finally, there seems to be one constant about Native history that remains forever inviolate: even when Native peoples are successful in filing claims or lawsuits, they generally gain very little. In fact, even when they do succeed sometimes they end up losing a great deal more than they actually secure.

4. THE INDIAN CLAIMS COMMISSION

From Hope to Reality

THE INDIAN CLAIMS Commission (ICC) was not an ideal mechanism that some had expected. But to others its creation was viewed as a godsend that at long last provided some promise of hope. Native peoples no longer had to fight individually to have bills introduced that would, if successful, allow them to file claim suits against the federal government. And no longer could single lawmakers block a tribe's right to present its claim before a court. All natives would now have an opportunity to have their claims heard by a commission empowered to hear their claims.[1] These hopeful prospects were somewhat tempered by the fact that the newly created commission was a federal agency, conceived of and staffed largely by non-natives whose ancestors had violated the rights of the now-petitioning Native groups. Would the commission actually benefit aggrieved Native peoples or, as had been the general rule so often in the past, would it be yet another instrument that fostered the interests of non-natives over aboriginal interests? There was much to be cautious about.

The ICC was initially composed of three members, who were appointed by the president with the advice and consent of the Senate. Early drafts of the act had called for one commissioner to be native, "but this requirement was bleached out of the final legislation."[2] At least two of the commissioners had to be attorneys, and no more than two could be members of the same political party. Though the act was passed on August 13, 1946, the first commissioners were not appointed until April 10, 1947. Edgar E. Will, a former lieutenant governor of Texas, became the first chief commissioner. He was joined by Louis J. O'Marr and William Holt. Interestingly, none of these men had any background in federal Indian law or policy. Their ignorance of this specialized area of law would presumably enable them to be unbiased in their decisions. This gross unfamiliarity was a common characteristic of virtually all commissioners until the late 1960s when the newly burgeoning principle of indigenous self-determination changed the paradigm and demanded that newly appointed commissioners have some grounding in the complex area of Native law, policy, and history.

The offices of the ICC were in Washington, D.C., but its members were free to travel for field hearings and to conduct on-site inspections. The commission first began to function in July of 1947. It had a staff of twelve, hardly a sufficient number to undertake the tasks before it. Twenty-three staff positions had been authorized initially, but not all received funding during the first year. In addition to this administrative staff, the commissioners were authorized to establish and staff an Investigation Division to assist them in discovering the pertinent facts about each claim brought before them. Much to the detriment of the commission and Native nations, the Investigation Division existed for years only on paper, largely because the litigating attorneys were reluctant to turn over the investigative functions to an independent body. The lawyers were determined to control this function themselves.[3] Nancy Lurie, a prominent anthropologist, who studied the ICC closely over a long period of time and served as an expert witness for several tribes, declared in 1985, "The greatest error of implementation of the 1946 act was the first commissioners' failure to establish the Investigation Division provided for in the act."[4]

Section 10 of the ICCA stipulated that claims could be brought before the commission "by any member of an Indian tribe, band, or other identifiable group of Indians as the representative of all its members." This controversial provision limited claims to those brought by or on behalf of Indian groups or organizations; it precluded claims by individual Indians. Congress feared that permitting individual claims would crowd the ICC's docket to such an extent that it would be impossible for the commission to function.[5] The restriction against individual claims had a profound effect upon many natives who were seeking redress, particularly those whose grievances related to abuses under the 1887 General Allotment Act. Since allotments involved individual ownership of property as opposed to tribal ownership, this type of claim was effectively foreclosed from any consideration.

The prohibition against individual claims was not the only problem emanating from Section 10. Difficulties often arose in an attempt to determine precisely what constituted "an identifiable group" of indigenous people. Unfortunately, the ICC was not consistent in its handling of this issue. Sometimes it would interpret the phrase broadly; at other times it would place a narrow constriction upon it. For instance, several tribes in the Pacific Northwest had been joined together by the Treaty of Medicine Creek and became known simply as the Medicine Creek nation. Yet when this unified group of Native peoples attempted to bring their grievances before the ICC, the commissioners required each of the groups that had formed the Medicine Creek nation to file individual tribal complaints. Similarly, the commission required the Chippewa, Ottawa, and Potawatomi tribes, who had merged into the United Chippewa, Ottawa, and Potawatomi nation, to individually file claims. In contrast, the Indians of California, a loose-knit coalition of many separate communities, were required to file claims collectively as one unit.[6]

Section 15 declared that each Native community or organization that brought a claim before the commission was entitled to retain the services of an attorney of its own choosing, hardly an earth-shaking proposition since within the Anglo-America system of law individuals have always been guaranteed the right to retain their own counsel. However, Section 15 went on to stipulate that the employment of attorneys would be subject to Sections 2103 to 2106 of the Revised Statutes, which required that all attorneys hired by Indian tribes be approved by the secretary of the Interior and the commissioner of Indian Affairs.[7] This was a practice that Congress insisted be satisfied. The alleged rationale behind this approval requirement was that it would protect Native peoples from potential abuses that might be foisted upon them by incompetent or otherwise unscrupulous attorneys.

To Indians, this provision smacked of paternalism and represented a continuation of federal domination over their personal and collective rights. A number of additional stipulations written into the law were designed ostensibly to protect the litigating Native communities, but they actually created an inherent conflict of interest between the plaintiffs' attorneys and their clients. Attorney fees, unless stated in an approved contract, were to be fixed by the commission and could not exceed 10 percent of the amount recovered in any case. Attorneys were permitted reimbursement of out-of-pocket expenses incurred in the litigation as long as those expenses were deemed reasonable. Furthermore, fees were to be handled on a contingency basis; that is, attorneys would be paid their money only if their client tribes won. This payment system was imposed to ensure that lawyers had an incentive to proceed with vigor and diligence. Attorney fees and expenses, therefore, were not to be paid until after a case had been concluded. But since most tribal nations lacked funds to pay for attorneys and Congress was reluctant to appropriate public funds, that "the only way to pay the attorneys was out of awards by the Commission for claims that assumed a 'taking' of Indian lands." "Contingent fee financing," in other words, "created a powerful incentive to prove the loss of as much Indian property as possible."[8]

The controversy over the role of attorneys and their fees entailed continuing problems that had periodically surfaced during the congressional hearings preceding adoption of the ICC. Another provision of the act, one that did not even mention attorneys, played an important role in this debate. Section 11 precluded the transfer of any case presently before the Court of Claims to the ICC. It has been argued that this provision was inserted because cases that were being argued before the Court of Claims permitted attorney fees that ranged upward of 25 percent of the amount the tribal nation would be awarded. Had these same claims been transferred to the ICC, attorney fees would have been restricted to the 10 percent limitation specified in the 1946 act. Vine Deloria has suggested that attorneys were instrumental in limiting the jurisdiction of the ICC to cases that arose prior to 1946 when the act was enacted. Cases arising after 1946 had to be presented to the Court of Claims, where once again the 10 percent fee limitation did not apply. "The high moral purpose of settling Indian claims," Deloria wrote, "boiled down in the end to a lucrative bonanza for a select group of attorneys possessing the special skills to practice Indian law and the career employees of the United States who saw the complicated Indian cases as a lifetime career in a specialized field."[9]

Beyond their fees, ICC attorneys, because of the manner in which they were hired, also typically operated from a mind-set that benefited the federal government as much as their indigenous client. Since "the attorneys must be approved by the United States before they can sue the United States on behalf of their Indian clients, they are a remarkably congenial group," Deloria observed. "One need only check the number of stipulations in the course of an Indian case to see that the tribal attorneys are most cooperative with the United States so that in many instances one could hardly say that an adversarial system of litigation exists."[10]

While the problem of legal representation as spelled out in the ICCA caused Native claimants real concern, it paled in comparison to the profound dissatisfaction they voiced over the types of remedies available to them. The ICCA appeared to provide a forum for a diversity of claims, but the vast majority of claims processed were claims for compensation related to land. Interestingly, "the underlying assumption—that the land itself would never be returned to its indigenous owners—is not discussed in the reported Commission and court decisions, the legislative history of the ICCA ('ICC Act') or the various amendments to extend the life of the Commission. The lack of commentary on this point masks its great significance."[11] It is significant, of course, because land is the foundation of indigenous identity and life ways. As Thomas Leubben points out, "The fact that the

ICC act did not empower the Commission to order the return of any land under any circumstances, and may even had foreclosed otherwise viable quiet title actions, predetermined that the 'justice' provided to Native Americans would be far from satisfactory."[12]

Although the decision not to return land to successful tribes was nowhere spelled out in explicit terms, several clauses in the act allude to monetary compensation as remedy. Section 19, for instance, reads that the "final determination of the Commission shall . . . include . . . a statement (a) whether there are any just grounds for relief of the claimant and, if so, the *amount* thereof" (emphasis added). Section 22 states, "There is hereby authorized to be appropriated such *sums* as are necessary to pay the final determination of the Commission" (emphasis added). From these clauses the commission inferred that the congressional intent underlying the act was to limit awards to those of a monetary nature.[13] Some Native peoples may have been satisfied with just monetary relief, but many other tribal nations expressed real dismay because their attachment to the land was intense and deep and they realized that in accepting money they were losing that which defined who they were. Money was viewed as an entirely inadequate remedy for such a fundamental depredation—the permanent loss of aboriginal homelands. Moreover, Section 2, clause 4 of the act empowered the commission with jurisdiction to adjudicate claims for "takings" of tribal lands. But at least 100 million acres of land for which Native nations received compensation by the ICC were never formally "taken" in any legal sense.[14]

The ICC was never intended to become a permanent fixture in the politico-legal arena. It was envisioned that the commission would hear those claims that arose prior to 1946, decide the cases expeditiously, and then shutter its doors and go out of business. Under the act, Congress had arbitrarily determined that all outstanding cases could be resolved within a ten-year period from the date of the commission's first meeting (Section 23). Realizing that the intricacies involved in preparing a claims case were terribly complex, tribal nations were given a five-year period in which to present their grievances before the commission (Section 5). After the expiration of five years, no further suits could be entertained by the commission.

The first problem that confronted a number of Native nations was that many of them never received any formal notice that the commission had actually come into existence, to say nothing of an explanation of the myriad procedures to follow in initiating a claim. The commission was charged with sending out a written explanation of the law to the recognized heads of every Indian tribe and band or to any other identifiable group of Indians existing as "distinct entities" (Section 13a). Notification was also to be sent to the superintendents of all Indian agencies. who, in turn, were to provide detailed explanations of the act and its procedures to the Native communities within their regions. In fact, this provision of the act was only partially met. According to one commentator, only seventeen tribes failed to initiate claims, either because they had none or because the timeline for submission would not be met.[15] This had a particular impact on those Indians living in *non-recognized* indigenous communities east of the Mississippi. With the exception of the Creek and Miami nations, who previously had brought suits before the Court of Claims, the unrecognized tribes of the eastern United States were virtually excluded from taking advantage of the act due to a lack of notification.[16] This failure to inform the Native peoples of the commission and its role was hardly an auspicious beginning for the commission.

Some of the early mistakes committed by the ICC might well be attributed to the fact that it was not only a new governmental body but also an experimental one. Still, its failure to notify all Native groups as to their rights under the 1946 act could hardly be excused. It was a stunning oversight and resulted in profound dissatisfaction within many Native communities. But as a new bureaucratic creation, the commission had few mechanisms in place and even fewer precedents on which to rely. Thus the commission was given the authority to chart its own course, and it did so by drafting its own regulations. Unfortunately, the commissioners chose to adopt a set of rules that had been used by the Court of Claims. It appears that the commission was heavily influenced by people who had had prominent roles in prosecuting Indian claims in the past. These connections, to attorneys and other who were active in the field of Indian claims, helped to "perpetuate an adjudicative environment in the Commission" in large part because there was a "carryover of personnel associated with such cases, i.e., the lawyers for the plaintiffs and those from the Department of Justice as defendants."[17] All of this meant that the commission functioned much more like a court than as a commission. As the commission itself once acknowledged: "[The] Commission was a court in fact and its method was adjudicatory. It functioned largely as did the Court of Claims but dealt only with Indian claims. Its expanded grounds of Government liability gave the Indian a wider scope of claims presentation and the potential for greater success in award recovery."[18]

The fact that the commission took on all the trappings and functions of a court is one of the principal reasons it failed to live up to expectations. Indeed, many believed that the establishment of the commission to be one of the more disheartening aspects of the entire indigenous claims controversy. All of this seemed in direct contrast to what Congress originally had intended. There had been earlier attempts to establish an Indian Court of Claims, but these efforts met with failure. Instead, Congress opted to create a commission to focus on both investigatory and adjudicatory functions. The desire for an investigatory component is one reason the 1946 act contained a provision calling for the establishment of an Investigation Division. A commission, lawmakers had concluded, could be more flexible than a court in dealing with the highly specialized and extremely complex subject of aboriginal claims against the federal government. Congress did not want the process to become burdened with the vast network of rules and technicalities that had so hampered the Court of Claims in its attempts to deal with similar grievances.

But this was not to be—and for several reasons. First, Section 20 of the act provided for both interlocutory (provisional) review and review on appeal by the Court of Claims and the Supreme Court.

Because of this, the commission had to compile an evidentiary record for each case and prepare findings of fact and conclusions of law. Second, in 1947 the commission adopted procedures that required it to function, essentially, as a court. Third, the first three commissioners were attorneys trained in regular judicial proceedings. Finally, the tribal attorneys also preferred a judicial setting that would enhance the need for their skills.[19]

As former commissioner John Vance noted, the "Commission has chosen to sit as a court, and, as a result, the Congressional mandate has been utterly frustrated."[20] This was clearly detrimental to Native interests. The adversarial system that the ICC adopted worked to the advantage of federal officials but severely disadvantaged Native claimants.[21] The system put into place was an alien system, not unlike the old Court of Claims, which couched everything in the language of Western law and relied on legal technicalities, doctrines, and ideas that in the past had proved so frustrating to indigenous claimants.

Within a short period of time Native peoples realized that the technical difficulties they had confronted in the Court of Claims were going to be continued at the new ICC. Indeed, the very first case decided by the commission—*The Western (Old Settler) Cherokee* case—provided a crystal clear example.[22] The Western Cherokee had alleged that a mistake had been made in the writing of their treaty, and they claimed damages under the "fair and honorable dealing" clause of the ICCA. The commission concluded, however, that the Court of Claims had decided this same fact situation involving the same parties at an earlier date; hence, it invoked the doctrine of res judicata. This concept stipulates that a fact once legally determined is conclusively binding between the disputing parties and may not be relitigated at a later date. Thus the historical record of the ICC, an entity created in an attempt to rectify past Indian grievances, began by denying the Western Cherokees access to the commission. Interestingly, the Court of Claims later reversed the commission's ruling, concluding that the Cherokee claim had been predicated upon a new cause of action set forth in the 1946 act, one that had not been considered in any prior Court of Claims case.[23] Thus, according to Harvey Rosenthal, the Court of Claims had moved powerfully to expand the very narrow determination of the ICC.[24]

The Struggle to Stay Alive

Few cases were filed with the ICC during its first years of operation. This was somewhat surprising given the vigor of the struggle that Native nations had waged in their attempts to get the 1946 act passed. The paucity of cases during these early years may be attributed, in part, to three reasons. First, tribal attorneys were cautious, wanting to see how the commission's early cases would be decided.[25] After observing the initial operations and attitude of the commission, lawyers would presumably be in a better position to formulate a successful litigation strategy for their clients. Second, many tribes struggled to find adequate legal representation. Finally, the commission learned that the work would be tedious and time consuming.

Since Indian complainants had only a five-year period in which to file their petitions, there was a barrage of filings just prior to the expiration date. The filing rush became so great that the number of cases submitted in the last six months was double the number filed during the preceding four and one-half years.[26] An attempt was made to extend the filing period for an additional year, but this proved unsuccessful. Ultimately, some 170 Native groups had filed 370 petitions, and these were divided eventually into more than 617 dockets during the life of the commission.

Congress felt that the commission, as originally conceived, would be able to complete its work within a ten-year period; thus the life of the commission was to terminate after a decade. As is the case with so many governmental programs, these congressional notions were far too optimistic. Administrative delay became the general rule that characterized much of the commission's operations. In drafting the 1946 law, Congress contemplated that the commission would make extensive use of its Investigation Division so that cases would not become bogged down in fact-gathering as had been the case with the old Court of Claims litigation.

Unfortunately, the commission failed to make use of the Investigation Division, and this contributed significantly to the slow pace of case consideration.[27] The records of the BIA, a major source of evidence, were also a major problem as they were in a chaotic state of organization. In addition, the General Accounting Office, which had assisted in searching records, suffered from inadequate staffing. The government was simply overwhelmed in preparing its defenses. In one eighteen-month period, it requested and received 6,451 days of delay in litigation.[28] Cases were further delayed because under the rules as promulgated by the ICC, either the Native claimants or the government could appeal to the Court of Claims and then to the Supreme Court on any part of a commission decision. This provided a field day for appeals since the commission broke down its hearing procedure into several major phases. Each of these could be appealed before proceeding to the next phase. These factors extended the amount of time it would take before the commission made a final decision.

The difficulties that confronted the ICC during its embryonic years, particularly the administrative delays, made it impossible for the commission to complete its work within the ten-year period allocated by the 1946 act. Given the complexity of many of the cases, it was probably folly to think the commission could resolve them within such a short time span. Nevertheless, the act specifically called for the commission to be terminated after ten years. Since the work of the commission was far from over at the end of ten years, it was necessary to return to Congress to seek an extension of the commission's life.

In 1955 the Senate considered a proposal to grant a five-year extension to the commission, but this measure died in committee. The same issue was raised, more successfully, in 1956, but it was a contentious battle. Much of the controversy revolved around a 1953 ICC ruling, *Otoe and Missouria Tribes of Indians v. United States*,[29] that permitted tribal nations to be compensated for the taking by the government of so-called Indian title (often referred to as unrecognized or aboriginal title). Before this decision, Native communities could assert claims only when the taking of Native land had been formally *recognized* by the federal government via treaty, statute, or court decision. There were vast Indian holdings that had never been formally *recognized* as belonging to Indian, but Native nations were precluded from prosecuting claims to these lands. The *Otoe and Missouria* decision, which was affirmed on appeal by the Court of Claims on May 3, 1955,[30] changed all of this and considerably expanded the territorial claims that Native communities could pursue. Strangely, less than three months earlier, through the Court of Claims ruling in 1955, the Supreme Court had issued a major decision involving Alaskan natives and their lands, *Tee-Hit-Ton v. United States*,[31] in which the High Court adopted a formal distinction between types of Indian property that dramatically reduced the amount of money awarded by the ICC.[32] This case allowed for the taking of a great deal of Alaskan native land. The Tee-Hit-Ton band was a small band of Tlingit Indians, and it had claimed that the United States had taken timber from its lands without compensation. But because the taking had occurred before August 13, 1946, the band could not sue under the ICCA "fair and honorable dealings" clause. In ruling against the Tee-Hit-Ton, the court made a sharp distinction between *aboriginal land*—which was land owned by the indigenous community since time immemorial—and *recognized land*—which was land conveyed to a Native community by an official act of Congress, treaty provision, or some other formal federal acknowledgment. Since the Tee-Hit-Ton had never signed a treaty with the United States and had no statutory or judicial recognition that their lands had been acknowledged by the federal government as belonging to them, the court held that they were not entitled to any compensation whatsoever. "Our conclusion," wrote Associate Justice Stanley Reed, "does not uphold harshness as against tenderness toward the Indians, but it leaves with Congress, where it belongs, the policy of Indian gratuities for the termination of Indian occupancy of government-owned land rather than making compensation for its value a rigid constitutional principle."[33]

This case sent shockwaves throughout Indian Country, particularly to the many tribes with claims pending before the ICC, many of them based on aboriginal title. Implicitly, Reed had said that all cases involving non-recognized Indian title would first have to be recognized by Congress before they could be submitted to the judicial process. More specifically, if the *Tee-Hit-Ton* precedent were strictly applied to the claims pending before the ICC, it was questioned "whether or not the decision might lead to exclusion of all cases of Indian title from the general jurisdiction of the commission."[34]

But when the Court of Claims upheld *Otoe and Missouria* in May 1955, it held that Indians could indeed pursue claims in the ICC using aboriginal or Indian title. Congress in enacting the ICC had fulfilled provisions apparently lacking in the *Tee-Hit-Ton* case. For example, *Tee-Hit-Ton* had not been decided under the ICCA. And the Court of Claims concluded that Congress expected the commission to resolve Native claims, including those based on their aboriginal Indian title. The Supreme Court subsequently declined to review the case. This was an important victory, if narrow and constrained; tribes basing their claims on aboriginal title still had to meet a number of court-defined criteria.[35]

When the debate on the extending the life of the ICC began in 1956, the Justice Department, fearing the potential consequences that might arise from the *Otoe and Missouria* decision, argued against extension. It advised Congress that the potentiality of awards from Indian claims might reach well into the billions of dollars even though by this date only $10 million had been awarded on a total of $800 million claimed.[36] Edgar Witt, who led the commission at that time, challenged the accuracy of the department's estimate, though he did admit that awards could easily rise given the vast acreage involved. As Witt noted in testimony before the House Subcommittee on Appropriations, "We have tried to keep in mind the interests of the taxpayers but also what is right for the Indians. . . . We [the U.S.] owed them a moral duty and some compensation for taking away from them the lands where we found them, from which they were then making their livelihood."[37]

When it appeared that the Department of Justice's attempt to sway Congress by manipulating the financial figures would not prevail, Assistant Attorney General Perry Morton sought to amend the bill so that the commission could not consider aboriginal claims based on or arising out of aboriginal Indian title except under certain specific conditions.[38] Otoe attorney Luther Bohanon used the commission's own statistics to show that the Department of Justice's efforts were wrongheaded and would "only be the basis of new claims to be filed before Congress in the future" if it were adopted.[39]

The Morton amendment alarmed Indian peoples around the country, and they mustered a determined campaign to defeat it. The Association of American Indian Affairs (AAIA), headed by Oliver La Farge, accused the DOJ of attempting to deprive "Indians of their rightful claims against the United States."[40] He noted that the DOJ had been "lobbying for weeks to frighten members of the Congress" and that the agency was so adamantly opposed to Indian claims that it fought vigorously against every claim "regardless of its merits."[41]

In an attempt to rebut the argument that future awards might run to billions of dollars, La Farge pointed out to the lawmakers that Indians so far had received less than 2 percent of the sums they had initially sought. To complement La Farge's testimony, the Inter-Tribal Council, representing a number of tribes in the nation, passed a resolution asking Congress to extend the life of the ICC as then constituted.[42] The Department of Interior also came out in opposition to Morton's amendment. Finally, on July 24, 1956, Congress passed H.R. 5565, extending the commission's life for an additional five years—minus the Morton amendment.[43]

In the late 1950s and early 1960s, the commission was not as productive or as efficient as many had hoped. Changes in its makeup slowed the pace of the commission considerably. In 1959 Arthur V.

Watkins of Utah, a former member of the Senate Committee on Indian Affairs, was appointed to the commission. For Native peoples this was an extremely disappointing appointment as Watkins, a confirmed assimilationist and therefore an avid supporter of termination policy, had never shown much support for indigenous peoples. During his term Watkins instituted a number of administrative changes—for example, set hearings by mutual agreement that expedited the commission's work and protected natives from being pressured into settlements.[44] But in general he supported the government's position whenever he could and even assaulted the ICC for its allegedly "extremely liberal and favorable attitude . . . toward Indian tribal clients."[45] Although the number of ICC decisions reached a nadir in 1962, things were dramatically reversed the following year when the number of cases resolved tripled in number.[46]

At the end of the five-year extension period, it was clear that more time was needed to clear up the commission's lengthy docket. By 1961, 471 of the 596 dockets remained unresolved. A brief legislative hearing was held in May of that year to determine if the commission should be granted a further extension, and everyone familiar with the process expected that this would happen. Congress's rationale in extending the commission an additional five years was clear. As indicated in a Senate report: "It cannot be stressed too strongly that the Claims Commission Act was passed by Congress to give the Indians their day in court to present their claims of every kind, shape, and variety. Until all these claims are heard and settled, we may expect the Indians to resist any effort to terminate federal supervision and control over them."[47] This statement was pregnant with multiple meanings and met the broad concerns of nearly everyone associated with the claims proceedings. The Indians, of course, were pleased with the additional time, and the congressional officials who were intent on Native assimilation acknowledged the need to satisfy Indian claims before they could make substantial progress on terminating the trust relationship and the reservation system. And so with little opposition, the commission received a second five-year extension.

Although the commission's case load was reduced during the second extension period, there was still insufficient time to bring the era of Indian claims to an end. Indeed, the commission would receive three more extensions. In 1967, during the debate on the third extension, the discussion did not revolve around the question of whether or not there should be an extension, but rather on just how long a period of time was needed for the commission to complete its work. Two-, five-, and seven-year periods were suggested as appropriate, but since the five-year term had become institutionalized, this time frame was agreed upon. The new law incorporated a trial calendar to make sure that the claimants presented their causes in a timely fashion. To help expedite the commission's work, since there were still 347 dockets pending, two additional commissioners were added, bringing the total to five members. The measure was enacted into law on April 10, 1967.[48] Interestingly, one of the new commissioners, appointed in 1969 by President Richard Nixon, was a Native person, Brantley Blue. Blue, an attorney and former judge, besides being the first indigenous commissioner, belonged to the Lumbee people of North Carolina, a non-federally recognized (though recognized by the state) tribal nation.[49]

By 1972, the ICC had forty-two employees and a budget of $1,045,000. Of its caseload, 164 claims had been dismissed, and 182 awards totaling $410 million had been issued. There were 264 pending cases.[50] This was the year the commission was supposed to bring its work to a conclusion, but once again it had to request an additional five-year extension from Congress. In 1968 the commission had embarked upon an expedited program in an effort to conclude its work by 1972, but staff shortages and unaccountable delays made it impossible. Chairman Jerome Kuykendall told Congress that if a fourth extension were not forthcoming, about fifty tribes "would not get their day in court."[51] Since the commission's productivity rate had increased significantly, with it accomplishing in five years 63 percent of the work accumulated in the previous two decades, Congress consented to yet another extension. The lawmakers insisted, however, that there would be no more extensions. Thus, the fourth renewal act became law on March 17, 1972.[52] Despite Congress's emphatic assertions, this extension would not be the last one granted.

The commission's work went rather smoothly during the fourth renewal period, but as it drew to a close, the commission once again sought an extension from Congress, this one for three years. The commission was joined in its lobbying efforts by a number of tribal nations and by the U.S. Court of Claims. Several reasons were given to justify a fifth extension. First, about 120 cases remained on the commission's docket. If no extension were granted, these would have to be transferred to the Court of Claims; this was viewed as an unmanageable number for the claims court to absorb. Second, the claims court's judges, unlike the commissioner's, lacked the expertise to handle complicated legal and historical cases. Third, it would be an injustice to the tribes with undecided cases if their cases were heard by a different body. Finally, the transference process would mean a further delay in concluding the cases.[53]

The debate over the fifth renewal continued for nearly eighteen months until a compromise was struck. The forces pressuring for an extension failed to secure the hoped-for three-year extension, but Congress did consent to extending the commission's life for a year and a half. Under the act that passed, the ICC was required to certify to the Court of Claims by December 31, 1976, those claims that could not be completed by September 30, 1978. This was the date the commission was to finally cease operations. When the ICC expired it left 68 dockets uncompleted, and these cases were automatically transferred to the Court of Claims. The ICC, conceived in 1946 to function for ten years, had its life renewed on five separate occasions and operated for thirty-two years.

The Commission: Jurisdiction and Powers

Throughout the years during which Native peoples and others pressured Congress to pass the ICCA, many feared that the legislature would create a largely symbolic body that would do little to address tribal grievances. Instead the lawmakers created an adjudicatory agency that possessed an impressive amount of power, even if its rulings barely addressed the many past depredations perpetrated against Native nations.

The jurisdictional powers of the commission were spelled out in Section 2 of the act, which authorized the commission to hear and determine five classifications of Indian claims:

> *Clause 1*: Claims in law and equity arising under the Constitution, laws, treaties of the United States, and Executive Orders of the President.
>
> *Clause 2*: All other claims in law or equity, including those sounding in tort, with respect to which the claimant would have been entitled to sue in a court of the United States if the United States was subject to suit.
>
> *Clause 3*: Claims which would result, if the treaties, contracts, and agreements between the claimant and the United States were revised on the grounds of fraud, duress, unconscionable consideration, mutual or unilateral mistake, whether of law or fact, or any other ground cognizable by a court of equity.
>
> *Clause 4*: Claims arising from the taking by the United States, whether as the result of a treaty of cession or otherwise, of lands owned or occupied by the claimant without the payment for such lands of compensation agreed to by the claimant.
>
> *Clause 5*: Claims based upon fair and honorable dealings that are not recognized by any existing rule of law or equity.

No claim accruing after the date of approval of the act (August 13, 1946) could be considered by the commission. The majority of cases that arose under Section 2 dealt with land problems. This may be why many people have referred to the commission as the Indian Land Claims Commission.

The first two clauses in Section 2 did not forge any new ground for Indian recovery. Under the first clause, natives were permitted to initiate claims "arising under the Constitution, laws, treaties of the United States, and executive orders." These were basically the same types of claims that Native communities had pursued under special jurisdictional statutes before passage of the ICCA. Now, however, the Indians could go straight to the commission seeking satisfaction. The Lakota Indians, for instance, brought suit under this clause to recover some $5,307,656 from the proceeds of 9,261,593 acres of land taken by the federal government pursuant to a treaty—but for which they had never paid for. While the Lakota initially prevailed in this litigation, they were unable to obtain a recovery because the Court of Claims in *Sioux Tribe of Indians v. United States*,[54] decided that the offsets involved in the case were greater than the monies initially awarded to the tribe. Clause 1 therefore provided no new ground for recovery; still, it was important in that it automatically invoked the jurisdiction of the ICC such that tribal nations no longer had to secure a special jurisdictional statute from Congress.

The second clause in Section 2 was similar to the first except that it defined the commission's jurisdiction so as to include claims "sounding in tort." Tortious injuries are private, civil wrongs inflicted upon a person. Negligence, for instance, would constitute an injury "sounding in tort." The second clause in the ICCA stripped away the immunity of the government in such suits so that Native nations, like whites, could bring suits sounding in tort against the federal government. The Creek nation, for instance, brought a suit against the federal government for a breach of its fiduciary duty in permitting a railroad to obtain a right-of-way across Creek lands without providing just compensation. The Creeks alleged that this constituted a tortious taking of their land. The Court of Claims, however, narrowly interpreted the Creek treaty in such a manner that it completely absolved the government from liability.[55] While the *Creek Nation* case actually arose prior to the passage of the 1946 act, it illustrates the type of tortious cases Native peoples sought to have redressed.

Unlike the first two, the last three clauses of Section 2 opened new opportunities for Native nations to sue the federal government. Clause 3 enabled indigenous communities to bring suits that would result "if the treaties, contracts, and agreements between the claimant and the United States were revised on the ground of fraud, duress, unconscionable consideration, mutual or unilateral mistake, whether of law or fact, or any other ground cognizable by a court of equity." This is quite a startling measure. It gave the ICC the power to affect the meaning of ratified treaties. Under normal circumstances this would be an impossibility. Constitutionally, not even the federal courts have the power to directly change or nullify a treaty. This can be done only through a subsequent treaty negotiated by the president or through unequivocal language in a federal statute. Yet in the 1946 act Congress vested the ICC with the power to remedy problems brought about in a treaty based on fraud or misrepresentation. It is important to note that the commission was not given the authority to revise a treaty per se. The act only provided the commissioners with the ability to grant relief by interpreting the circumstances "as if" the treaty would have been revised. As Ralph Barney, chief of the Indian Claims Section of the Department of Justice, pointed out, treaties have "always been considered a political matter completely outside the scope of judicial inquiry. And technically this separation of powers has been preserved [in the act] for you will notice that the Commission and the courts are not given authority to actually revise the treaty but only to grant relief 'as if' the treaty were revised."[56]

This major addition to the 1946 act provided Indian claimants with a ground for recovery that had never before existed. Treaties could no longer be interpreted with a mechanical rigidity that often prevented Indians from prevailing regardless of the fraud that had been perpetrated against them. It is interesting to note that claims based on "unconscionable consideration," a jurisdictional ground urged upon the commission by attorney Glen Wilkinson, found their way into the final act. Ultimately this meant that even in the absence of fraud or mistake, natives could recover as long as they could prove that there was a "very gross" discrepancy between the value of the land conveyed and the amount of money the tribe received for that land. Such activity constituted a transaction based on unconscionable consideration, and clause 3 afforded Native nations a new remedy to deal with this type of problem.

The fourth clause inserted into the jurisdictional powers section dealt exclusively with the problem of aboriginal lands. It provided a remedy for claims "arising from the taking by the United States, whether as a result of treaty of cession or otherwise, of lands owned or occupied by [Indians] without the payment for such lands of compensation agreed to by the claimant." Since most tribal claims were predicated upon land transactions, this became a very important provision. Indeed, the Department of Justice opposed this clause with such vigor that it fought to have it excluded from the act when it was being considered for extension in 1957.[57] What at first sight appeared to be a rather straightforward and simple provision ultimately became mired because of two controversial phrases—"from time immemorial" and "Indian title"—with which the commission and the Court of Claims had to wrestle. Interestingly, neither of these two legal phrases is found in the wording of the 1946 act.

The phrase "from time immemorial" at times has caused significant interpretive problems in indigenous claims litigation. Historically the relationship of Native nations to the federal government was conditioned largely by precedents established by the Spanish, French, and, of course, the English prior to the founding of the United States. Since each of these international states only sporadically recognized the territorial rights of indigenous peoples as the original occupants of the land,[58] it was held that petitioning Native communities should have to prove possession of their aboriginal land right by resting that title on "actual, exclusive, and continuous use and occupancy 'for a long time' prior to the loss of the property."[59] Defining Indian territory together with problems of proving continuous "use and occupancy" of those lands clouded a good many legal proceedings. Fortunately, the commission ultimately began to focus its investigations less on the notion of "from time immemorial" and more on those periods of time when Native lands were lost or ceded to the federal government.

More important than the phrase "from time immemorial" was the concept of "Indian title" or "aboriginal title," as defined by the ICC and the Court of Claims. In determining whether a Native nation could be compensated for the unlawful taking of land by the federal government prior to the passage of the ICCA, the Court of Claims concluded that only those Indian lands that had been formally recognized as such by the federal government would qualify for compensation. The court distinguished between "recognized title," that is, Indian ownership of land formally acknowledged as such in a treaty or statute, and "unrecognized title," frequently called "Indian title" or "aboriginal title." As noted earlier, in 1954, the Court of Claims in *Tee-Hit-Ton v. United States* concluded that Congress was liable to compensate Indians only for the loss of federally recognized lands; there was no legal obligation to reimburse Native communities for the loss of "Indian title" lands since the tribal rights in these cases were only the rights to "use and occupy" territory and not to the property value of the land.[60] Additionally, Congress was determined to be the institution to determine whether or not Native nations should be compensated for their losses—not the courts. Recovery by Indians thus became a matter of political grace and not one of law.

This grave injustice toward Indian nations was corrected by clause 4 of the ICCA. The narrow rule of recovery as spelled out in *Tee-Hit-Ton* was jettisoned by the Court of Claims in view of the new grounds for recovery found in clause 4. Focusing on the notion that natives could bring claims against the government "as a result of treaty of cession or otherwise," the Court of Claims in 1955 found that this was sufficient to permit recovery even when the land in question was based upon non-recognized title.[61] The presence of clause 4 in the 1946 act therefore provided Indian nations with a firm basis for relief that had not existed prior to the passage of the act.

The final jurisdictional clause in Section 2 permitted Indian tribes to base their claims against the federal government on a lack of "fair and honorable dealings not recognized by any existing rule of law or equity." This provision had the potential to encompass a large number of violations from treaty abrogations to virtually any transaction where the federal government, as trustee, might have dealt unfairly with their Indian trust beneficiaries. The Department of Justice vigorously opposed including this section in the law, asserting that liability should be limited to legal violations and not based upon moral claims. During the congressional hearings, however, John Collier argued that a considerable "number of claims and grievances do not grow out of the legal facts but essentially out of the moral parts of the record. There are a great many valid claims, valid humanely and morally, but as such have no basis in law."[62] Nancy Lurie reinforced this thinking in commenting on the failure of the Geronimo's Apaches to secure a claim award despite all that they had endured as prisoners-of-war during their years of confinement: "It is possible that faced with hundreds of claims, the Commission simply panicked at the prospect of trying to put a price on mental anguish and similar intangibles and beat an expeditious retreat to high, legalistic ground to avoid the quagmire of moral questions."[63]

Native peoples were not hesitant to use clause 5 as a basis for rectifying some of the past governmental depredations, but their efforts proved to be largely fruitless. The massacres of natives at Sand Creek in 1876 and Wounded Knee in 1890 were thought to be valid grievances that could be pursued under clause 5, but the commission viewed these complaints as "individual claims," not national claims, and as therefore not compensable under the 1946 act. The injuries, in the commissioners' view, had been incurred by individual Indians and not tribal entities. It mattered little that the government may have dealt with the Indians on less than fair and honorable terms. As long as the claims were viewed as individually based, they fell outside the purview of the ICCA.

Although the potential was there, few claims were filed under this controversial clause. The constrained interpretation that the commission gave to the "fair and honorable dealings" provision moved tribal attorneys to concentrate their efforts more on the first four clauses in the act. Every creative effort brought under clause 5 seemed to end in failure. In 1968, for instance, the Gila River Pima–Maricopa Indian Community brought a cause of action before the commission for damage allegedly incurred as a result of government failure to provide adequate education and medical services. The tribe's leadership claimed that this qualified as a claim based upon a lack of "fair and honorable dealings" not recognized by any existing rule of law or equity.[64]

The Gila River people lost this case. The Court of Claims, in hearing the appeal from the ICC decision, argued that there was nothing in the history of the 1946 act to suggest that "claims this broad were intended to come within the broad grant of jurisdiction to the Commission."[65] The thrust of the ICCA was not to remedy all of the damages to Native peoples that had flowed from the history of United States Indian policy. As Judge Philip Nichols, Jr., put it in his concurring opinion, the ICC was not meant "to be the arbiter of every possible dispute that might have arisen between the United States and the Indians in 170 years of history, or that it was to settle every grievance."[66] The government, the court held, had not, in fact, assumed any obligation as a "guardian" to the members of this tribal nation. And since the Indians had not been able to prove that the government had failed to fulfill "whatever it was required to do" in meeting its obligations to the Indians, it had not violated the fair and honorable dealings section of the ICCA. Thus, the kinds of complaints the natives were alleging needed to be channeled through the political processes, not through the ICC or the Court of Claims.[67]

There was great disappointment among Native nations that more could not be accomplished under clause 5. This was only part of the story. There were other categories of claims that also fell outside the scope of coverage under Section 2. All grievances where a state government possessed jurisdiction over a subject matter were excluded from consideration. This, by the way, is why few eastern Indian land claims were filed with the commission.[68] Claims arising out of the 1887 General Allotment Act were also excluded as these were viewed as being individually based claims and not "tribal" in nature. And finally, claims arising after the year 1946 fell beyond the jurisdiction of the ICC. These post-1946 claims, however, could go before the Court of Claims without first obtaining a special jurisdictional statute from Congress.

The powers that Congress had bestowed upon the ICC initially seemed most impressive. In addition to the general authority that the commission assumed in clauses 1 and 2, new and vibrant powers found their way into the 1946 act in clauses 3, 4, and 5 of Section 2. But the actual amount of power wielded by the commission proved to be much less than envisioned after a series of self-assumed subtle and restrictive interpretations that the commission arrived at during its early years of operations. As Thomas Leubben poignantly observed, many of the commission's decisions were tortuous efforts on the part of the commissioners that gave the appearance of justice but actually perpetuated substantial injustices. "Given the underlying assumptions and objections that informed the ICC process," Leubben continued, "political termination and cultural assimilation—and the complete failure of that judicial process and its associated political process to address the injustice of unlawful appropriation of Native American ancestral lands, it is no surprise that many tribal plaintiffs were dissatisfied with their ICC 'victories.' "[69]

The hope that many Native nations initially saw in the impressive array of jurisdictional powers that Congress had bestowed on the commission began to diminish as soon as that body began to function. If Justice Oliver Wendell Holmes was correct when he said that the life of the law is not logic but experience, then Native nations, rather than feeling hopeful, should instead have been extremely skeptical, given what their relationships with the federal government had been like in the previous century and a half.

5. THE INDIAN CLAIMS COMMISSION

Its Politics and Operations

A CURSORY READING of the legislative hearings that led to the passage of the Indian Claims Commission Act (ICCA) reveals three fundamental purposes. First, the claims problems confronting Native peoples were of sufficient magnitude to justify the creation of a distinct mechanism to address their resolution. Second, the procedures and structural apparatus established to deal with these problems were to be straightforward and guarantee indigenous nations a prompt and fair hearing. And finally, the 1946 act was to bring about a final resolution of aboriginal claims within a reasonable period of time. What could be more self-evident? Congress created the ICC, provided it with an Investigation Division to assist in the gathering and processing of all the pertinent historical and legal data, and empowered the commission with the authority to bring this persistent and critically important issue to a fair and just conclusion. At the time of its enactment, the process sounded perfectly feasible. But implementing it proved far more difficult than anyone had imagined.

Problems surfaced immediately and continued to plague the commission throughout its existence. The commission, partly as a result of inexperience, committed a number of errors and made policy decisions during its early years, some of which had a devastating impact on Native nations. Take the issue of notice, for instance. The idea that people affected by a law should be given ample notice is thought by most to be an elementary and essential concept in the American political and legal system. Yet a large number of indigenous nations were never notified either of the existence of the ICC or of the procedures to follow to initiate a case. As noted in chapter 4, the commission charged the Bureau of Indian Affairs with the obligation of notifying Native peoples, bands, and other identifiable groups, but the bureau chose to communicate only with Native nations that were formally recognized by the federal government. This precluded a number of aboriginal groups, particularly those east of the Mississippi River, from ever receiving any formal notification. The Creeks and Miamis, both of which had brought cases before the Court of Claims, were the only exceptions to this grievous BIA decision.

To compound this negligence, the BIA drafted its procedural guidelines in such a manner as to place the initiation of claims cases in the hands of attorneys. Lawyers, in effect, not Native governments, were empowered to decide what types of grievances would be taken before the commission for resolution.[1] Native nations were thus precluded from drawing up their own complaints or even from speaking for themselves. The attorneys were their spokespersons. This persistent reliance on non-Indian legal authority was not limited to pre-trial activity; litigating attorneys also assumed a dominant role in charting the internal procedures of the commission. The legal profession imposed upon the commission a network of forms, procedures, and language that only lawyers could comprehend and manipulate. As John T. Vance, a former commissioner noted, the commission, at the request of the lawyers who practiced before it, provided a bewildering series of hearings on Native title, value, offsets, and attorneys' fees that fueled the complexity of the ICC to the disadvantage of Native peoples. The commission, in fact, waited "for the claimants' attorneys and the lawyers for the Department of Justice to present the issues and the evidence to the Commission." Although nothing in the act required the tribal claimants to have lawyers represent them, "no claim made any progress unless the claimants were represented by a lawyer."[2] Vance also argued that the commission fastidiously followed outdated and discriminatory procedures in line with past jurisdictional acts and out of keeping with the intent of the ICC—even though such adherence clearly frustrated Native nations and the will of Congress.[3] By any measure, it was a Euro-American process, with the rules and procedures having been established by, and largely for, non-Indians.

The Three-Phased Hearing

If an aboriginal community had a bona fide claim and was able to muster the wherewithal to bring a cause of action before the ICC, it then had to navigate successfully a series of three separate hearings before receiving a monetary award. In the first phase, referred to as the *title phase*, Native claimants had to prove that they were legally entitled to come before the commission as a plaintiff. This required the Native nation to prove that it was an identifiable group rightfully descended from those who had previously used and occupied the lands in question. This was no easy task. It required the group to demonstrate that it was a recognizable Indian community and not just a collection of individual tribal members who sought redress under the ICCA, which was particularly difficult when the aggrieved Native group was viewed as little more than an obscure band or village that had been "conveniently" combined into a formal tribe by the federal government. Indeed, the very concept of what constituted a "tribe" became unduly complicated because of federal officials' insistence on using this problematic term. As Alfred L. Kroeber, a leading anthropologist, had observed: "The more we review aboriginal America, the less certain does any consistently recurring phenomenon become that matches with our usual conventional concept of tribe; and the more largely does this concept appear to be a white man's creation of convenience for talking about Indians, negotiating with them, administering them—and finally impressed upon their own thinking by our sheer weight."[4]

The problem of identifying what constituted legitimate Native groups eligible to pursue claims under the ICC posed difficulties both to the commission and to the Court of Claims. Even expert witnesses who testified on the issue could not reach agreement since their testimony was no more dependable than the scattered bits of information available to them.[5] As one author put it, "One scholar's tribe is another scholar's band; some writers have used the terms synonymously; other anthropologists distinguish different types of tribes and bands depending on their historic origin."[6] For instance, in one controversial decision, the expert witnesses had great difficulty in determining whether the Kootenai people of Idaho, who had brought a claim against the United States, was part of or politically distinctive from the Kootenai inhabiting Montana, a group bringing a separate claim against the government.

It was not uncommon for a single Native nation holding a common territory to divide into separate groups, such as the Sac and Fox, Iowa, Potawatomi, and Winnebago. On other occasions, separate aboriginal groups located on a single reservation would sign a multilateral treaty with the U.S. and thereafter be recognized for political purposes as a single polity. But although the treaty might have established a consolidated tribal council, the legislative body did not necessarily represent the original component tribes. This type of complex historical situation led to the establishment of such communities as the Confederated Salish and Kootenai tribes and the Confederated Tribes of the Colville Reservation, among others.[7] The legal and political merging of historically differentiated Native peoples was particularly evident in the Northwest where there was a tendency on the part of the federal government to combine a number of small tribes into a single larger entity for administrative and economic purposes and to then place them all on a single reservation. How were "consolidated" reservation communities to be identified for purposes of bringing suits before the commission? Should they be required to go forth on the basis of their historical and original national, band, or village status, or should they be instructed to file suit as a larger, formal collective entity?

The decisions of the ICC and the Court of Claims created far more questions than they answered from the standpoint of instructing Native communities in how best to proceed. The difficulties encountered by some of the aboriginal peoples in California are a testimony to this.[8] Native groups in California were so numerous that it was extremely difficult to identify claimants by band or village affiliation. Hence, Congress created a class referred to as "Indians of California," which included all Indians living in California as of 1852 as well as their descendants who inhabited the state in 1928. Having been artificially classified as a legitimate entity, the Indians of California were then granted the right to bring their collective grievances before the ICC.[9] The commission, however, threw out the suit after concluding that the Indians of California were not an "identifiable group" within the meaning of the ICCA.[10] On appeal, the Court of Claims reversed, holding that in the ICCA Congress had clearly accepted the idea that there would be claims coming before the commission that could not be presented by a single tribe or band. By adding the phrase "other identifiable groups," the Congress, the Claims Court held, "intended to enlarge the category of groups of Indians entitled to present claims for hearing and determination."[11] The grievance procedure, therefore, was not to be limited solely to groups existing at the time when the claim arose, and the court said the provisions of the law should be "liberally construed" to benefit the natives.[12]

Other attempts to consolidate claims under the umbrella of a formal collective indigenous body were less successful. The Anishinaabe people, also known as Ojibwe or Chippewa, had sought to bring a common claim before the Court of Claims. The Court of Claims, however, required each of the Chippewa (the name used most often at that time) grievances to be broken into separate claims that corresponded to the injuries suffered by each of the related bands.[13] The Ottawas, likewise, had a similar experience when they attempted to bring a joint grievance before the ICC.[14] They were told by the commissioners that "claims are now maintainable only by the successors in interest of the respective bands of Ottawa, and recoveries are to be had, if any, to the extent of the interest or ownership by such respective bands of the lands involved and made the basis of claims."[15]

Interestingly, the inconsistent manner in which the commission and the Court of Claims approached this problem provided some

Native segments with a device they could use to exclude certain Indian groups from participating in the claims process. A historical example is useful to show how this situation originated. In 1814 the federal government attempted to move the Creek Indians out of their original homelands in Georgia and Florida to a new territory west of the Mississippi, in what would later be called Indian Territory (present-day Oklahoma.) Some Creeks refused to move and thus became known as the Eastern Creeks. Eventually the western-situated Creeks filed a claim with the ICC. The Eastern Creeks, who had maintained no discernibly distinctive political organization, attempted to intervene in the suit. But their western relatives protested, arguing that the Eastern Creeks were a separate Native polity and should not be allowed to join the suit. The commission upheld the position of the Oklahoma Creeks, finding that the Eastern Creek were nothing more than individuals attempting to take advantage of the claims process. The exclusionary strategy of the Oklahoma Creeks appeared to be successful. But when the issue was appealed to the Court of Claims, the commission's decision was reversed. The Claims Court, in an opinion by Judge Benjamin Littleton, concluded that the Eastern Creeks had been an integral part of the Creek nation at the time the claim arose in 1814 and while no longer formally organized, they still qualified as an "identifiable group" of Indians under the ICCA.[16]

When an aboriginal community was able to demonstrate that it legally fell within the category of an "identifiable group" of Indians, it then faced the burden of proving that it exclusively used and occupied a definable territory from "time immemorial." This could be proved only by examining the totality of facts and circumstances of each case.[17] But if the federal government, however, could demonstrate that more than one Native people had used a particular area, the "exclusivity" argument became invalid and the claim was denied.

Exclusive use and occupancy was thus very hard to prove. "Most Indians were organized in small, localized, autonomous units ranging in size from the single family to multiple-family groups and each unit habitually exploited specific areas in their food quest. Rarely did a group's numbers exceed 500, with only a few reaching 2,000 or more."[18] To qualify for occupancy, a Native community's land use had to be consistent, in either a continual or a seasonal sense, and the use had to have been of vital importance to the economy of the group's members. Significant problems of proof arose, of course, because indigenous peoples generally did not view property or ownership in the manner of non-natives. Historically, Native peoples were willing to allow shared use of their territory so long as the sharing did not infringe upon their own usage of the land or resources appurtenant to the land.[19]

The notion of exclusivity was much more widely utilized in Western society than in aboriginal society. Proof of exclusivity was further complicated by the additional requirement that the lands in question had to have been held by the Native group from "time immemorial." This posed a profound problem for a large number of indigenous nations, many of whom who lived a somewhat mobile existence within an expansive territory.

Vast amounts of data and numerous expert testimonials were required to deal with these issues. In an effort to bring some order to this empirically chaotic world, a number of anthropologists, historians, and what would come to be called ethnohistorians[20] were called upon to assist in the gathering and evaluating of evidence. Not surprisingly, both the Native peoples and the federal government carefully selected experts who would present their evidence in the best light. A number of commentators have, in fact, suggested that Congress created the Investigation Division of the commission to undertake this task. Unfortunately, the Investigation Division never became fully operational. It was little more than a paper apparatus, left to atrophy for years for want of work.

The first phase of the commission's hearings posed a heavy burden on aboriginal communities to legitimize their rights to the land, and the second phase of the proceeding was equally taxing. It was during this phase that hearings were held to determine the value of the land involved; hence, it was referred to as the *land valuation phase*. Determining the value of a tract of land is not a task easily fulfilled, particularly if the land transaction occurred in the distant past.

In the land valuation phase, the fair market value of the land was to be fixed at the time the land was originally taken or sold. Thus, if a Native community ceded land to the United States in, say, 1843 but had never received payment, it could sue the federal government before the ICC. If the suit was brought in 1950, the commission, in determining the value of the land, would assess its value *at the time the land was ceded*, thus its value in 1843, not in 1950. This held true even regardless of the fair market value of the land in 1950. Leubben argues that the undervaluation of land was the second most difficult problem confronting Native groups, next to the refusal of the ICC to return any land to tribes. The total amount awarded before the ICC transferred its unresolved cases to the Court of Claims in 1978 was a little more than $818 million. "The total value," said Luebben, "would have been many times that amount if awards had reflected the actual value of Indian losses."[21]

Trying to ascertain the fair market value of a piece of property that was disposed of over one hundred years ago is more an art than a science. As Thomas Le Duc noted, remote "retrospective appraisal is not, and cannot be, an exact science. Every parcel of land is unique and so is every moment in time."[22] Whenever the government condemns property through its power of eminent domain, for instance, it usually bases the compensation rate upon the idea of fair market value. But sometimes a market does not exist. How, then, does one determine fair market value? The suggestions have been many and varied. Some are so technical that they defy comprehension. One approach suggested by the Justice Department was to "assign as the value of the land the capital sum whose income at 5 percent would produce the cash value of contemporary army rations for the number of Indians known to have occupied the land at the time of session."[23] Fortunately, the Supreme Court had previously held in *United States v. Miller*[24] that trying to ascertain the meaning of fair market value as a legal term involved "at best, a guess by informed persons." Subsequently, in *Otoe and Missouria Tribe v. U.S.*[25] the Court of Claims followed suit and rejected the fair market value phrase as being too cumbersome and awkward.

In attempting to arrive at this "informed guess," appraisers used as many indicators as possible. Factors such as the area involved, records showing the quality of other land available and sold, and consideration of economic conditions of the time were used in an effort to ascertain the value of the land at the time of the taking. The difficulties posed by this substantial problem led the litigating parties in many instances simply to enter into compromise agreements. Under these circumstances the fair market value of the land would simply be stipulated to the commission by the parties.[26] No compensation, however, was awarded for the potential profits natives might have earned had they been able to hold on to their lands. When, for example, the Lakota and the natives of California lost title to their original homelands, in part because of gold rushes, they received no compensation whatsoever for the staggering amount of gold taken from their former territories.[27] And the ICC included no authorization to adjust awards based on inflation. The devaluation of awards by inflation was extreme. As an example, "an award of one U.S. dollar for the value in 1871 would be equal to U.S. $7.88 in 1979 if adjusted for inflation."[28]

The stakes in these land valuation hearings were high, largely because of the enormous scale of the acreage involved. The Crow, for instance, brought a claim before the commission for over 30 million acres of land in Montana and Wyoming.[29] The Kaw tribe sought compensation for well over 6 million acres in Kansas;[30] the Red Lake, Pembina, and White Earth bands of Ojibwe for over 7 million acres in Minnesota and North Dakota;[31] and the acreage involved of the Native communities in California were for a staggering 70 million acres.[32] Expert witnesses had an overwhelming charge in trying to ascertain the *fair market value* of such large amounts of property, particularly since the land transactions had occurred decades in the past—the Crow claim dated to 1868; the Kaw nation to 1846; and the

Red Lake band to 1863. This factual reality required the commissioners to revisit the nineteenth-century real estate markets in an attempt to determine the value of the land at the time it was transferred from indigenous to non-indigenous hands.

The commission also confronted the problem of how to determine precisely how much land should be included in the Indian holdings. In resolving this issue, the commissioners adopted a formula that slightly favored Native communities. The Department of Justice and its experts had promoted a criterion that would apportion the amount of land according to the area needed to supply a tribal community's daily needs. The commission, however, opted for an older more culturally based theory that viewed land use in terms of a Native people's way of life.[33] They also acknowledged that some of the lands claimed by the Indians were used less intensively, but this, it was determined, did not detract from their usefulness to the Indians.[34]

Several types of cases came before the ICC regarding land valuation. If, for instance, aboriginal land had been taken without any compensation whatsoever, the injury to the Indians was clear. There only remained the task of ascertaining the fair market value of the land at the time of the taking. But what if the land was taken and the full price had never been paid by the government, or as was more frequently the case, what if the price agreed upon had been too low? This latter type case, which usually came to the commission under the "unconscionable consideration" clause of the ICCA, posed a serious problem. How was the commission to determine an award under those circumstances? In *Osage Nation of Indians v. United States*,[35] the commissioners devised a strategy that required Native communities to show that the difference between the fair market value of the land at the time of the taking and the amount paid to the Indians was "very gross" before recovery could be had. The difference between the two prices, said, the court, had to be sufficiently large to be considered truly unconscionable. In fact, the commission never formally established any precise rules concerning the difference between the sale price and the fair market value. However, over the years "few agreements were deemed unconscionable if the market value, as determined by the commission, was not at least double the price."[36]

The "very gross" standard used by the commission was terribly imprecise. Indeed, some commentators have argued that to "impose such a requirement is entirely inconsistent with the intent of the policy to compensate *all* proved claims" (emphasis in original).[37] In analyzing the problems inherent in this test, Sandra Danforth, for instance, concluded that in adhering to this standard, "the Commission [felt] it must deal with questions of payment in terms of an ill—but restrictively—defined moral basis, rather than on a more straightforward consideration of equity."[38] The ambiguity of the "very gross" criteria resulted in a number of commission decisions being appealed to the Court of Claims. Despite the commission's clinging to this narrow interpretation of "unconscionable," the Court of Claims occasionally found that its institutional conscience was easily shocked, thereby facilitating a somewhat greater Indian recovery.[39]

The third and final phase of a claims hearing was referred to as the *offset phase*. Once the commission found the federal government liable and assessed the value of the damages to which an aboriginal nation was entitled, it then had to determine if there were any offsets to be deducted from the award. As noted earlier, Congress probably would not have passed the ICCA without an offset provision, since there was great concern among lawmakers that the total amount to be paid on Indian claims could be of astronomical proportions. As John White noted, "It's as if the government was expressing a willingness to correct the error of its ways—providing the effort wasn't too costly."[40]

Offsets included any funds, property, or services given to or expanded gratuitously for the benefit of a Native community by the federal government. The government's rationalization was that if "Indians had received proper compensation for their lands initially they would not have needed subsequent gratuities."[41] Offsets were therefore viewed as part of the price that the U.S. paid for the land. This was nothing more than a legal fiction, of course, but like the legal fiction of the "doctrine of discovery"—how does one "discover" an already inhabited land-base?—it had a profound and immediate impact upon the awards judgments Native peoples received.[42]

The ICCA did, however, exclude certain types of governmental expenditures from falling within the offset category. Money spent to relocate a Native people from one place to another at the request of the federal government did not qualify as an offset. Nor were agency or other administrative, educational, health, or highway expenditures included. In addition, most of the appropriations given to aboriginal communities under the Indian Reorganization Act of 1934 were also excluded.[43] In their final report in 1978, the commissioners pointed out that the act actually "eliminated for offset purposes about one-fourth of the more than fifty categories of gratuities."[44] The key to determining if a gratuity qualified as an offset was predicated upon whether the negotiations between the Native nation and the U.S. "in good conscience [warranted] such action."[45] The phrase "in good conscience" is significant.

The burden of identifying what constituted gratuitous offsets was extremely difficult. Most of the work in this area was handled by the Indian Tribal Claims branch of the General Accounting Office, though after 1965 the task was assigned to the General Services Administration. These governmental agencies were charged with making exhaustive searches of tribal records, invoices, vouchers, and accounts that sometimes dated back more than a hundred years. The paperwork involved frequently overwhelmed the agency's small bureaucratic staff that was charged with making these determinations. In 1976, the ICC reported that its records had been combined into thirty-nine volumes, each averaging about 500 pages. And what was the ultimate purpose of these detailed endeavors?—to minimize the amount of money that the federal government was required to pay to Native nations for past transgressions.

These three phases formed the obstacle-laden path that indigenous nations had to take in order to have their grievances redressed. Three separate and difficult phases had to be navigated—the title phase, the land valuation phase, and, finally, the offset phase. There was, moreover, one additional hearing—a gathering at which the commission decided the expenses and attorney's fees that would be allowed. The entire process, of course, once it had been completed, was subject to an appeals process to the Court of Claims. The appeals process not only lengthened the time period required before tribal nations received their award, if they were entitled to one, but was quite costly.

The right of appeal to the Court of Claims was particularly important to Native nations during the early years of the commission's existence. Despite the fact that Congress had attempted to provide a broad forum for the handling of Native claims, the commission construed its functions narrowly during its embryonic days in existence. Because of this, the Court of Claims stepped forward to assume a leadership role in bringing about what it thought to be the original intent of Congress. This became quite apparent in two of the commission's earlier decisions that were appealed to the Court of Claims. In the first of these cases, *Osage Nation v. United States*,[46] the court announced that it intended to meticulously examine the fact findings in the cases it received on appeal. In particular, the court noted that it would look to see if (1) the commission's findings of facts were supported by substantial evidence, and (2) whether the commission's conclusions of law were valid and supported by the findings of facts.[47] Anticipating possible criticism of this position, the court noted that the commission's jurisdiction did "not embrace matters of a technical or highly specialized character." In any event, the Court of Claims possessed as much expertise as did the commission so that its judicial scrutiny was entirely warranted.[48]

The Elusive Evidentiary Problem

The criticism by the Court of Claims of the commission's fact-finding performance was of considerable importance. There were several important factors that contributed to the success or lack thereof that the commission experienced in obtaining evidence—expert witnesses, geographical inaccuracies, prejudice, and the Investigation Division.

The Role of Expert Witnesses. The very nature of the claims brought before the commission was such that they presented enormous problems of proof. The passage of time and the unavailability or inadequacy of evidence and documentation posed very real problems to the commission. Julian H. Steward of the University of Illinois noted, "Virtually no evidence presented in these cases can properly be called 'primary evidence,' 'first-hand knowledge,' or 'an eyewitness account.' "[49] Hence, it was necessary for the commission to rely heavily upon expert witnesses as an aid to determining the facts of a particular case. As a general rule, an ordinary witness is not permitted to state his or her opinion in a judicial proceeding. Testimony must be confined to those facts that have been personally observed. If the commission had to rely upon ordinary witnesses for its evidence, it could have shuttered its doors the day after it opened for business. Because of the impossibility of relying on observation, the commission had to turn to the use of "expert" witnesses to assist in the gathering and analysis of evidence even though "their testimony was really no more dependable than the fragments of oral, written, and physical information available to them."[50] Under the old rules of evidence, to qualify as an expert, a person had to employ his or her skill professionally or commercially. But by the time the ICC was under way the criterion for an expert had shifted and seemed to revolve around whether, on the subject involved, the tryier of fact could receive significant help from the person acting as an expert witness.[51] Thus, not all witnesses need fall within the category of professionals, though most did. As Helen Hornbeck Tanner, a frequent expert witness and a trained historian noted in a retrospective assessment, "I had been told that, in all the early cases brought before the Indian Claims Commission, the expert witnesses were eminent anthropologists with established reputations and connection with prominent educational institutions. Apparently, I was the first historian to turn up in court, and somehow a doctoral degree from Michigan proved to be a sufficient qualification to be accepted as an 'expert' on four Indian tribes. I wondered whether there were any specific 'credentials' for an expert witness."[52] Unfortunately for the commission, expert testimony was still new in the field. The Court of Claims had used anthropological testimony on only three occasions in the past and thus no precedents had been formally established. The role of the expert witness—whether they were ethnohistorians, archaeologists, or historians—was a new one.[53] But new or not, the commission had to aggressively move in the direction of using these experts extensively, for without their services the commissioners' task would have been extremely difficult.

The social scientists who appeared before the commission as trained experts did so in two distinct fashions. First, they presented opinions that were derived from a set of observable facts. The experts stated their perceptions of the facts and then presented opinions based upon those observable facts. This was no small charge. Experts in Indian claims cases seldom dealt with primary evidence, that is, raw data that could be perceived by the physical senses and that had measurable and distinctive characteristics.[54] Instead, secondary sources were frequently relied upon to determine the nature of aboriginal societies—informant's knowledge from parents or grandparents, contemporary observations of travelers, the views of Indian agents, among others. This evidence was presented according to the expert witnesses' personal perception of the situation.

The second approach used by expert witnesses was even more complicated. Under this method, the experts based their opinions on "an assumed state of acts not within [their] personal knowledge."[55] This testimony was usually predicated on a hypothetical question in which the truth of the facts was assumed. The expert witness was then asked to state his opinion on the basis of the hypothetical situation. Since so many of the grievances experienced by Native peoples revolved around transactions conducted generations earlier, this method of obtaining evidence from expert witnesses was frequently used. This type of evidence was accepted because the expert witness, unlike ordinary witnesses, was not bound by the hearsay rule.[56]

Most of the expert witnesses who appeared before the ICC were inexperienced. Few had testified before formal judicial bodies, and they often found themselves confronted with difficult and awkward situations. A number of problems resulted from the fact that neither the attorneys nor the expert witnesses spoke a common professional language or viewed concepts from the same perspective. Moreover, there were immense semantic difficulties. Attorneys spoke their own legal jargon, which was altogether distinct from the nomenclature of social scientists like anthropologists and ethnohistorians. Expert witnesses often found themselves forced to assume a deferential role both to the adjudicatory process and to the attorneys who largely controlled the claims arena. This is how Helen Tanner, a historian with a Ph.D. from the University of Michigan, described one of her early experiences as a witness: "When the federal government defense attorney began the cross-examination, I concentrated on giving a clear and accurate account of where tribal people lived and hunted and also where they fought the Americans, mostly in Ohio. After several minutes, when I thought that the grilling was over, the lawyer suddenly exclaimed, 'I move that all this testimony be stricken from the record as incompetent, irrelevant, and immaterial.' Though usually tolerant, I have a short fuse when it comes to personal honor and integrity. I did not hear past 'incompetent' and was instantly on my feet, pounding the table and shouting, 'I have never been called incompetent in all my life, and I am not about to take it here!' "[57]

Expert witnesses, of necessity, had to rely heavily upon Native informants and early historical sources because it was impossible to produce direct observations. Thus, the social scientists faced a daunting task in their efforts to translate complex testimony and fragmentary and dated historical records into the rigid legal demands of lawyers and the adversarial claims process.

Besides the frustrations experienced by expert witnesses, many anthropologists and ethnohistorians also experienced internal and ethical dilemmas. Some witnesses felt that social scientists should not get involved with partisan issues or take a position that might affect their relationship with a particular Native people. Some academics refused to get involved and were unavailable for testimony. In contrast, another group of scholars became so close to the particular indigenous people whom they had long studied that they felt morally and ethically bound to aid them in their quest for legal justice and economic and social well-being. These individuals were, therefore, reluctant to testify for the government. Most, however, probably would not have hesitated to go before the commission in support of the Native community they worked closely with.

Closely related though distinct from this group of social scientists were those anthropologists and ethnohistorians who essentially offered their services to the highest bidder. They became engaged by one side or the other and directed their scholarly endeavors to the group paying their fee.

Finally, there existed expert witnesses who believed their duty was simply to present the most accurate picture possible and let the trier of facts decide the case. These witnesses were committed to that elusive realm referred to as "value-free science." Since calling this type of witness to the stand could be somewhat risky in that their testimony might damage one's position, these allegedly value-free scientists were only rarely sought out. A competent attorney knows precisely how the expert he is calling is going to testify, and it would be folly to take chances on a witness who might enunciate a surprising position that could harm the attorney's case.

The difficulties arising from the use of expert witnesses in claims hearings posed serious problems, which were compounded by the kinds of evidence used in the proceedings. Getting immersed in the nature of evidence is a fairly dry and pedantic adventure. There are several types of evidence admissible:

1. Any official letter, paper, document, map, or record in the possession of any officer, department, court, or committee of Congress that can support an Indian claim so long as it is relevant to the proof of the claim.

2. Evidence that is admissible under either statutes of the U.S. or the rules of evidence of federal courts, as well as relevant portions of depositions or transcripts of testimony from other trials in federal courts to which natives are a party.
3. Contemporaneous statements by authorized government representatives and official reports, records, and statements by Indians that were recorded in minutes of councils with government representatives.
4. Materials and documents relating to events prior to the signing of a treaty with a Native nation, as well as those accords negotiated subsequent to it.
5. Testimony of natives about their tribal history when it was corroborated by other evidence.
6. Testimony of expert witnesses to interpret documents and materials.[58]

Although these categories appear to be rather broad, the quality of admitted evidence often had limitations. We have already referred to the problem of the advanced age of much of the data. Many aboriginal claims were over one hundred years old, and oftentimes germane materials had been lost or were in such poor condition as to not be useful. As there were usually few, if any, living witnesses to the events under consideration, the fragmentary documentary record was all that was available.

Geographical inaccuracies are the second factor that contributed to the struggles by Native peoples to mount their evidentiary arguments. As the Court of Claims noted in *Confederated Tribes of Warm Springs Reservation v. U.S.*,[59] historic accounts "often speak in general terms inasmuch as their compilers were seldom versed in geography; they also speak with inexactitude on the nature of the use and occupancy by various tribes." In a case involving the Yakima tribe, the boundaries of the disputed area did not fit within the language of the treaty that governed this nation's cession of land.[60] According to the court, the surveyor's markings and notes taken six years after the 1855 treaty were uncertain as to the location of the mouth of the river, and this location was crucial to the amount of land credited to the Indians. "Since the maps are but imprecise sketches with scanty nomenclature and markings, they do not provide certain guidance," said the court.[61] Nevertheless, it was determined that the ICC was in the better position to interpret the 1855 map, and thus its reading of the cartographic record was accepted over that of the Yakima's. The court decided that since it could not precisely determine the location it would still draw the boundary line to exclude the land claimed by the Indians. This was not an uncommon practice.

Prejudice is a third limitation that affected the quality of evidence. The historical materials examined had in almost every case been written by non-natives. Hence, they were frequently written in prose that reflected the ethnocentric mindset of the chronicler, and only rarely presented an indigenous perspective on the events in questions. Orality was the dominant means through which much indigenous history was retained. And while oral evidence could be introduced in claims proceedings, it had to be corroborated by documentary evidence, evidence which usually came from non-native sources. In *Pueblo de Zia v. U.S.*, for example, the U.S., as appellee, went so far as to argue that oral testimony was "literally worthless and was justifiably *not given any weight* by the Commission."[62] The Court of Claims held, however, that oral evidence was entitled to "some" weight and could not be completely ignored or discarded.[63] Thus, securing reliable historical evidence was a major hazard for both Native nations, expert witnesses, and the ICC.

The Investigation Division. Many of the problems plaguing the commissioners in their attempt to deal with evidentiary issues were self-imposed. Although a number of the difficulties inherent in dealing with aged evidence were not easily resolvable, some issues could have been minimized had the commission made better use of its Investigation Division (ID). Section 13 of the ICCA anticipated the evidentiary problem and permitted the commissioners to establish an investigative arm. The act, however, did not mandate that every claim be referred to the ID; rather, the commissioners were authorized to exercise their discretion in deciding whether to refer a claim to the ID.

Originally, the commission created little more than a skeletal outline for the division. It was to be composed of a chief investigator and a single staff attorney. When the division's first chief left, he was not replaced. Instead, the commissioners began to assign members of their own legal staff as attorney-investigators. Most of the ID's intended functions were simply abandoned. Indeed, the division, with no staff positions, did little more than mail out inquiries to the various Native nations. The commission had decided early on that it would not serve as a primary fact-gathering agency. Rather, it let the opposing attorneys obtain the necessary evidence. The commission, by its own volition, decided to relegate itself to an adjudicatory body performing few investigatory functions.

Occasionally, however, the ID was moved to act. In a few instances, circumstances arose whereby Native communities came before the commission without legal counsel, and in a few situations the commissioners were faced with cases where for inexplicable reasons the tribe's attorney had resigned. These cases could proceed only if someone on the commission staff undertook the case for the tribe. Under these rare circumstances the ID was momentarily active.[64] The commissioners also called upon the ID if they felt that not all of the evidence in a particular case had been uncovered. Under these circumstances, the commissioners would either direct the respective attorneys to undertake a further investigation or instruct the ID to enter the case in the capacity of amicus curiae, otherwise known as a *friend of the court*.

Perhaps the greatest impediment to the full development and implementation of the ID was the opposition voiced by legal counsel. Most of the attorneys simply did not want to rely upon the findings of an independent agency. There was also the fear that use of an independent investigation division could prolong hearings. Attorneys might constantly object to the findings and seek to have them struck down. Arthur Watkins, a former commissioner, pointed out that our "experience is that the parties would take exception to whatever was reported unless it was in their favor. If they didn't approve of the investigation reports they would undoubtedly move to strike them from the record. All of these items would be time-consuming and could easily add another five to ten years to the life of the Commission."[65] Watkins went on to point out that there was little demand from the natives or their attorneys for information from "our very limited investigations. A few Indians have mentioned it to us recently, but when we have explained the situation to them they seemed to be satisfied."[66] The point was also raised that many natives opposed greater reliance upon the ID simply because it was a federal agency, and the level of distrust felt toward such units remained very high.

As a result of the unwillingness of the commissioners to fully staff and support the ID, notwithstanding Congress's intentions and the support of Secretary of Interior Harold Ickes, many commentators have suggested that this was a major shortcoming of the commission.[67] Testimony to this effect may be found in the occasional reprimands that the Court of Claims directed to the commission for its failure to maintain a high level of excellence in the investigative area.

John Vance, a former commissioner, argued for many years that greater emphasis should have been placed upon the role of the ID. He believed that *all* claims should have been referred to the division. Furthermore, Vance said that he would have authorized the ID to employ anthropologists, historians, ecologists, land appraisers, and any other personnel necessary to thoroughly complete an investigation. The ID, having concluded its search, would then submit all of the pertinent evidence to the commission for its decision. If the commissioners concluded that the findings were proper, then it would conduct a hearing where the interested parties could appear before the commission's final determination.[68] Vance's recommendations, however, were never fully implemented. The legal profession was simply too entrenched within the claims network, and it was unwilling to relinquish control over the investigation functions.

The unavailability of governmental fact-finding made claims litigation much more expensive for Native peoples because it put the burden of finding and paying for experts on them. Lieder and Page suggest that "the failure to establish an Investigation Division wasn't significant because of the possible impact on the quality of the presentation of Indian claims, but because of what it indicated about how the Commission would function. It might be called a Commission, but it would operate almost exclusively like a court."[69]

Administrative Problems

The burdens that confronted the ICC commissioners were not limited to politics, evidence, or inexperience. Administrative problems plagued the commission from its inception. The amount of work involved was enormous and would have overwhelmed anyone attempting to resolve indigenous grievances. An executive decision-making body of three was woefully insufficient to the daunting and ponderous workload. Not until 1967 did Congress add two additional members to the organization staff. The 1967 law also called for the creation of an Office of Chief Counsel to supervise the activities of the staff.

At this time a number of adjustments were made in an effort to make the commission's operation more efficient. Under the new rules only one commissioner was required to be present at a trial. This permitted the commissioners to increase the number of hearings, at least partially expediting the time frame for completion of the commission's workload.[70] Pre-trial conferences, previously held infrequently, were encouraged and were to be accompanied by several new procedures designed to shorten the length of trials. These steps helped to strip away the many peripheral issues the attorneys tended to insert into their pleadings. Facts could now be stipulated and the key issues identified, reducing trial time considerably.

In another attempt to streamline the administrative operations of the claims hearings, expert witnesses were required to submit their written testimony in advance of a hearing. This shortened trial time by eliminating the long and often rambling dissertations by the cadre of social scientists testifying for either a Native nation or the federal government. During the early 1960s Congress created a revolving fund by which to pay expert witnesses. Earlier it was not uncommon for expert witnesses to be hired by Native nations on a contingency fee basis, a process that had a tendency to cloud the credibility of the witnesses since "any potential expert who wishes to testify—whether for professional or financial reasons and who knows how the system works accepts an engagement with the understanding that his view should support the client who retains him."[71]

The revolving loan fund not only minimized the problem of potential witness bias, but it afforded a number of the more impoverished Native communities an opportunity to hire witnesses, a key benefit that had been beyond their financial capability in the past. The fund was originally set at $900,000 and provided for interest-bearing loans for Native nations that could not afford to employ witnesses. The loans were to be repaid out of the proceeds of any judgment a tribe might receive on its claim against the U.S. The Expert Assistance Loan Fund became operational in 1963 and was fully subscribed within a period of two years. By 1973 the fund had increased to $2.7 million.[72]

In 1959, former Senator Arthur V. Watkins of Utah was appointed to the commission. Watkins, who had never been viewed as a champion of aboriginal rights—he had, in fact, played a central role in the development of the termination policy that was then in effect—did introduce some significant administrative alterations to the commission's operations. Previously, Native and government lawyers would decide when hearings should be held. Watkins created a regular calendar that was used to schedule hearings, placing control of the commission's most important work back into the hands of the commissioners. Continuances, a practice that had been badly abused, were to be tightly controlled and granted only in dire emergencies. As Robert Barker noted, "In the past, defendant [attorneys have] in several cases waited until the tribe has put out its evidence, only to ask for a long continuance to prepare its case-in-chief on the same issue. This not only departs from due process, but breeds delay and irresponsibility in the extreme."[73]

The issue of appeals also posed difficulties to indigenous claimants. During the commission's infancy, no appeal could be taken to the Court of Claims until all three phases of the hearing process had been completed, which created a hardship for many Native nations: they were required to wait until the proceedings concluded before filing their appeal. An appeal sometimes took an additional three years before the claim was settled. In 1960 Congress adopted an amendment that permitted the parties to initiate an interlocutory appeal (an appeal prior to the final judgment). The process eased the burden carried by the indigenous claimants.

A final procedural problem concerned the paucity of compromised settlements in Native claims cases, despite the fact that the 1946 act provided for such settlements. The Department of Justice, however, never embraced compromise settlements and failed to initiate any such settlement agreements.[74] Assistant Attorney General Edwin L. Weisl noted, "It is the long-standing policy of the Department of Justice in all cases in which money judgments are involved not to make settlement offers on its own, but to await them from the other side."[75] Congress was clearly displeased as lawmakers felt that compromised settlements could shorten the life of the commission, and so it amended the ICCA, stipulating that if a claim was not ready by its calendar date, with an allowance for a maximum of one year for continuance, it was to be dismissed with prejudice unless a compromise was in the process of being negotiated.

Thus, by the 1960s the commission began to place greater emphasis on compromised settlements. Under the new system, compromises had to receive the approval of the Native groups involved before they could be considered by the commission. This procedure was incorporated to prevent Native governments from bringing suit against the federal government if at a later date they became dissatisfied with their settlement.

Tribal nations had good reason to be suspicious of negotiated settlements during the early days of the commission's operations. In one case involving California's Native peoples, a compromise of some magnitude was negotiated involving approximately 500 distinctive aboriginal groups and entailing about 70 percent of the land in the state. This was one of the largest single cases ever to come before the ICC. When the natives were asked their views on the arrangement, a number were quite dissatisfied. Sandra Danforth described the commission's antics in its effort to reach a compromised solution thus:

> The Commission made a formal decision to submit a settlement to the claimant, Pitt River Indians of California (one component of the "Indians of California") in a meeting of the tribe at Altruas (California). The Bureau of Indian Affairs prepared a list of tribal members and sent out notifications. The meeting rejected the settlement. Thereafter, admittedly upon the urging of the attorney for the Pitt River Indians, the Commission changed its decision in order to provide for a mail ballot for those who had not voted at the meeting. Incidentally, the proposition submitted by mail was different from the proposition submitted at the meeting, and the mail ballots were sent to 100 or more people than were on the list to be invited to the meeting. The Bureau then announced that the total ballot narrowly approved the settlement.[76]

In an effort to crystallize its support of compromise, the commission spelled out its support of such settlements in *Omaha Tribe v. U.S.*: "Indian claims, many of which originated more than a century ago, are difficult to prepare for presentation to the Commission, and it is almost as difficult to prepare a defense against them. Then there are the matters of trial, preparation of briefs, considered by the Commission, rendering of judgments, possible appeals, perhaps retrial if the Commission is reversed, or at least additional hearings, etc. And these activities are time-consuming and require large expenditures of money." The court went on to note that the most unfortunate part was the long delay in bringing claims to a conclusion. "Many of the original petitioners . . . as well as some of the attorneys involved, have passed on to their eternal rewards before their claims were finally adjudicated. The legal maxim, that 'justice delayed is often justice denied,' seems appropriate at this point. With all this in mind we urge that more compromises be entered into in situations where they are possible of accomplishment."[77]

The commission's preference for negotiated settlements was an important step that helped to expedite the resolutions of some aboriginal claims. Fortunately, Congress and the commission were prudent enough to require tribal approval such that the compromises better reflected the needs and desires of the Native claimants and were not just the tools by which attorneys could bring a case to a close and collect a hefty fee.

The ICC was operational for thirty-two years. Thirty-two years filled with many failures and some successes. For many Native nations, the ICCA was little more than a hollow and largely unjust experience. Their hopes for bona fide, satisfactory, and lasting settlements were not achieved because of the multitude of fact-based, procedural-based, and narrow interpretive commission interpretations and findings. Many Native nations also experienced internal divisiveness as a result of the claims process, with many being divided into contending political and economic segments during the long years of litigation.[78]

Economically progressive tribal citizens usually wanted the claims settled quickly. More culturally oriented adopted a more patient profile and demanded a full accounting of the unethical and sometimes patently illegal acts that had been committed against their nations, their resources, and their meager remaining lands by agencies of the federal government. More important, and not surprisingly, the more staunchly cultural Native citizens aspired not for monetary settlements but felt morally and legally entitled to call for the return of their land, notwithstanding the ICC's rejection of that possibility. Their calls for land were unheeded at the time but remained a driving force among Native nations. In fact, land restitution was a principal factor animating not only the Oglala Lakota activists and their allies during the Wounded Knee takeover in 1973[79] but also a number of eastern Native nations in Maine (see chapter 6), New York, Massachusetts, South Carolina, and others who took advantage of historic laws, treaties, a changed political landscape, and their own sharp memories to push hard for an actual return of land, federal recognition, and compensation.

Many commentators have failed to grasp the essential nature of indigenous legal claims. The ICC's decisions did not extinguish the treaty rights of Native peoples. Indeed, the commission never examined most of these rights. According to Vine Deloria, Jr., all the commission accomplished, in the cases where the Native peoples were successful, was to provide some compensation to tribal nations for the "real-estate-contract aspect of the treaties." The issue of political status and sovereign rights of the tribes remained largely unresolved. As Deloria went on to note, rather than "finally settling the Indian claims against the United States, the Indian Claims Commission [worked] merely to clear out the underbrush and allow the claims created by the forced political and economic dependency during the last century to emerge."[80]

There were some positive results from the ICCA and the commission's decisions (see table 3). Collectively, the commission and the federal government paid to Native nations slightly over $800 million through 274 awards, not nearly as much as they might have received but an economic stimulus nonetheless. A total of 204 claims were dismissed. The largest award, some $35 million, went to the Kiowa, Comanche, and Apache of Oklahoma in 1974. As meager as these funds were in comparison to what was irretrievably lost, they were desperately needed and contributed to tribal economic development. Furthermore, the commission's activities raised the consciousness of segments of the American public with regard to aboriginal peoples and their distinctive histories and intergovernmental relations with states and the federal government.

Table 3 Indian Claims Commission: Fiscal Year Totals of Dockets Completed and Awards

	Number of Dockets Completed, 1947–1978				
Fiscal Year	By Dismissals	By Awards	Number of Awards	Total Amount of Awards (in dollars)	Cumulative Total of Awards (in dollars)
1947	—	—	—	—	—
1948	—	—	—	—	—
1949	7	—	—	—	—
1950	12	—	—	—	—
1951	7	2	2	3,489,843.58	3,489,843.58
1952	8	3	3	2,998,220.02	6,488,063.60
1953	7	—	—		6,488,063.60
1954	8	1	1	927,668.04	7,415,731.64
1955	4	1	1	864,107.55	8,279,839.19
1956	1	3	3	1,515,494.95	9,795,334.14
1957	12	1	1	433,013.60	10,228,347.74
1958	10	4	4	6,860,238.54	17,088,586.28
1959	12	2	1	3,288,974.90	20,377,561.18
1960	7	13	8	21,588,007.51	41,965,658.69
1961	5	5	5	14,926,255.11	56,891,823.80
1962	5	2	3	18,063,859.65	74,955,683.45
1963	9	8	9	18,319,187.20	93,247,870.65
1964	7	9	11	15,796,254.69	109,071,125.34
1965	7	27	17	57,019,352.93	166,090,478.27
1966	2	12	11	38,701,569.58	204,792,047.85
1967	2	7	6	21,497,766.74	226,289,814.59
1968	3	23	16	43,576,732.73	269,866,547.32
1969	23	24	20	32,025,817.01	301,892,364.33
1970	2	14	13	44,254,099.43	346,146,463.76
1971	4	20	16	46,621,560.61	392,768,024.37
1972	11	14	10	33,078,111.56	425,846,135.93

continued

1973	11	32	18	40,837,122.35	466,683,258.28
1974	11	24	20	46,409,564.06	513,092,822.34
1975	3	9	7	35,945,458.57	549,038,280.91
1976	—	15	11	63,055,867.25	612,094,148.16
July–Sept. 1976	—	5	4	27,825,465.90	639,919,614.06
1977	—	11	12	67,604,270.07	707,523,884.13
1978	4	31	24	110,648,722.51	818,172,606.64
Total:	204	342	274		

Source: Indian Claims Commission, Final Report (Washington, DC: Government Printing Office, 1978).

Additionally, the ethnohistorical data accumulated during the thirty-two years of the commission's existence contributed significantly to an understanding of indigenous–non-indigenous relations, and a new field of study, ethnohistory, was established. In 1954 ethnohistorians then created an academic journal, *Ethnohistory*, which provided an important outlet for some of the incisive scholarship generated during these and later years.[81] In 1955 an entire issue was devoted to Native claims. Indeed, as Christian McMillen indicated, this period of time provided Native nations as well as society at large with a deeper history of indigenous peoples and their unique political and proprietary relations with the U.S., which would not have been available in the absence of the ICC, and the ICC became a model for other nations in their dealings with indigenous peoples.[82] These were not insignificant accomplishments from the federal government's perspective. The concluding comments in the commission's final report in 1978 provide an interesting commentary on these controversial years.

> This struggle for perpetuating Indian culture and settling tribal claims has run through American history for almost 150years. Possibly it will continue for another century or until America finds an accommodation with these internal wards.

> There is no easy solution to this problem or maybe no solution at all. For, at best, the existence of a tribal society within the borders of a highly individualistic and technical culture is tenuous. It is not that the tribal society materially threatens the technological way of life, but that it presents a moral threat to settled myths. It keeps an unpleasant past alive and presents challenging questions for the future. Perhaps it is time to appreciate that the triumphs of the frontier period were mitigated by the sordid dealings with the Indians. . . . The Indian Claims Commission went a long step in this direction [righting old wrongs] but could offer only money. Other remedies to the unresolved problems between the Government and the Indians may now be found.[83]

From an indigenous perspective, however, Leubben's closing comments more accurately describe the ICC years:

> The way Indian land claims were litigated in the ICC is a scandal of historic proportions and sobering failure of advocacy. A careful analysis of the history of the ICC casts a harsh light on the American myth of a political system devoted to the highest standards of justice and fairness under law. It demonstrates how illegitimate political goals and priorities can be masked by legal procedure. In the end, the ICC significantly met the needs and achieved the objectives of the dominant culture at great cost to Native Americans. The ICC established a body of Indian law that is contrary not only to ordinary US constitutional and property law, but also to established norms of international human rights. It contributed to the deeply flawed nature of what is called in the United States, "federal Indian law." This reality has left Native Americans with countless compelling, unresolved moral claims, and little hope of satisfactory resolution in US courts or political forums.[84]

6. THE RESURGENCE OF EASTERN NATIVES

The Maine Indian Claims Settlement Act of 1980

BEFORE THE 1970S, with a few aboriginal exceptions, Native nations living east of the Mississippi were virtually ignored by federal officials, state governments, and the majority of non-Indians. This naiveté or benign neglect of Native nations and their relation to their historic lands was forever altered beginning in 1975 when an important federal appellate case—*Joint Tribal Council of the Passamaquoddy Tribe et al. v. Morton et al.*—was handed down.[1] This decision, involving the Passamaquoddy, Penobscot, and Houlton band of Maliseet peoples of Maine, initiated a third flank of indigenous land claim attacks that eventually included a number of other eastern Native nations: the Narragansett of Rhode Island; the Wampanoag of Gay Head, Massachusetts; the Schagticoke and Western Pequot of Connecticut; the Oneida, St. Regis Mohawk, and Cayuga of New York; the Catawba of South Carolina; the Chitimacha of Louisiana; the Seminole and Miccosukee of Florida; and the Pamunkey of Virginia.[2] (See table 1 for a listing of a number of these distinctive claims.) The claims of these indigenous peoples had not been served by the Indian Claims Commission because their land losses had occurred not because of federal action but as a result of actions by individual states, cities, or individuals.

These cases, with exception of the Chitimachas', originated in the thirteen colonies after they achieved statehood. Those governments "dealt directly—and, it is asserted, illegally—with Indian nations during the early history of the Republic."[3] The Native nations in these cases had argued, and continued to insist, that the states had unlawfully purchased or otherwise secured title to much of their aboriginal territory in direct violation of the Trade and Intercourse Act of 1790. This act had stated that any land transactions involving aboriginal peoples and other parties had to be supervised and approved by the federal government. Furthermore, this law, as the court held in *Passamaquoddy*, protected all indigenous nations, even those that were unacknowledged or not federally recognized, as were the three Native nations of Maine at the time of their lawsuit.[4]

The most important difference between eastern Indian land-claims cases and those heard in the Indian Depredations arena, the Court of Claims, and the Indian Claims Commission is that under the Trade and Intercourse Act, Native nations could, in fact, sue, negotiate, or seek direct presidential action to have some portion of their lost lands restored. The Narragansett people of Rhode Island were the first eastern nation to have their land claim formally settled. In 1978 Congress enacted P.L. 95–395,[5] a negotiated accord between the Narragansett people, the State of Rhode Island, and the town of Charlestown, accomplished with the direct consultation and consent of President Jimmy Carter. The act restored to the Narragansett 1,800 acres of land —900 of which came from the state and 900 of which were purchased from landholders by the federal government. Additionally, a $3.5 million settlement fund was set up in the U.S. Treasury to implement the act's provisions. As part of the arrangement, all other land claims by the Narragansett were formally extinguished.[6]

Other eastern land claims cases have since been settled—the Mashantucket Pequot of Connecticut in 1983; the Seneca nation of New York in 1990; and the Mohegan of Connecticut in 1994—but some others are still being contested. A particularly bitter case involves the Oneida people of New York and their sister communities in Wisconsin and New London, Ontario. The three communities initiated their lawsuit against two counties in New York in 1970 for some 6 million acres.[7] They alleged the lands had been taken in treaties with the State of New York between 1785 and 1846 in violation of the Trade and Intercourse Act. A three-decade-long-long legal battle found the Oneida successful in their land pursuit in two early Supreme Court cases—*Oneida v. Oneida* (1974)[8] and *Oneida v. Oneida* (1985)[9]—but ultimately defeated in a third High Court ruling in 2005, *City of Sherrill v. Oneida Indian Nation.*[10]

In the third case, the city of Sherrill had sought to evict the Oneida for nonpayment of taxes on land the nation had recently reacquired. The Oneida argued that the repurchased land constituted Indian Country and could not be taxed, but the Supreme Court rejected their argument, holding that the Oneida's land claims in New York were barred by the passage of time.[11] *Sherrill* has established a devastating precedent that implicates all other similarly situated Native land claims that are rooted in historic wrongs against Native nations.

The largest and, arguably, most substantial victory by eastern Native communities was the effort by the three[12] small Native nations of Maine to recover some of their lands and secure other important rights. The Department of Justice, in fact, early in the land claims process characterized this case as "potentially the most complex litigation ever brought in the Federal courts with social and economic impacts without precedent and incredible potential litigation costs to all parties."[13]

Historical Background

The Passamaquoddy, Penobscot, and Maliseet were strong societies in the colonial period and had consented to fight alongside the Americans in the Revolutionary War. In 1777 George Washington had sent a representative to negotiate an alliance with the leaders of these nations. In the ensuing accord, ratified on June 23, 1777, the Americans pledged to protect the lands and to provide supplies to the natives if they agreed to assist the Americans in their war against the British.

After the war's conclusion, the newly formed federal government reneged on many of the treaty provisions it had made with the Native nations, essentially abandoning the protectorate position it had pledged to maintain. The first Trade and Intercourse Act, enacted by Congress in 1790—originally limited to a two-year time period but renewed several times and finally codified in 1834[14]—it was designed broadly to regulate trade with Native peoples, and it prohibited the unauthorized purchase of tribal lands by individuals or states. Unscrupulous non-Indian traders and unauthorized land purchases were exacerbating tensions with Native peoples, who were finding their proprietary rights and properties often subject to non-Indian confiscation or exploitation, a situation that frequently led to hostilities.

The act expressly prohibited all Native land sales that had not been approved by the federal government, but as Jack Campisi has pointed out, this presented significant problems to the thirteen original states as they claimed preemption (first purchase) rights to tribal lands within their borders.[15] The 1790 law provided no opportunity for states to negotiate with Native peoples. This led to the first modification of the act in 1793: it maintained the prohibition against unauthorized purchases of Indian land but also forced states to explicitly declare their interests in Native lands so that federal officials could make sure they were present for any future transaction.

Both before and *after* the Trade and Intercourse Acts were approved, the Commonwealth of Massachusetts—which then had jurisdiction over what later became Maine—negotiated six treaties with the Penobscot: on August 30, 1786; September 29, 1794; August 8, 1796; June 29, 1818; and two on August 17, 1820—one with Massachusetts, the other with Maine. The Passamaquoddy and Maliseet participated in only one treaty with the state—(the September 29, 1794, accord.

The September 29, 1794, treaty, featuring all three Native nations and Massachusetts, was both a land cession and land reservation treaty between state officials and tribal representatives, with the Passamaquoddy surrendering all but 23,000 acres of their "right, title, interest, claim or demand of any land or lands, lying and being within the said Commonwealth of Massachusetts; and also engaging to be peaceable and quiet inhabitants . . . without molesting any other of the settlers of the Commonwealth."[16] There was, however, no direct federal involvement or oversight in these or subsequent treaty negotiations; a clear violation of the main provisions of the Intercourse Act.

The Claims Begin

In the 1950s, John Stevens, a Passamaquoddy political leader, received some important historical documents—copies of early treaties, letters from George Washington, and so on,—which convinced him to more fully investigate his ancestors' land title. As he researched the treaty and statutory history of his people, he realized that they and the other tribal nations of Maine had been illegally deprived of title and jurisdictional control to much of their aboriginal lands. Initially, Stevens pursued a negotiated resolution in the hope that some of the land would be returned, but these efforts proved unsuccessful. The Passamaquoddy then sought legal advice and eventually engaged the services of Thomas N. Tureen, a recent law school graduate.[17]

Tureen, later joined by Francis J. O'Toole, vigorously researched the historical, legal, and political background of the Passamaquoddy people's relationship with the British, the colonies, and the State of Maine and determined that they and the Penobscot had a bona fide land claim against Maine, concluding that "it is apparent that the State of Maine cannot claim the nonexistence of the Passamaquoddy's as a basis for usurping the paramount power of the federal government" and "consent by the federal government, therefore, must be found for the making of the 1794 treaty by Massachusetts with the Passamaquoddy Tribe."[18]

Thus in February 1972 the Passamaquoddy requested that the commissioner of the Bureau of Indian Affairs bring a lawsuit on their behalf against the State of Maine under the Trade and Intercourse Act. On March 24 the commissioner did, in fact, recommend to the solicitor of the Department of the Interior (DOI) that the lawsuit be instituted. He wanted the action initiated prior to July 18, 1972, at which time the suit would be barred by a special statute of limitations for actions seeking damages resulting from trespass on restricted

Indian lands. Despite the commissioner's urging, the DOI refused to file on the tribe's behalf on the grounds that as a non-federally recognized Native nation, the Passamaquoddy had no trust relationship with the United States and therefore the federal government was under no obligation to sue the state on their behalf. Insisting that it had not reached this decision "lightly" and that it was well aware that its action would most likely prevent the nation from pursuing its claim against the state in federal court, the department maintained that it was constrained by the fact that the federal government had never negotiated any treaties with the tribe and thus no trust obligation had been established. "We are," said the department's officials, "led inescapably to conclude that the Tribe's proper legal remedy should be sought elsewhere."[19]

The Passamaquoddy, frustrated by this decision, filed a lawsuit against the federal government, identifying the secretary of Interior, Rogers C. B. Morton, the attorney general of the U.S., and the U.S. attorney for the district of Maine as defendants. Maine was allowed to intervene as a party defendant. After hearing all the evidence, Judge Edward T. Gignoux emphatically disagreed with the federal government's primary contention that there was no trust relationship between the parties. He stated, "In the only decided cases to treat this issue, the Court of Claims has, in a series of decisions during the last ten years, definitively held that the Nonintercourse Act imposes a trust or fiduciary obligation on the United States to protect land owned by all Indian tribes covered by the statute,"[20] which included the Passamaquoddy people, even though they had never been explicitly recognized by the federal government.

The U.S. promptly appealed this ruling, but in December 1975 the Court of Appeals for the First Circuit issued a unanimous decision affirming Gignoux's opinion. Judge Levin H. Campbell, held that the Nonintercourse Act did, in fact, apply to the Passamaquoddy; that a trust relationship had therefore been established; and that Congress had never expressly terminated its trustee role vis-à-vis the tribal nation. And since it had been stipulated that the Passamaquoddy were a bona fide "tribe" in both a racial and cultural sense, there was no question in the judge's mind that it existed as a "distinctly Indian" community.[21]

After extended delays, the Department of Justice concluded that the Native nations did, indeed, have valid claims for the territory they had lost as a result of Maine's actions. The validity of the claims rested upon several key elements: (1) that the claimants were bona fide "tribes" within the meaning of the Trade and Intercourse Act; (2) that the land claimed by the Indians was covered under the act as "tribal" land; (3) that the U.S. had never consented to the tribe's alienation or transference of their title to the state; and (4) that the trust relationship between the federal government and the natives had never been formally disavowed by the U.S.

The State of Maine countered with its own set of arguments, namely, (1) that the Trade and Intercourse Act had never been intended to apply to the thirteen original colonies once they had achieved statehood; (2) that, even if it did apply, the Indians had transferred title of their lands to Maine before the Intercourse Act became effective in 1790; and (3) that in ratifying the Articles of Separation, by which Maine was separated from Massachusetts and admitted to the Union in 1820, Congress impliedly approved all the treaties Massachusetts had negotiated up to that time.[22]

After this series of events, three methods of settlement were open to the contending parties. First, there could be an out-of-court settlement, negotiated between the federal government's executive branch—subject to congressional approval—and the Native peoples. Second, Congress could act directly, without negotiating with the tribes. This would serve to extinguish all aboriginal title asserted by the tribes and would retroactively ratify all the invalid treaties through which tribal land had been transferred to the state. Third, the land conflict could be settled in federal court. The Department of Justice was particularly opposed to this method, characterizing the Maine case as "potentially the most complex litigation ever brought in the Federal courts with social and economic impacts without precedent and incredible potential costs to all parties."[23] This conclusion was based on the sheer enormity of the claim, the number of people living in the disputed area, and the nature of the legal issues involved.

The tribes, Maine, and the federal government eventually decided that a negotiated settlement would be the most appropriate method for resolving the dispute for several reasons: the process would be less time-consuming, it would allow for greater flexibility, and it guaranteed direct participation by all parties involved. The possibility of protracted litigation was particularly unnerving to the state, local governments, and non-Indian landowners: real estate markets had been paralyzed, insurance companies refused to insure property titles, municipal bond sales had stalled, and unemployment had increased.[24]

The Penobscot's and Passamaquoddy's original claim was for 12.5 million acres of land—approximately two-thirds of the State of Maine—and $25 billion in damages and accumulated rents. It quickly became apparent, however, that the federal government would never support such a vast claim, regardless of its validity. After negotiations with federal officials, the two Native nations reduced their claims to a targeted area ranging from between 4 to 8 million acres.[25]

Recognizing the potential for significant federal liability as a result of the land claim, President Jimmy Carter on March 12, 1977, appointed a special representative, William B. Gunter, a Georgia supreme court justice, to study the case and propose recommendations. Gunter had planned to retire from the court at the end of March, but he accepted the assignment as a favor to President Carter, with whom he had been lifetime friends.[26]

On July 15, 1977, Judge Gunter submitted his recommendations to Carter. In essence, he proposed the following:

1. The immediate return of 100,000 acres of land to the two tribes by the state, with the U.S. being the trustee of the Indians' territory.
2. An appropriation of $25 million for the use of the tribal nations, the money to be administered by the Department of the Interior.

3. Full federal recognition of both Native communities, thus making them eligible for all BIA benefits.
4. Long-term options of purchasing, at fair market value, an additional 400,000 acres of land with the assistance of the secretary of the Interior granted to the tribes.
5. Congressional extinguishment of all aboriginal title of the two tribes in Maine and all claims under the Trade and Intercourse Act.

Gunter suggested that if the tribes did not consent to the proposal, Congress should step in and extinguish all aboriginal title except those held in public ownership by the state. The tribes could then pursue their claim to the state-owned land, securing the land if they won and nothing if they lost. If Maine refused to agree to the proposal, $25 million would be appropriated to the tribes for their use, title to all privately owned land would be extinguished, and the tribes could pursue their claims to state-controlled lands in federal court.[27]

The recommendations drew a decidedly mixed reaction from the parties. President Carter confidently expressed the view that Gunter's proposal was "fair, judicious, and wise," Maine was reluctant to embrace it fully, and the two tribes felt it was simply unacceptable. Negotiations continued between tribal leaders and their attorney and a White House working group, which included representatives from the Office of Management and Budget and the solicitor of the Interior Department. Several months later, in February 1978, an agreement was reached with the two tribes that involved a partial settlement of the claim and the provision of federal services.[28]

A joint memorandum of understanding was formally released on February 10 by the White House. According to the agreement, the federal government would pursue a legislative package that would give the tribes $25 million in exchange for the Indians allowing other claims to be extinguished, thus clearing title to over 9 million acres of the original 12.5 claimed. The other 3.3 million acres remained in dispute, and other issues, such as the tribes' expectation that they could still receive state services, remained unresolved. But all claims against householders, counties and municipalities, and small business owners would also be cleared under the joint agreement.[29]

In March 1979 representatives from the major parties met at the Interior Department. Each side and its respective legal team agreed to review the draft legislation prepared by the department's solicitor and reconvene in a few weeks with comments and suggestions. Even as these final negotiations were taking place, two court cases, *Bottomly v. Passamaquoddy Tribe*[30] and *State of Maine v. Dana*,[31] provided the tribal nations with solid support for their position as sovereign bodies. In *Bottomly*, the U.S. Court of Appeals for the First Circuit held that the Passamaquoddy tribe benefited from the doctrine of sovereign immunity and could not be sued without its express consent. In *Dana*, a decision by the Supreme Judicial Court of Maine, the court reaffirmed the 1975 *Passamaquoddy* decision, which had declared that the Maine tribes were entitled to federal protection and that their lands constituted "Indian Country," as that term was understood in federal law. As a result of that depiction, the state court held that the 1885 Major Crimes Act, an act that provided the federal government with jurisdiction over several selected crimes, prevented the State of Maine from exercising jurisdiction over the crime of arson, which had allegedly been committed by two Passamaquoddy members.

In March 1980 an agreement was tentatively reached by the negotiating parties. A month later, on April 3, Maine's governor, Joseph Brennan, signed into law the Maine Implementing Act. This act, however, dealt only with jurisdiction as it would apply to the tribes and the state, and its effectiveness was contingent on a second piece of legislation that still had to secure congressional approval and ratification. In June, Senators William Cohen of Maine and George Mitchell of South Dakota introduced S. 2829. Later that year, Representatives David Emery and Olympia Snowe introduced H.R. 7919.

During Senate hearings held in July it became apparent that S. 2829 was a far more flawed piece of legislation than the House version, and the decision was made to muster support for the

H.R. 7919. As hearings in the House of Representatives proceeded, it became evident to many that H.R. 7919 was not a perfect solution to this complicated claim, but it had the support of a majority of those in Congress, elected tribal officials, Maine's elected officials, and the paper companies.

But there was also resistance. It came mostly from more traditionally minded tribal members, who were supported by lawyers with the Indian Law Resource Center. Robert T. Coulter, the executive director of the center and counsel for the traditional tribal members, gave eloquent testimony against both H.R. 7919 and S. 2829.

Coulter contended that the bills were procedurally being moved too fast and that his Native clients had not had ample time to consider the complex issues. He also noted that while the Penobscot population numbered more than 1,500, only 395 of the tribe's members had actually cast votes on the proposed settlement. Furthermore, he stated that many of the tribe's members never received word that the referendum was being held; that the ballots had not been secret; and that there were no safeguards to prevent possible fraud or improper influence. One of the most damning factors, however, was that the bill (S. 2829) as finalized was "a new bill; it [was] not the same bill that was submitted to the referendum."[32]

Coulter continued, saying emphatically: "Let me be clear; there is no question about whether or not we can make our views known here; the question is whether the people of the Passamaquoddy Tribe and the Penobscot Nation have ever had a chance to fairly evaluate the legislation and fairly speak their minds about it, to fairly consent to it or reject it. We say we have not had that opportunity, and there is nothing that we can do here; there is nothing that we can submit to you that will change that."[33] Coulter also emphasized that the bills would leave the Native communities in an overly dependent position vis-à-vis the federal government, with the secretary of Interior maintaining too much discretionary authority over the money his office would be holding in trust for the tribes. Finally, Coulter and his clients feared that the bills allowed for far too much municipal and state interference in the internal affairs of the three Native communities.[34]

There were other voices of discontent with the final version of the legislation. Alexander Tallchief published a short essay in May 1980, just months before passage, in which he raised serious questions about the proposed settlement. He suggested that the tribes had missed an opportunity to dramatically strengthen their sovereign status and clarify their relationships with both Maine and the federal government. Tallchief argued that the three small nations had been favorably positioned to push for a treaty relationship with the United States and a sufficient land base with complete territorial jurisdiction.[35]

Instead, the proposed settlement, in Tallchief's view, had multiple flaws that would inhibit genuine indigenous self-determination. These included the following. First, that the tribes would actually have less sovereignty than other federally recognized tribes because of the prominent jurisdictional role Maine would have over some of their internal affairs. Second, although the secretary of Interior would receive $54.5 million to purchase land for the tribes, the time frame and conditions for such land transactions were far too vague. Third, since the settlement was in the form of a congressional act, Congress would retain the authority to unilaterally modify its provisions. Finally, and echoing one of Coulter's complaints, Tallchief also noted that the power of secretary of Interior to hold the $27 million "in trust" for the tribes was a situation ripe with opportunities for governmental abuse.

Continuing, Tallchief identified additional problems with the legislation. For example, when reservations were actually established for the tribes, those territories, according to the act, could still be "taken for public uses consistent with the Maine Implementing Act or the laws of the United States." This reality would leave the tribes with a very tenuous land status. In addition, the tribes' members and their lands—with a few important exceptions, such as criminal offenses committed by tribal members against other tribal members, juvenile offenses of tribal members, small claims civil actions, and Indian child custody proceedings—were still to be subject to Maine's civil and criminal jurisdiction. And finally, from Tallchief's perspective, the most debilitating aspect of the proposed measure was that it incorporated the Maine Implementing Act, a lengthy document that defined the relationship between the state and the tribes. This act would effectively give the state the authority to create an Indian territory. Thus the tribes effectively "become creatures of the state of Maine."[36]

Despite the serious concerns raised by these two knowledgeable commentators, H.R. 7919 sailed through the hearings virtually unscathed. The final legislation was signed into law by President Carter on October 10, 1980.[37] In signing the act, Carter boasted, "This is a great day for all the people of Maine, for the Indian tribes involved, for Maine's landowners, and also a good day for the Congress of the United States, because they are all satisfied with the Settlement Act. Because we have a Settlement Act," he continued, "rather than a lengthy and extremely costly litigation, a mutual consent agreement, rather than acrimonious debate and further division among the people of Maine," the president emphasized that the legislation would lead to improved tribal-state relations and would substantially improve the socioeconomic situation of the Native peoples.

The act contained sixteen major sections and was thirteen pages long. It extended federal recognition to the Passamaquoddy, Penobscot, and the Houlton Band of Maliseet; established a land acquisition fund of $54.5 million to be used by the three tribes to purchase 300,000 acres of land that would be placed under federal trust protection; established a settlement fund of $27 million to be divided equally between the Passamaquoddy and the Penobscot peoples and held in trust by the Interior secretary (these funds could not be taxed and interest was to be paid quarterly); extinguished all remaining land claims of the three groups; and authorized the State of Maine to continue to wield broad civil and criminal jurisdiction over the tribes' members and their lands, notwithstanding their new status as federally recognized tribal communities. Although the

Houlton Maliseets received some $900,000 for land trust acquisition, unlike the other two tribes, they did not secure municipality status in relationship to Maine and they did not benefit from the $27 million trust fund.

While the three Native nations certainly emerged from these negotiations in an improved financial, territorial, and political position, arguably the State of Maine reaped even greater benefits. First, the federal government, not the state, paid the $81 million settlement cost. Second, the state secured clear title to all of the remaining land under its jurisdiction. Third, with the tribes having received federal recognition, the state effectively terminated its own Department of Indian Affairs, thus "divesting itself entirely from 150 years of supervision of some of the poorest Native populations in the country."[38] Finally, although the state no longer maintained any direct responsibility to the indigenous population, it nevertheless retained extensive jurisdictional authority over both aboriginal lands and the peoples of those lands. In effect, although receiving a measure of federal recognition as a result of the settlement act's passage, the three Native nations still found themselves treated for many purposes as if they were "state" Indians. Any federal law, for instance, enacted after October 10, 1980, for the benefit of Indians which would "*effect* or *preempt* the laws of the State of Maine 'shall not apply within the State of Maine, unless [it] is specifically made applicable within the State.' "[39]

In the decades since the act was passed, the three Native peoples have realized that the act has constrained their efforts to become more economically self-sufficient and to be recognized and respected as bona fide sovereign nations. For example, when the Passamaquoddy sought to enter the field of legalized gambling in the early 1990s, after seeing the economic benefits accruing to the Pequot and other Native nations, they were rebuffed by the federal courts. In 1996 the Court of Appeals for the First Circuit in *Passamaquoddy v. Maine*[40] upheld a district court ruling that the 1988 Indian Gaming Regulatory Act was not applicable to the Maine tribes because of the stipulation in the 1980 settlement that no federal Indian laws would affect or preempt

Maine law unless made "specifically applicable" to Maine. As a result, the Passamaquoddy were not entitled to an order that would compel the State of Maine to negotiate a compact for Class III gaming, the most lucrative of all gaming opportunities.

Despite that setback, the Passamaquoddy continued to lobby at the state and federal level for some form of gaming, and in the summer of 2010 they succeeded in securing the right to open a high-stakes bingo operation, which is considered Class II gaming and does not require a tribal-state compact. This business will operate on tribal land at Indian Township in Washington County. The tribe leased fifty Class II gaming machines, which are similar in appearance to slot machines. Their use was authorized by a recently enacted state law that went into effect July 15, 2010.[41]

According to Jack Campisi, who has worked with a number of eastern Native communities, the Maine land claims case was significant for several reasons. First, it demonstrated that negotiations were a critical part of the claims process and helped lead to the compromise legislation that was finally approved. Second, and most obviously, this process would not have been possible without direct federal involvement. The courts, notes Campisi, were the initial catalyst, forcing both the executive and congressional branches to get involved in resolving the dispute. Third, when the Supreme Court declared that the Trade and Intercourse Act applied even to non-recognized Native communities, it was a major development that dramatically altered the terrain of indigenous-state relations, as it widened the number Native communities eligible for direct political relations with the federal government. And finally, "the will to settle, on the parts both of the state and of the tribes," was most important, and it exceeded even "the desire to win the lawsuit."[42]

Despite the improved relationship between the tribes and the state, other scholars maintain that the settlement act needs to be amended because under the current scenario none of the Native nations benefit from genuine self-government because of the political power Maine retains. The nations lack the authority to manage relations with government employees; they are denied the right to regulate on-reservation activities that affect their territory and natural resources; and Maine is not required to consult or secure the consent of the nations before engaging in activities that may adversely affect tribal resources or lands.[43]

Interestingly, Maine is the only state thus far to have endorsed the United Nations Declaration on the Rights of Indigenous Peoples, adopted in 2007. Maine's legislature expressed its support for this important convention in 2008—signifying that it has the capacity to embrace global indigenous self-determination. Future events will determine whether such international support will be extended domestically to the small nations within Maine's borders.[44]

7. THE *COBELL* TRUST FUND LITIGATION AND SETTLEMENT

An "Accounting Coup"[1]

ON JUNE 20, 2011, federal district judge Thomas F. Homan held a fairness hearing during which he heard arguments from the lawyers representing Elouise Pepion Cobell and a half million Indian plaintiffs and from lawyers representing the Departments of Interior and Treasury in *Cobell v. Salazar.* As part of the hearing Judge Homan also received objections from some members of the plaintiffs' class in connection with the class action settlement on Indian trust management approved by Congress on December 7, 2009. That settlement, in which the U.S. agreed to pay the Indian plaintiffs and their attorneys $3.4 billion, was followed by multiple delays and nearly a year of hearings and deliberation before Congress enacted the Claims Resolution Act of 2010,[2] legislation that expressly "authorized, ratified, and confirmed" the settlement. Although sanctioned by Congress and then signed by President Barack Obama on December 8, 2010, the settlement required Judge Homan's final approval as it had been introduced in his court. Homan's ruling concluded a nearly fourteen-year litigation and political odyssey unlike any that had previously come before the federal courts, the Congress, or the executive branch.

The scope, length, and complexity of *Cobell* case mark it as a most extraordinary lawsuit, and the distinguishing factors are many. First, the lawsuit, originally filed on June 10, 1996, by Elouise Cobell, Mildred Cleghorn, Thomas Maulson, James Louis LaRose, and Earl Old Person on their own behalf and on behalf of some 500,000 other

Indian trust beneficiaries, was the largest class action suit ever certified against the U.S. Second, the nearly 15 years that it was before the courts and Congress spanned the tenure of three presidents and four secretaries of the Interior and Treasury and generated over 3,600 docket entries, 250 days of hearings and trials, 80 published opinions—10 of which were federal appellate rulings—1 en banc petition to the Circuit Court for the District of Columbia, and 2 petitions for writs of certiorari to the U.S. Supreme Court.[3]

Third, the litigation produced several contempt rulings for several secretaries of the Interior and Treasury. Fourth, the ultimate settlement was not so much a claim for just compensation or money damages; it was a claim for an accounting of moneys already in the account awarded by the trustee—the federal government—for receipts and disbursements representing the trust corpus (the body of property for which the trustee is responsible) held for the benefit of nearly half a million individual Indians who retain some 11 million acres of land that is held in trust by the federal government.[4]

Lastly, the final settlement figure of $3.4 billion for the Native plaintiffs and their legal team represented the largest settlement ever approved against the federal government. This figure, however, was much reduced from the original estimate of $176 billion. A time line of this historical claims action is summarized in table 4.

At the heart of this most complex litigation lay a central concept in this turgid area of study—the trust doctrine. The concept of *trust* is multifaceted and complex, encompassing, in one commonly understood definition, a notion of federal responsibility to assist indigenous peoples in the protection of their lands, resources, and cultural heritage through policy decisions and management actions that affirm the distinctive political, legal, and moral relationship between the federal government and indigenous nations as set forth in the U.S. Constitution, diplomatic arrangements (i.e., treaties), statutes, executive orders, and court decisions. The trust doctrine, along with treaties and congressional plenary power, is a foundational concept underlying the relationship between Native nations and the federal

Table 4 *Cobell* Time Line

1820	U.S. begins holding tribal funds in trust.
1828	Henry Rowe Schoolcraft complains of Bureau of Indian Affairs mismanagement of Native lands andw resources.
1831	*Cherokee Nation v. Georgia* handed down by the Supreme Court. Many commentators suggest that the federal trust doctrine originates in this opinion because of language referring to Native nations as "domestic-dependent" peoples and analogizing the relationship between natives and the U.S. to one that "resembles that of a ward to his guardian."
1861	Congressional investigation of the Interior Department's "abstraction," a euphemism for "theft," of some $2.5 million in Indian trust bonds.
1887	General Allotment Act.
1910	Congress authorizes federal officials to deposit Indian monies into bonds.
1915	Report by the Bureau of Municipal Research critically examining the BIA's poorly managed financial affairs.
1934	Indian Reorganization Act renews perpetual trust status on all remaining and future Indian lands.
1938	Congressional act that authorizes the deposit and investment of Indian funds by the federal government on behalf of Indian beneficiaries.
1983	BIA hires Price Waterhouse accounting firm to analyze the management of the Indian trust fund.
1989	Senate report on fraud and corruption in Indian Country.
1992	Congressional Committee on Government Operations produces a detailed report titled "Misplaced Trust: The BIA's Mismanagement of the Indian Trust Fund" that assails the BIA's accounting problems.

1994 Congress enacts the American Indian Trust Fund Management Act

1996 Elouise Cobell and the Native American Rights Fund file class action lawsuit.

Transfer from BIA to Office of Special Trustee to oversee and manage the trust funds.

2004 The American Indian Records Repository is opened in Lenexa, Kansas, where inactive trust fund records are to be stored.

2005 Congress proposes initial bill to legislatively settle the *Cobell* conflict.

2006 District Judge Royce Lamberth is removed from the *Cobell* case for allegedly being "biased" against the Department of Interior.

2008 District Judge James Robertson, who replaced Lamberth, finds that the Indian plaintiffs are entitled to a mere $455.6 million in restitution.

2009 *Cobell v. Salazar* reverses Robertson's decision and holds that Indian beneficiaries were entitled to an accounting.

Congress preliminarily approves the *Cobell* settlement for $3.4 billion.

2010 Congress formally approves and President Barack Obama signs the *Cobell* settlement into law.

2011 U.S. District Court for the District of Columbia gives final approval to the *Cobell* settlement in June.

Elouise Cobell dies of cancer in October before receiving any compensation for her pivotal part in this longstanding issue.

2011 Several appeals are filed by Native plaintiffs challenging the *Cobell* settlement.

2012 Forty-one Native nations that had filed separate lawsuits against the U.S. for mismanagement of monetary assets and natural resources agree to a $1 billion settlement, to be divided among the nations.

2012 The four appeals filed by individual natives failed in the courts, thus opening the door for the class members to begin receiving their payments in December.

---

government. But despite its foundational quality, there is no universally agreed-upon definition of what the federal trust relationship entails. In fact, there are many questions about this important concept that remain largely unanswered. Consequently, uncertainty and ambiguity reign supreme when an effort is made to gain a clear understanding of what the trust doctrine actually means.

Different Tributaries of Trust

A majority of political and legal commentators, jurists, and federal policymakers posit that the trust doctrine is an ancient and entrenched, if ambiguous, presence overarching the indigenous-federal relationship. The trust doctrine has been delineated in three different ways. First, it is found in the international law doctrine of trusteeship, initially broached in papal bulls (policy statements issued by the pope) and related documents dating to European nations' first encounters with indigenous societies in the fifteenth and sixteenth centuries when European secular and religious officials assumed a theoretical, if not actual, protectorate position vis-à-vis aboriginal peoples based on their alleged physical, cultural, technological, and religious inferiority.

Second, there is an implied notion of trust evident in the many treaties and other diplomatic arrangements negotiated among Native nations, European states, and later the U.S. In many of these contractual compacts tribal nations sold varying amounts of land to purchasing states. These negotiations formally recognized the sovereign status of the indigenous parties, and, in addition, the Native peoples received various goods, exemptions, and protections. Hence, the tribal nations had the legal expectation and moral assurance that the federal government would fulfill the pledges and provisions made in exchange for the massive land exchanges.

Third, a number of Supreme Court opinions have held that the federal government has a general trust relationship to indigenous peoples and that the U.S. is the trustee of indigenous lands and resources, meaning that the federal government is supposed to act in good faith, with extreme loyalty, and in the best interests of the Native nations and individual natives. The Supreme Court case typically cited as initiating the trust doctrine is *Cherokee Nation v. Georgia.*[5] In this ruling Chief Justice John Marshall observed in dictum that the relationship between Indian nations and the U.S. "resembles that of a ward to his guardian." Although this was merely an analogy, it is considered by many commentators to be the basis of the trust doctrine.

In addition, Congress, through major policies (e.g., the Snyder Act of 1921) and specific acts (Civilization Act of 1819), and the president, via specific policy pronouncements and executive orders, have underscored the unique legal and moral relationship between the federal and tribal nations. With so many sources contributing to an understanding of the federal trust doctrine, it is not surprising that there is significant ambiguity surrounding the concept. This is not an insignificant issue, given the symbolic and substantive importance of trust to the indigenous-nonindigenous political relationship. Ironically, while the federal government has a generalized duty to act in good faith toward Native peoples, specific tasks are not necessarily required. In other words, while the trust obligation sometimes includes implied rights (e.g., a tribal nation has a right to water even though the treaty/agreement makes no direct mention of a water entitlement), tribes and individual Indians cannot insist that the U.S. carry out a specific activity unless the treaty, agreement, or statute expressly states what the obligation or commitment is.

For example, in *Lyng v. Northwest Indian Cemetery Protective Association*,[6] a coalition of three Northern California tribes, several organizations and concerned individuals, and the State of California sought to prevent the U.S. Forest Service from constructing a road through a portion of a national forest that was considered sacred by the Indians and deemed to have vital importance to the other respondents. The Indians and their litigant partners asserted that the Forest Service's decision to construct the road violated the First Amendment's free exercise clause, the American Indian Religious Freedom Act (AIRFA; 1978), several environmental laws and other statutes, and the federal government's trust responsibilities to the Indians.

The Supreme Court denied each of these claims and declared the Forest Service's decision in keeping with the land-use policies of the federal government, even in the face of incontrovertible evidence that the road's construction would have "devastating effects on traditional Indian religious practices." In denying that the government's trust responsibilities precluded such irreparable damage to the tribes and individual Indians, the Supreme Court, at least by implication, muted the force of the trust doctrine and specific laws, like the AIRFA, that were intended to provide a statutory measure of protection for Native practitioners of traditional religions. In effect, the *Lyng* ruling held that because the trust doctrine was not constitutionally based, it was not enforceable against Congress or, in this case, a federal agency, and since the U.S. "owned" the lands found in national forests, it had the inherent right to do what it wanted with those lands.

More recently, in a 2011 case, *Jicarilla Apache v. United States*,[7] the Supreme Court profoundly narrowed the meaning of the trust doctrine in a manner that essentially allowed the federal trustee, in this case the Department of the Interior, to invoke the attorney-client privilege to withhold documents requested by the Jicarilla Apache in their suit against the federal government. The Jicarilla Apache live on a 900,000-acre reservation in New Mexico that contains timber, gravel, and oil and gas reserves. The proceeds generated from exploiting these resources are held in trust by the federal government for the tribe. In 2002 the Jicarilla filed suit, arguing that the Department of Interior had mismanaged their funds by failing to invest them properly, by failing to maximize the returns on their funds, by having invested too heavily in short-term annuities, and by having failed to pool the trust fund with other tribal trusts.[8]

Between 2002 and 2008, the U.S. and the Jicarilla engaged in alternative dispute resolution (trying to negotiate a settlement before pursuing litigation) in an effort to resolve the tribe's claims. Although the federal government turned over many documents during the discovery phase of the proceeding, it withheld from the Jicarilla's legal team some 226 "potentially relevant documents" and invoked the attorney-client privilege as the basis for this withholding.[9] The government later released 71 of the documents but refused to surrender the remaining 155 records.

In a devastating opinion written by Associate Justice Samuel Alito, the High Court invoked the doctrine of virtually absolute congressional plenary power—that the Congress has nearly untrammeled authority over all Indian affairs—and, remarkably and quite possibly for the first time, opined that the trust relationship actually spawned from the idea of legislative plenary power, leaving Native nations with little recourse. Alito declared that because the "Indian trust relationship represents an exercise of that [plenary] authority, we have explained that the Government 'has a real and direct interest' in the guardianship it exercises over the Indian tribes; 'the interest is one which is vested in it as a sovereign.' . . . This is especially so because the Government has often structured the trust relationship to pursue its own policy goals. Thus, while trust administration 'relates to the welfare of the Indians, the maintenance of the limitation which Congress has prescribed as a part of its plan of distribution is distinctly an interest of the United States.' "[10]

In other words, while affirming that a general trust relationship did exist (citing *U.S. v. Mitchell*)[11] and that the U.S. had "moral obligations of the highest responsibility and trust" (citing *Seminole Nation v. U.S.*),[12] Alito refused to apply the normal law exception to the attorney-client privilege rule because the U.S. was asserting its sovereign interest in this case, and the Jicarilla were precluded from advancing a position contrary to that of the government. According to Alito's opinion, the federal government assumed only those specific trust responsibilities for Native peoples that were explicitly laid out in congressional statutes or administrative regulations.

In another powerful blow to the trust doctrine, Alito maintained that "while one purpose of the Indian trust relationship is to benefit the tribes, the Government has its own independent interest in the implementation of federal Indian policy." As such, "when the Government seeks legal advice related to the administration of tribal trusts, it establishes an attorney-client relationship related to its sovereign interest in the execution of federal law. In other words, the Government seeks legal advice in a 'personal' rather than a fiduciary capacity."[13]

Finally, and in keeping with the Roberts court's narrowly construed meaning of trust, Alito, in a comment reminiscent of Justice Sandra Day O'Connor's previous statement in *Lyng* about the U.S. being the "owner" of the national forests and therefore entitled to build a road if it wanted to, said that "by law and regulation, moreover, the documents at issue in this case are classed 'the property of the United States' while other records are 'the property of the tribe.' . . . [W]e consider ownership of the resulting records could be a significant factor in deciding who 'ought to have access to the documents.' . . . In this case, that privilege belongs to the United States."[14]

Thus, there remains substantial tension between how the federal government articulates and exercises its trust relationship with Native peoples—particularly when it is conducted in a paternalistic manner over tribal and individual Indian lands and resources—and how it supports indigenous self-determination and self-governance, which presumably means that Native nations and individual tribal citizens should be positioned to make the major decisions regarding their resources.

Historical Background to Indian Trust Accounts

It is in the diplomatic record— the hundreds of treaties, accords, alliances, compacts, contracts, and agreements dating from the early 1600s to the contemporary era[15]—that we find the most important means through which foreign powers, and later the U.S., agreed to engage in the trust protection of indigenous resources that would be held for the benefit of both Native nations and individual tribal citizens.

The earliest treaties between Native nations and the U.S., from 1778 through the early 1800s, dealt mostly with the establishment of peace and friendship, military alliances, territorial boundaries, trade relations, and land conveyances and did not specifically provide that the federal government hold funds in trust for tribal nations, but this changed in 1820. In that year the U.S., for the first time, adopted the policy of holding some tribal funds—those belonging to entire Native nations—in trust.[16]

As federal power waxed and Native power waned, treaties gradually came to include provisions that specifically referenced the federal government assuming the role as designated trust agent for Native nations and individual Indians. For example, in 1832 the Chickasaw people, in Article 11 of the treaty negotiated on October 20 and proclaimed the following year, insisted on the creation of a "perpetual fund" from the proceeds of the land they were selling to the United States. An extended quote from this provision shows the beginnings of an explicit trust relationship and the manner in which it was projected to unfold, with the Chickasaw eventually gaining sufficient knowledge and skills to assume complete control of their own money:

> And for that purpose they [the Chickasaw] propose to invest a large proportion of the money arising from the sale of the land, in some safe and valuable stocks, which will bring them in an annual interest or dividend, to be used for all national purposes, leaving the principal untouched, intending to sue

> the interest alone. It is therefore proposed by the Chickasaws, and agreed to, that the sum to be laid out in stocks as above mentioned, shall be left with the government of the United States, until it can be laid out under the direction of the President of the United States, by and with the advice and consent of the Senate, in such safe and valuable stock as he may approve of, for the use and benefit of the Chickasaw nation. The sum thus to be invested, shall be equal to, at least three fourths of the whole net proceeds of the sales of the lands; and as much more, as the nation may determine, if there shall be a surplus after supplying all the national wants. . . . At the expiration of fifty years from the date, if the Chickasaw nation shall have improved in education and civilization, and become so enlightened, as to be capable of managing so large a sum of money to advantage, and with safety, for the benefit of the nation, and the President of the United States, with the Senate, shall be satisfied thereof, at that time, and shall give their consent thereto, the Chickasaw nation may then withdraw the whole, or any part of the fund now set apart, to be laid out in stocks, or at interest, and dispose of the same, in any manner that they may think proper at that time, for the use and benefit of the whole nation.[17]

Likewise, the U.S. Congress, as early as 1790[18] sought to strike a balance between extinguishing Indian title for expanding white settlement and providing a measure of assurance to Native nations that their remaining property would be protected. The Indian Trade and Intercourse Acts, a series of temporary laws that began in 1790 and culminated in a permanent codification in 1834,[19] contained language designed to shield the tribal communities from scheming non-Indians who might seek to defraud tribal members of lands or other resources.

In 1824, John Calhoun, without express congressional approval, created the Bureau of Indian Affairs in the War Department. Headed by Thomas L. McKenney, it was charged with overseeing the appropriation for annuities and current expenses, analyzing and approving vouchers for expenditures, administering the funds authorized by Congress to "civilize" the Indians, and dealing with sundry other responsibilities.[20] Notwithstanding treaty and statutory provisions, and despite the bureau's presence, indigenous peoples and their resources continued to be the focus of intense desire, appropriation, and abuse by federal, state, territorial, and individual interests.

In 1828, Henry Rowe Schoolcraft, an ethnologist, explorer, and participant in many treaty negotiations, commented on the already problematic ability of the BIA to properly fulfill its basic financial trust obligations to Native peoples. He opined, "The derangements in the fiscal affairs of the Indian department are in the extreme. One would think that appropriations had been handled with a pitchfork. A correspondent writes: 'For 1827 we were promised $48,000 and received $30,000. For 1828 we were promised $40,000 and have received $25,000; and, besides these promises, were all the extra expenditures authorized to be incurred, amounting to not less than $15,000. It is impossible this can continue.' And these derangements are only with regard to the North. How the South and the West stand it is impossible to say. But there is a screw loose in the public machinery somewhere."[21]

Four years later, on July 9, 1832,[22] Congress authorized the president to appoint a commissioner of Indian Affairs to direct and manage all Indian affairs under the guidance of the secretary of war. And on June 30, 1834,[23] Congress statutorily established what is the organic law of the BIA when it created the Department of Indian Affairs. The department, then in the War Department, would be relocated in 1849 to the newly established Department of Interior, where it has been ever since.[24] This was a major structural and perceptual shift—from war to interior resource management—and coincided with another shift in the 1840s, a congressional act which declared that monies owed to tribal nations and their leaders should now be paid directly to family heads and other individuals. Felix Cohen says this action "was the first in a long series of statutes designed to individualize tribal property."[25]

Beginning in the 1830s and continuing for several decades afterwards, many tribal trust funds were invested in state bonds. This was a fulfillment of the federal government's treaty and statutory obligations to invest the funds. Ironically, the investment of these tribal moneys generated vital capital for some state governments—among them Missouri, North Carolina, Tennessee—with the money being used for railroad and canal securities. A major congressional investigation in 1861 revealed that $2.5 million in bonds, held by the Interior Department on behalf of numerous Native nations, had been fraudulently "abstracted"—a euphemism for stolen—from Interior. Representative Isaac N. Morris, who chaired the select committee charged with investigating the so-called abstract Indian trust bonds noted at the conclusion of this report that the committee "begs leave to suggest that the fluctuations of the stock market, and the delay and uncertainty in the collection of the interest on the bonds, seem to demand some further legislation in regard to the Indian trust fund, as a measure of obvious justice and humanity to the Indians."[26]

During the next few decades the federal government gained vast swaths of Native land via treaties. Tribal nations, reeling from military engagements, depopulation resulting from the spread of communicable diseases, and policies like the development of the reservation system, had little choice but to surrender title to much of their territory in exchange for U.S. guarantees to protect the remains of tribal sovereignty and with the federal government, as trustee, pledging to protect the drastically diminished remainder of Native property and to provide other services and benefits as well.

The unilateral cessation of treaty making with Native nations in 1871, a constitutionally problematic action[27] on the part of the legislative branch since it effectively deprived the president of one of the enumerated powers that office was authorized to exercise, set the tone for a decade of activity in the 1880s that dramatically and devastatingly redefined the status of Native nations. The internal and external sovereign powers of indigenous peoples were further diminished through the imposition of policies that aimed to destroy their national identity by forcibly Americanizing (via boarding schools and law-and-order rules and regulations), Christianizing (via missionary activity), and individualizing (via land allotments) Native peoples. The cumulative impact of this powerful confluence of coercive assimilative policies and laws was profound. The individualization of Native lands, in particular, warrants our attention, as the allotting process was the dominant agent creating the conditions that ultimately culminated in the *Cobell* lawsuit.

The Allotting of Native America

With the adoption in 1887 of the General Allotment Act—also popularly known as the Dawes Severalty Act—Congress inaugurated a policy that led to individual allotting agreements for specific tribal nations and finally to the individual allotment of formerly communal reservation lands to tribal citizens. The avowed rationale behind this policy was that by insisting that individual Indians learn to farm, become private property holders, and eventually acquire U.S. citizenship, they would more easily be assimilated into the American polity. Such an attitude, of course, presumed that Indians desired to become farmers, that they would be accorded all the tools necessary to make the required social, economic, and cultural changes necessary, and it clearly assumed that the Native nations' communal, non-Christian lifestyles were inappropriate and warranted obliteration.

By the time the allotment policy was terminated by the Indian Reorganization Act in 1934, 118 of the 213 reservations had been allotted, resulting in the loss of some 90 million acres of Native territory. On the reservations allotted, and after the parceling out of individual plots—which were to be held in trust by the federal government for each allottee—household heads received 160 acres, single persons over eighteen years of age received 80 acres, and those under eighteen secured 40 acre tracts. All remaining lands were declared "surplus" and were put up for purchase by non-Indians, creating a convoluted checkerboard ownership pattern on these reservations. The money generated by these sales was placed with the U.S. Treasury, to be managed and invested for the benefit of tribal nations and individual tribal members.

The loss of so much land was devastating, and the allotment process had another destructive consequence: fractionation. As successive generations of Indian heirs came to hold allotted lands, the original 160-, 80-, and 40-acre tracts became subdivided, with some parcels having hundreds of owners. The fractionation problem multiplied exponentially, since each individual Indian property owner was likely to have more than one heir.

As the allotting process unfolded, with the U.S. eventually holding some 46 million acres in trust for Native nations and another 10 million acres for individual Indians, the BIA, as the primary trust agent for Native peoples, was charged with managing the funds, the lands, and the related assets for the tribal nations and for the individual allottees. The income generated from federal management of the Indians' oil, coal, timber leases, and so on was to be paid into a trust account maintained by the Treasury Department and then paid out to the Native holders of individual trust accounts. The Department of the Interior was charged with monitoring the records and keeping those accounts current. Our focus in this chapter, per the *Cobell* case, is on the bureau's management of Individual Indian Money (IIM) accounts, not on tribal accounts.

As individual Native nations and their citizens gradually were ensnared by the federal government's allotment process, individual Indian allottees, whose variable acreage was to be held in trust for at least twenty-five years or until the secretary of Interior determined their competency, soon realized that virtually all decision-making authority regarding their lands and the funds generated by those lands rested not with them but with their national trustee, the secretary of Interior, or, in most cases, the secretary's designate, the local Indian agent or the reservation superintendent.

Since wardship and incompetency were the dominant federal perceptions of Indians in the early part of the twentieth century, it came as no surprise when Congress, on June 25, 1910, enacted a law authorizing local Indian agents, reservation superintendents, and other disbursing agents of the BIA to "deposit Indian moneys, individual or tribal, coming into his hands as custodian, in such bank or banks as he may select," although certain requirements had to be met.[28] This was the first in a series of laws, the others being adopted in 1918[29] and in 1938,[30] in which the secretary of Interior was empowered with significant discretionary authority to deposit individual trust money in banks of his choice, under rules he prescribed, so long as it was "for the benefit of individual Indians."[31]

The financial problems in the BIA identified by Henry Rowe Schoolcraft in 1828 had increased exponentially by the early 1900s, as the Department of Interior wielded virtually absolute power over the rights, resources, and cultural identities of Native peoples. As a result, in 1914, a Joint Commission to Investigate Indian Affairs, consisting of six federal lawmakers—three senators and three representatives—was created to critically examine the BIA's business and accounting methods. The commission retained the services of a New York–based firm, the Bureau of Municipal Research (BMR), to conduct a detailed study of the BIA's financial systems and to make recommendations on how to improve matters.

The BMR produced a thorough study of the BIA's accounting systems and found them severely wanting. In a brief introduction, the report's authors highlighted the unique political and legal status of Native peoples: "The need for special care in management of Indian affairs lies in the fact that in theory of law the Indian has not the rights of the citizen. He has not even the rights of a foreign resident. . . . He himself is considered a ward of the United States. His property and funds are held in trust. Both of these facts place the Government in the position of a guardian charged with extraordinary care."[32]

In frank language, the authors declared that the bureau's problems were myriad and that Native resources and funds had been abused for over a century. The following excerpt highlights some of the central problems identified:

> What is of special interest in this inquiry is to note the conditions under which the Indian Office has been required to conduct its business. In no other relation are the agents of the Government under conditions more adverse to efficient administration. The influences which make for infidelity to trusteeship, for subversion of properties and funds, for violation of physical and moral welfare have been powerful. The opportunities and inducements to peculation are much greater than those which have operated with the ruinous effect on other branches of public service and on the trustees and officers of our great private corporations. . . . In the first place, the machinery of the Government has not been adapted to the purpose of administering a trust. In the second place, there has been little sympathy or favorable opinion to demand that an effective business machine he developed. In fact, the public opinion which has dominated the Government has been either hostile or passively indulgent of abuse. This is one side of the picture. On the other side, behind the sham protection which operated largely as a blind to publicity, have been at all times great wealth in the form of Indian funds to be subverted: valuable lands, mines, oil fields, and other natural resources to be despoiled or appropriated to the use of the trader and large profits to be made by those dealing with trustees who were animated by motives of gain. This has been the situation in which the Indian Service has been for more than a century—the Indian during all this time having his rights and properties to greater or less extent neglected; the Guardian, the Government, in many instances, passive to conditions which are attributed to his undoing.[33]

In language that would be reprised time and again until the end of *Cobell*, The authors of the BMR report graphically stated:

> And still, due to the increasing value of his remaining estate, there is left an inducement to fraud, corruption, and

> institutional incompetence almost beyond the possibility of comprehension. The properties and funds of the Indians today are estimated at not less than one-thousand millions of dollars. There is still a great obligation to be discharged, which must run through many years. The Government itself owes many millions of dollars for Indian moneys which it has converted to its own use, and it is of interest to note that it does not know and the officers do not know what is the present condition of the Indian funds in their keeping. Every community bordering on Indian lands still has in it persons who are using every influence at their command to obtain official action to the end that they may get possession of Indian lands. Great corporations maintain lobbyists and unprincipled agents with a view of getting concessions, leases, and legislation which are favorable to their own selfish purposes but unfavorable to the Indian.[34]

After completing a comprehensive review of the bureau's financial affairs, the investigators proposed a set of constructive recommendations, which had they been fully implemented and institutionalized might have corrected the most egregious problems. They urged a systematic reorganization and revision of methods: that in making the changes called for, the units of organization designed to exercise "guardianship" be kept separate from those units charged with fulfilling the functions of "trusteeship"; that bureau personnel follow the merit system and not be political appointees; that there be greater control over contracting and purchasing relations; that provisions be made for more economical means of purchasing and distributing supplies, materials, and equipment; and that a system of double entry accounting be installed that would insure complete and accurate reports for all interested parties.[35]

Such a system would have been especially beneficial for individual Indians whose monies derived from one of eight sources—(1) sales of allotments, (2) timber sales on allotments, (3) rentals of Indian allotments for agricultural purposes, (4) rental of allotments for mining purposes, (5) mineral royalties from allotments, (6) earnings from Indian students, (7) miscellaneous individual monies, and (8) bank account interests.[36]

Despite the clarity of this report and the litany of useful recommendations offered, conditions for individual Indian account holders were not improved. Three years later, section 28 of the 1918 annual Indian Appropriation Act authorized the secretary of Interior to segregate from tribal funds the monies of individual tribal members, which were to be deposited to the individual's credit in banks selected by the secretary.[37] The banks selected were to pay interest at a reasonable rate on these accounts, and the secretary was authorized to invest the trust funds in U.S. government bonds. Although this seemed like a responsible, if paternalistic, gesture, it was some years—not until 1966[38]—before the bureau exercised the full range of investment power authorized by this and later statutes, for example, the 1938 act, that superseded it in authorizing the deposit and investment of Indian funds.[39]

In 1934, Congress, at the behest of that singular figure John Collier,[40] enacted the Indian Reorganization Act (IRA), finally ending the allotment process and the coercive assimilation of Native peoples.[41] But the damage caused by six decades of ham-fisted federal policy was incalculable, with most reservations having been allotted, resulting in more than 40 million acres placed in the allotted category and another 22 million being declared "surplus" and open for non-native settlement.[42] The IRA, arguably the most important law as regards Native peoples of the twentieth century, contained a number of crucial provisions: (1) it formally prohibited the further allotment of Indian lands; (2) it prevented the transfer of Native land to entities other than the tribal nation itself; (3) it authorized the secretary of Interior to create new reservations or add lands to existing reservations; (4) it encouraged Native nations to adopt constitutions, bylaws, and charters of incorporation; (5) it authorized funds for educational loans; and (6) it established a revolving credit fund for economic development purposes.

Another major provision, and the most important one for our purposes, was section 2, which indefinitely extended the federal government's trust protection over any Indian lands held under trust status. This provision enshrined in law an exquisite tension that still permeates indigenous status—on one hand, Congress, through the IRA, sought to revise and support indigenous self-determination; on the other hand, the perpetual trust status of remaining Native lands (and future lands) reiterated to tribal nations and individuals that federal officials would continue to wield extraordinary authority over their most essential resources, funds, and territories.

When Congress cloaked what remained of Indian Country in a state of perpetual trust, the federal departments placed in charge of carrying out the government's trust obligations were Interior and Treasury. The BIA and the Department of the Interior are responsible for managing trust lands, handling leases of land transfers, and collecting the income generated off the trust lands. The Treasury Department is required to hold and invest the Individual Indian Money (IIM) accounts and is responsible for accounting and managing the funds in those accounts.[43]

Notwithstanding the explicit statutory, regulatory, and treaty charges, financial and accounting problems festered in both departments, and individual Indian account holders suffered accordingly. As one congressional committee report noted in 1992, "Scores of reports over the years by the Interior department's inspector general, the U.S. General Accounting Office, the Office of Management and Budget, and others have documented significant, habitual problems in BIA's ability to fully and accurately account for trust fund moneys, to properly discharge its fiduciary responsibilities, and to prudently manage the trust fund."[44]

By the early 1980s, the financial failings of the BIA had become so profound and concerns and complaints from Native nations and individuals so vociferous that the bureau was compelled in 1983 to hire an accounting firm, Price-Waterhouse, to analyze how it was managing the Indian trust fund, which by this time had grown to include an estimated 250,000 IIM accounts and accounts for 254 Native nations. By the time it was completed in 1984, Price-Waterhouse's study filled twelve volumes. In summary, the report called for the bureau to (1) define responsibilities of trust fund financial management officials; (2) prepare an up-to-date policy and procedures manual for the central office and agency offices; (3) segregate the tasks of investment and management and security custody; (4) establish an ongoing audit function; (5) implement a single trust accounting system; (6) implement an improved system for tracking expected income; (7) implement a deposit reporting service; (8) modify cash deposit procedures by establishing more local depositories and instituting fund concentration accounts using a balance reporting service with a major commercial bank; and (9) consider a shift of BIA disbursement activities to a commercial bank.[45]

But rather than heed this list of recommendations to address its own management and accounting problems, the BIA, then led by Assistant Secretary of Indian Affairs Ross Swimmer (an enrolled Cherokee), a conservative, focused almost exclusively on the final recommendation—shifting BIA disbursement to a commercial bank—in other words, privatizing financial management of the Indian trust funds.[46] In fact, between 1987 and 1989, the bureau spent great amounts of money and time attempting, according to congressional officials, "inappropriately and unsuccessfully," to transfer the Indian trust fund to the private sector.[47] Such activities prompted several congressional oversight committee investigations of the bureau's IIM mismanagement in the late 1980s, culminating in a thorough and highly critical report in 1992 by the House Committee on Government Operations, provocatively titled "Misplaced Trust: The BIA's Mismanagement of the Indian Trust Fund."[48]

In 1994, Congress intervened once again by enacting the American Indian Trust Fund Management Reform Act.[49] This act clearly stipulated that the secretary of the Interior had trust responsibilities to Native nations and individual Indians and that those included, but were not limited to, providing adequate systems for accounting for and reporting trust fund balances; providing adequate controls over receipts and disbursements; determining accurate cash balances; and establishing consistent policies and procedures for trust fund management and accounting, among others.[50] Another major thrust of this act was the creation of the position of special trustee for American Indians. The special trustee, a presidential appointee, had the broad charge of overseeing the trust administration process. Within a year of his or her appointment, and in consultation with Native nations and tribal organizations, the trustee was to submit a comprehensive strategic plan for all phases of the trust management business cycle.[51] Despite this act's provisions, very little changed in the BIA or Treasury Department, compelling a passionate lawyer and a leading Indian legal interest group to pursue litigation as a means to secure a proper accounting of IIM accounts.

Elouise Cobell—the Head of the Class

Elouise Pepion Cobell, a Blackfeet Indian from Montana, was born into a family that stressed the value of education. She began reading old back issues of the Sunday *New York Times* as a third-grade student. As a young woman, she went to business college and then enrolled at Montana State University. She held jobs in Denver and Seattle before working her way back to the Blackfeet Reservation. In due time, she was hired as the Blackfeet tribe's treasurer, and in this capacity she began to learn about how broken the BIA's IIM account system was.[52]

In 1982, Cobell participated in the founding of an organization called the Native American Finance Officers Association, an organization formed by finance officers, treasurers, and comptrollers from over fifty Native governments. These individuals were dedicated to "the improvement of the quality of financial management of tribal government and the promotion of their fiscal integrity."[53] By 1986, Cobell vice president of this organization, while still working as her nation's treasurer. In her dual capacity, she testified before the Select Committee on Indian Affairs, which held an Indian trust fund oversight hearing in September 1986. Her brief testimony, based on her years of experience in tribal financial accounting, offered suggestions that might ameliorate some of the BIA's shoddy accounting practices, including the need for direct tribal involvement in financial planning. She said: "We offer the following suggestions for Federal consideration: that tribal consulting, briefing, and training sessions are necessary on any new operational requirement resulting from private sector management; assistance to tribes in defining and establishing custom tailored investment objectives should be made available; assistance to tribes in selecting any new investment portfolio options resulting from tribal management should also be made available; development of effective tribal budgeting, forecasting, and financial planning systems is a threshold. Information resulting from these functions is fundamentally necessary so that investment managers may develop and recommend the best portfolio options for tribal investment; improvements to the BIA's current investment coordinator systems are necessary so that its investment directions to any future contract manager will reflect tribal investment performances and cash requirements."[54]

She continued her investigation of the BIA's and Treasury's dysfunctional financial and accounting systems, she was soon convinced that the federal government owed IIM account holders and tribal nations an enormous amount of money: the mismanagement of Indian monies was profound and had lasted for so many generations. Through her collaboration with other tribal accountants she "untangled a messy history of Indian trust monies dumped in the U.S. Treasury's general fund, where they could be used for the latest weapons system or for bailing out the Savings and Loan industry."[55] Cobell continued to approach federal lawmakers for relief, but by 1996 it was evident to her and others that more drastic action was required. After having been rebuffed by federal officials one too many times, Cobell and four other individuals—Earl Old Person,[56] James Louis LaRose, Thomas Maulson, and Mildred Kleghorn[57]—represented by the Native American Rights Fund (NARF) of Boulder,

Colorado, filed a class action lawsuit on June 10, 1996, on their own behalf and on behalf of over 300,000 (later revised to 500,000) similarly situated individual Indian trust fund beneficiaries, in the federal district court in Washington, D.C. The named defendants in the suit, in their official capacity as the trustee delegates of the U.S., were Secretary of the Interior Bruce Babbitt, Assistant Secretary for Indian Affairs Kevin Gover, and Treasury Secretary Robert E. Rubin.

Royce C. Lamberth, appointed as judge for the district court in 1987, was assigned the case. He would shepherd it for the next decade, writing numerous opinions that generally favored the Indian plaintiffs. On June 11, 2006, Lamberth was unceremoniously removed from the case by the Court of Appeals for the District of Columbia Circuit at the request of the government's lawyers[58] on the grounds that his hostility toward the Interior Department had clouded his ability to issue fair judgments. The appellate court concluded that since "reasonable observers must have confidence that judicial decisions flow from the impartial application of law to fact, not from the judge's animosity toward a party—we conclude, reluctantly, that this is one of those rare cases in which reassignment is necessary."[59] This was only the second time in the history of the District of Columbia circuit that a judge had been removed in a civil case "and the first time in history that a judge was removed based upon statements made in reaching his decision."[60]

The Litigation Begins

A tedious review of all litigation generated by this complicated and lengthy lawsuit—the 3,600 docket entries, 250 days of hearings and trials, 80 published opinions, and so on—would require a massive tome. For our purposes we will, of necessity, utilize a more generalized perspective of the litigation/settlement. A broad focus on the eddies and tides generated by the lawsuit will provide more than sufficient evidence of the tortuous route traversed by the Native plaintiffs, the federal judges, and the federal trust agents.

Elouise Cobell and the 300,000 to 500,000 IIM account holders alleged in *Cobell v. Babbitt*[61] that the U.S—through the Departments of Interior and Treasury—had profoundly mismanaged its trust obligations and had been doing so for a very long time. The mismanagement, they argued, included failures in maintaining an adequate accounting and records system, failing to invest the funds in the accounts prudently, failing to make timely and accurate reports to Native beneficiaries, and refraining from self-dealing.[62]The Native plaintiffs also charged that the secretaries of these two departments had destroyed records that violated the trust relations, failed to account to the trust beneficiaries, and had "lost, dissipated, or converted to the United States' own use the money of the trust beneficiaries" while also conspiring to "prevent the Special Trustee from carrying out his duties to correct unlawful practices and procedures with regards to IIM accounting."[63]

The plaintiffs sought relief in each of these areas, and they also requested a full accounting and recovery of court costs, expert costs, and attorneys' fees. Specifically, the plaintiffs presented evidence that "there were at least 15,599 duplicate accounts with the same number; there were more than 54,000 accounts, containing over $46 million, for individuals with no address or no correct address; and there were more than 21,000 accounts with more than $36 million for persons who had died; at least 2,400 of these were foreclosed estates, yet more than $600,000 due to heirs under such estates had still not been distributed."[64]

The defendants, Secretaries Bruce Babbitt of Interior and Robert Rubin of Treasury and Assistant Secretary Kevin Gover, asked Judge Lamberth to dismiss the case, claiming that the district court lacked jurisdiction and that the government had not waived sovereign immunity. More damningly, the government sought to abolish the rights of the plaintiffs ever again to seek redress in the courts by seeking summary judgment on all of their claims.[65]

Judge Lamberth quickly denied the government's motion for summary judgment as "premature" and said the Indian plaintiffs were not seeking money damages but were pursuing an accounting because the account balances had been misstated. Using an analogy, Lamberth said, "The plaintiffs liken the status of the accounts to the loss of a checkbook. That is, the money is in the account but the ledger cannot be properly kept, so the stated balance is incorrect. In the plaintiff's view, they only seek to balance the checkbook, not add any money to the checking account."[66]

On May 5, 1998, Lamberth bifurcated the trial into two phases, with Phase 1 to focus on reforming the management and accounting of the IIM trust funds and Phase 2 to address the historical accounting of those accounts. The Phase 1 trial of *Cobell v. Babbitt*[67] began in June 1999 and concluded on December 21, 1999. In this case Lamberth ruled that the government did indeed have a fiduciary duty to render an accurate accounting of all money in the IIM trust, which it had failed to do. Lamberth graphically stated, "It would be difficult to find a more historically mismanaged federal program than the Individual Indian Money (IIM) trust. The U.S, the trustee of the IIM, cannot say how much money is or should be in the trust. As the trustee admitted on the eve of trial, it cannot render an accurate accounting to the beneficiaries, contrary to a specific statutory mandate and the century-old obligation to do so. More specifically, as Secretary Babbitt testified, an accounting cannot be rendered for most of the 300,000-plus beneficiaries, who are now plaintiffs in this lawsuit."[68]

Lamberth went on to explain how and why the government's violation of its fiduciary duties was more violative than other types of trust arrangements: "The United States' mismanagement of the IIM trust is far more inexcusable than garden-variety trust mismanagement of a typical donative trust. For the beneficiaries of this trust did not voluntarily choose to have their lands taken from them; they did not willingly relinquish pervasive control of their money to the United States. The United States imposed this trust on the Indian people. As the government concedes, the purpose of the IIM trust was to deprive plaintiffs' ancestors of their Native lands and rid the nation of their tribal identity. The United States reaped the 'benefit' of this impulse program long ago—sixty-five percent of what were previously tribal landholdings quickly opened up to non-Indian settlement. But the United States has refused to act in accordance with the fiduciary obligations attendant to the imposition of the trust, which are not imposed by statute."

In short, Lamberth held that the United States was in breach of its trust duties to render an accurate accounting of all the money in the IIM trust. He did acknowledge that the government had recently taken substantial steps to rectify its more egregious flaws, for example, establishing a high level implementation plan, but he refused the plaintiffs' call to appoint a special monitor to oversee the case. He did, however, insist that his court would retain jurisdiction over the case until he felt the government was in full compliance.

The government's shortsighted response to this decision was an appeal to the U.S. Court of Appeals for the District of Columbia.[69] Federal attorneys argued that Congress had included no deadlines in the 1994 American Indian Trust Fund Management Reform Act and had left it up to the government to decide on the timing of the needed trust fund reform. In other words, the U.S. maintained that there had been no breach of trust because the government was free under the 1994 act to do whatever it wanted. Also, the government argued that the IIM beneficiaries had no judicially enforceable right to an accounting at all. But the court of appeals, speaking through Circuit Judge David B. Sentelle, broadly upheld Lamberth's decision, stating that (1) the district court could consider beneficiaries' claims absent final administrative action, given unreasonable delay by government officials; (2) secretaries' fiduciary obligations toward beneficiaries predated the American Indian Trust Fund Management Reform Act; (3) fiduciary duties owed by the secretary of the Interior included the duty to perform adequate historical accounting; (4) fiduciary duty to provide accounting was judicially enforceable; (5) secretary of the Treasury breached his fiduciary obligations toward beneficiaries when he failed to maintain documents necessary to perform accounting; and (6) appropriate relief included remand so that secretaries could begin to discharge duties found by the court, retention of jurisdiction, and ordering secretaries to file quarterly status reports.[70] The case was remanded back to Lamberth for additional proceedings.

With Phase 1 completed, Judge Lamberth transitioned to Phase 2, which was focused on an historical accounting. But this phase would prove far more difficult to address because the government was unable to submit—at least in forms acceptable to the court—plans for reforming the account management system and for providing a comprehensive historical accounting.[71]

In fact, in April 2001, just two months after the court of appeals ruling, Judge Lamberth, with the consent of both sides, appointed a court monitor, Joseph S. Feiffer III, to review all Interior Department trust reform activities and report to the court. A year later, the court reappointed Keiffer, over the government's objections. In September 2002, the court held the Secretary of Interior Gale Norton and Assistant Secretary of Indian Affairs Neal A. McCaleb in contempt of court for having committed "fraud upon the court" for having withheld important information regarding the pace of reform taking place at the Department of Interior.[72] On appeal, the Court of Appeals for the District of Columbia Circuit in 2003 vacated the contempt ruling,[73] holding that Lamberth had improperly imposed criminal rather than civil contempt on Secretary Norton. But the court did not set aside Lamberth's numerous findings of federal misconduct.

Also in 2003, Lamberth made two decisions that intensified the tension between him and the government's lawyers. First, in July he ordered the Interior Department's communication system to be immediately disconnected from the Internet because he believed the integrity of the system had been compromised, which endangered vital records of the department pertaining to the case. Second, in September he issued a structural injunction giving the court broad oversight authority to ensure that the department carried out the necessary accounting for IIM accounts and that it reform its system for managing them. He ordered the Interior Department to conduct a transaction-by-transaction accounting, retroactive to the General

Allotment Act of 1887, of all of the IIM accounts. Lamberth wanted this completed by the end of 2006.

Interior officials were irate at both of these decisions, arguing that, on one hand, they were crippling the department's work in the case of the disconnect from the Internet and, on the other, they were financially problematic—with the government's lawyers claiming that the accounting would cost "between 9 billion and 12 billion, and even then it would not be able to meet the court's requirements or its aggressive timeline."[74] Lamberth admitted that the accounting would be costly, but he firmly believed the Indian plaintiffs were entitled to it: "The hardship to the IIM beneficiaries that would result from a further delay of the long-promised accounting of their trust fund is simply beyond the pale. Many of the beneficiaries live at a subsistence level, and depend on their IIM trust fund checks in order to purchase basic necessities such as food and drink. The delay of an adequate accounting of their funds therefore directly affects their basic ability to survive. Although neither the imposition of additional tasks upon an administrative agency nor the requirement that taxpayer funds be made available to fund such tasks represent insignificant hardships, both of these must be weighed against the personal interests in life and health of an estimated 300,000 to 500,000 American Indians."[75]

Congress, at the Interior Department's behest, stepped in on November 10, 2003, and enacted an appropriation rider that stayed the effect of Lamberth's accounting order until 2005, or until the lawmakers more clearly outlined the department's accounting obligations under the American Indian Trust Fund Management Reform Act of 1994. The general view was that Congress had acted against Lamberth's injunction because of the enormous cost, upwards of 6 billion, that it would have taken to fulfill the comprehensive accounting he had called for. But J. D. Hayworth (R. AZ), and a supporter of the Indians, declared the rider a "poison pill that was added to the legislation in blatant violation of House rules and protocol."[76] Congress, however, would not be dissuaded from cost concerns, and two subsequent appropriation bills limited the funds available to the department for the historical accounting to 58 million for 2005–2006.[77]

In December 2004, the Court of Appeals for the District of Columbia Circuit emphatically struck down nearly all of Judge Lamberth's injunction.[78] The three-judge panel held that (1) in keeping with Congress's directive in the appropriation rider, the Department of Interior could not be compelled to perform any historical accounting; and (2) they also generally overturned Lamberth's injunction calling for the department's systemic reform, holding that the judge by making "claims of broad programmatic failure" rather than specific agency actions, had strayed into territory reserved for executive or legislative action. The circuit court, did, however, uphold Lamberth's requirement that Interior submit a plan specifying how it would comply with its fiduciary obligations.

In February 2005, Judge Lamberth issued another structural injunction regarding the historical accounting he was still committed to.[79] And again, the D.C. Circuit, in November, reversed Lamberth's injunction, asserting that he had "completely disregarded relevant information about the costs of the injunction."[80] Declaring that the Department of the Interior's costs to comply with Lamberth's ruling had risen from "$335 million over five years to more than $10 billion, and that Lamberth had ignored that, the circuit court said the judge had "abused [his] discretion by reissuing the injunction."[81]

After this latest decision, in December 2005, Cobell and her legal team offered to settle the dispute with the government for $27.5 billion, although they believed they were entitled to well over $100 billion. But the department rebuffed the offer, despite the fact that by this time the United States had spent over $100 million in litigation costs and a like amount in accounting efforts.[82]

The Department of Interior, which had previously sought to have Lamberth removed from the case, ratcheted up its assault on the judge. On July 11, 2006, its efforts were rewarded when the Court of Appeals for the District of Columbia Circuit found that the district court had abused its discretion in ordering the Department of Interior to disconnect from the Internet; ordered the court to vacate an order requiring the department to include in any communication to class members a warning that information provided about trust matters might be unreliable; and invented the ultimate rationale—removing Lamberth from the case for "bias" in having accused the department of racism.[83]

To support this rare action to reassign a case, the circuit court quoted at length from Lamberth's July 12, 2005, decision in *Cobell v. Norton*.[84] A few choice quotes from Lamberth's ruling provided the court with the evidence they felt proved the judge had surrendered the ability to act impartially and to render fair judgment:

> At times, it seems that the parties, particularly Interior, lose sight of what this case is really about. The case is nearly a decade old, the docket sheet contains over 3000 entries, and the issues are such that the parties are engaged in perpetual, heated litigation on several fronts simultaneously. But when one strips away the convoluted statutes, the technical legal complexities, the elaborate collateral proceedings, and the layers upon layers of interrelated orders and opinions from this Court and the Court of Appeals, what remains is the raw, shocking, humiliating truth at the bottom: After all these years, our government still treats Native American Indians as if they were somehow less than deserving of respect that should be afforded to everyone in the society where all people are supposed to be equal.[85]

> Alas, our "modern" Interior department has time and again demonstrated that it is a dinosaur—the morally and culturally oblivious hand-me-down of a disgracefully racist and imperialist government that should have been buried a century ago, the last pathetic outpost of the indifference and anglocentrism we thought we had left behind. But these are only examples. The entire record in this case tells the true story of Interior's degenerate tenure as Trustee-Delegate for

> the Indian trust—a story shot through with bureaucratic blunders, flubs, goofs and foul-ups, and peppered scandals, deception, dirty tricks and outright villainy—the end of which is nowhere in sight. Despite the breadth and clarity of this record, Interior continues to litigate and relitigate, in excruciating fashion, every minor, technical legal issue. This is yet another factor forestalling the final resolution of the issues in this case and delaying the relief the Indians so desperately need. It is against this background of mismanagement, falsification, spite, and obstinate litigiousness that this Court is to evaluate the general reliability of the information Interior distributes to IIM account holders.[86]

In one final extended quote cited by the appeals court, Lamberth forcefully sought to identify the factors that he believed had led the Department of Interior to act so callously toward Native individuals:

> While it is undeniable that Interior has failed as a Trustee-Delegate, it is nevertheless difficult to conjure plausible hypotheses to explain Interior's default. Perhaps Interior's past and present leaders have been evil people, deriving their pleasure from inflicting harm on society's most vulnerable. Interior may be consistently populated with apathetic people who just cannot muster the necessary energy or emotion to avoid complicity in the Department's grossly negligent administration of the Indian trust. Or maybe Interior's officials are cowardly people who dodge their responsibilities out of a childish fear of the magnitude of effort involved in reforming a degenerate system. Perhaps Interior as an institution is so badly broken that even the most well-intentioned initiatives are polluted and warped by the processes of implementation. The government as a whole may be inherently incapable of serving as an adequate fiduciary because of some structural flaw. Perhaps the Indians were doomed the moment the first European to set foot

> on American soil. Who can say? It may be that the opacity of the cause renders the Indian trust insoluble.[87]

Such intense language convinced the appeals judges that Lamberth's "professed hostility" toward Interior was such that reassignment was necessary, given that "justice must satisfy the appearance of justice."[88] But even with Lamberth gone, the judges concluded their ruling by reminding the government that it remained "in breach of its trust responsibilities" and that it had an obligation to find a remedy to its "deplorable record."[89]

Congress Becomes Active

By 2005, it was clear to Senators John McCain and Byron Dorgan, leaders of the Senate Committee of Indian Affairs, and Representatives Richard Pombo and Nick J. Rahall II, of the House Resources Committee, that something more needed to be done. These four sent a request to the *Cobell* plaintiffs, tribal nations, individual allottees, and various Native organizations requesting a set of principles that would guide the lawmakers' drafting of legislation to provide an expeditious and fair resolution of the trust issue. In response, a Trust Reform and *Cobell* Settlement Workgroup was organized by the National Congress of the American Indians and the Inter-Tribal Monetary Association that included all the groups and individuals named above. On June 20, 2005, the workgroup drafted fifty "Principles for Legislation" grouped into four categories: (1) historical accounting and individual Indian trust accounts, (2) reforming the individual and tribal trust systems, (3) Indian land consolidation, and (4) individual Indian resource management claims.[90]

The congressional response was S. 1439, the Indian Trust Reform Act of 2005. An identical measure, H.R. 4322, was introduced in the House, to address settlement of the *Cobell v. Norton* litigation. While the two bills were essentially a rough sketch of a comprehensive settlement, McCain, in introducing the bill in the Senate, said it would create a settlement fund and direct the secretary of the Treasury to develop a formula for distributing the funds to the beneficial owners of IIM accounts in full settlement for losses, errors, and unpaid interests. The legislation was also designed to reform the trust management system, restructure the BIA under an under secretary for Indian Affairs, and phase out the Office of Special Trustee. During a Senate Indian Affairs hearing on July 26, 2005, Cobell offered a mixed response to the proposed legislation, complaining that it would not uphold the victories she and her partners had achieved in the courts to date and that it would, in fact, terminate the court's oversight in the case, that it failed to set an actual amount for the settlement fund, and that it would not dramatically improve the supervision of individual Indian trust accounts by providing an explicit definition of the government's trust duties.[91]

With Congress now engaged, the Bush administration also stepped up. On March 1, 2007, Secretary of Interior Dirk Kempthorne and Attorney General Alberto R. Gonzalez, in a letter to the congressional leaders who had introduced the legislation, indicated that the White House was prepared to commit $7 billion on a multiyear basis to settle the litigation provided that it cover "all existing and potential individual and tribal claims for trust accounting, cash and land mismanagement, and other related claims, along with the resolution of other related matters" like trust reform, improving information technology, among others.[92] At the time, there were some 250 additional trust cases pending, and Gonzalez himself had previously noted that the federal government's liability for all claims of trust mismanagement could exceed $200 billion. The Department of Interior's personnel had earlier stated that *Cobell* alone could cost somewhere between $10 billion and $40 billion.[93]

New Judge, Different Results

On January 30, 2008, Judge James Robertson, assigned to the case after Lamberth's abrupt dismissal in 2006, issued his first ruling.[94] He sharply rejected the Interior Department's historical accounting plan, finding that it was legally inadequate regarding the years and accounts covered. But he also chastised Congress for not providing the department with sufficient funding to conduct a thorough trust accounting. He then ordered a hearing to formulate a process that would culminate in an appropriate remedy for the plaintiffs.

Cobell and associates said that $58 billion was needed, though that figure was later reduced by the plaintiffs to $46.85 billion. The government rejected these figures. It calculated that plaintiffs were entitled to only $158.7 million, although on appeal in 2009, the U.S. contradictorily declared that the Indians were entitled to nothing.[95]

Judge Robertson issued his decision on the remedy on August 7, 2008, and awarded the plaintiffs a grossly reduced figure of $455.6 million in restitution.[96] According the government the benefit of the doubt in nearly every aspect of the case. Robertson found that the plaintiffs had failed to substantiate their argument that the government withheld or diverted approximately 30 percent of the total receipts. "Yes," said Robertson, "the United States government spills billions of dollars a year, loses money to fraud, waste, and abuse, and generally mismanages its affairs. But the Indian trust has been repeatedly audited, and while each of those audits has been qualified . . . no audit report states or hints at the disappearance of anything close to thirty percent of trust receipts."[97] He went on to note that "they [the plaintiffs] were not able to prove any *bias* that would render it [the government's statistical model] fundamentally unsound" (emphasis his).[98]

Robertson, in fact, chided the plaintiffs' statistical model, asserting that it could not be considered because, for instance, it was inconsistent—accepting the government's estimate of receipts but not of disbursements, which reflected "a super-strong interpretation of the presumption against the breaching trustee that cannot be equitably applied to the trusts at issue here."[99] In a final blow to the plaintiffs, the judge declared that, jurisdictionally, even if the Indians had been able to prove that the government had benefited at their expense, their calls for restitution were barred by the doctrine of sovereign immunity.

Robertson's two decisions were soon vacated by the U.S. Court of Appeals for the District of Columbia in its tenth opinion in this multiyear suit, in July 2009 in *Cobell v. Salazar.*[100] Chief Judge Sentelle wrote that Robertson had "erred in freeing the Department of Interior from its burden to make an accounting." The case was sent back to the district judge with the demand that the lower court "provide the trust beneficiaries the best accounting possible, in a reasonable time, with the money that Congress is willing to appropriate."[101]

Final Settlement and Aftermath

This latest ruling combined with the presidential election of Barack Obama, who had pledged to resolve the *Cobell* lawsuit, revived interest in a negotiated settlement. After several months of intense negotiations, on December 7, 2009, the parties arrived at two agreements: a comprehensive class action settlement agreement (Settlement Agreement); and an agreement on attorneys' fees, expenses, and costs (Agreement on Attorneys' Fees). Both agreements required congressional authorization. Over the course of a year, several deadlines were missed as the settlements underwent intense scrutiny at congressional hearings and numerous meetings. Congress finally authorized the settlement through the Claims Resolution Act of December 8, 2010.[102] President Obama signed it into law immediately.

The total amount of the settlement was $3.412 billion, an amount greatly reduced from the $46.85 billion the plaintiffs had sought the previous year but substantially larger than Judge Robertson's proposed $455 million in 2008. The settlement monies were to be divided into three separate funds. First, a $1.412 billion Accounting and Trust Administration Fund would be paid directly to class members, with an estimated $377 million proposed as payment to settle historical accounting claims, after deduction of court approved fees, incentive payments, and expenses of administration. Second, a $100 million Trust Administration Adjustment Fund, to be used to increase the minimum payment made to members of the class. And third, a

$1.9 billion Tribal Land Consolidation Fund, to be held and administered by the Interior Department to purchase fractionated interests in trust or restricted lands from individual Indians.[103]

The $1.412 billion was to be distributed to class members in two stages. Stage 1 payments would settle the historical accounting claims—those individuals who had an account open in the government's system as of October 25, 1994 (the date the American Indian Trust Fund Management Reform Act was passed). Each member of this class will receive a check for $1,000 in lieu of the Department of Interior providing a historical accounting. Members of this class were not allowed to opt-out; they had to accept this payment. Stage 2 payments, minus the cost of settlement implementation, would be distributed pro-rata, with payment calculated on the activity in the beneficiary's trust account over a ten-year period. These class members could opt-out of the settlement by providing a written request to be excluded within ninety days of notice. Five hundred dollars was set as the minimum payment to be awarded to those who agree to this settlement, though many will receive $1,500, and some much higher amounts.[104]

When the final settlement was approved in July 2011 incentive awards were made to the four original plaintiffs, led by Elouise Cobell. She was set to receive $2 million; James Louis LaRose was to get $200,000; and Penny Cleghorn and Thomas Maulson were each to receive $150,000.

The funding of the other major account, $1.9 billion for the Trust Land Consolidation Fund, was deemed essential since fractionation of individual allotments, which resulted in thousands of undivided beneficial ownership interests, is a major impediment to effective economic development, tribal jurisdiction, and trust administration.[105] The monies in this fund will be used to buy fractional interests in trust and restricted lands from owners who agree to sell. These lands would be returned to tribal control to aid in consolidation. As an additional incentive to class members, the Settlement Agreement created a $60 million scholarship fund for

Native students to defray the cost of attending post-secondary academic and vocational institutions.

Finally, the settlement included a commitment by the Department of the Interior to establish a National Commission on Indian Trust Administration and Reform to oversee the department in its accounting for and management of individual trusts in the future. On November 30, 2011, Secretary Salazar named the five members—all natives—of this commission, whose job will include delivering, within two years, a report designed to make federal trust administration "more transparent, responsive, customer friendly and accountable" in managing these funds and assets.[106]

The separate agreement on "attorney's fees, expenses, and costs" was also dealt with. The amount the attorneys were to receive was to be determined by the district court, which had overseen the case. The government's lawyers argued that Cobell's legal team should not receive more than $50 million, but the district judge on December 10, 2010, awarded the plaintiffs' attorney team $99 million as "fair and reasonable fees, expenses and costs for work through December 7, 2009."[107] That amount was to be paid out of the Accounting and Trust Administration Fund and it was not to be appealed.

Cobell's lawyers, however, filed an appeal and challenged that figure, arguing that the amount was far too little for the work they had done during the previous fourteen years. Asserting that "class counsel have achieved a 'stunning' landmark victory in this case and through their efforts, approximately $9 billion in tangible benefits have been conferred on the plaintiffs' classes," they stressed that "a fee award of $223 million, plus expenses and costs of $1,276,598, is in accordance with controlling law and within this court's discretion."[108]

Cobell's lawyers faced a weltering tide of complaints by Indian beneficiaries, federal lawmakers, and others who maintained that this much larger figure would cause profound harm to the interests of those Indian class members who stood to gain least from the settlement. Byron Dorgan of North Dakota, chairman of the Senate Committee on Indian Affairs, declared, "It's a profound disappointment to me that the lawyers are trying to go beyond the agreement reached by Congress," adding that it was a "cruel irony that the very lawyers who were supposed to be fighting for Indian interests are now chipping away at their justice."[109] Kimberly Craven, a Sisseton-Wahpeton tribal member and a potential class beneficiary, was also deeply troubled by the attorneys' actions. "The lawyers get congressional approval of the settlement by promising fees would be under $100 million, and are now pulling a bait and switch at the expense of Indians and taxpayers."[110]

The *Cobell* settlement still required final approval by the U.S. District Court for the District of Columbia before it would go into effect. On June 20, 2011, District Judge Thomas Homan held a Fairness Hearing, during which counsel for both parties and objections from members of the plaintiff classes were heard. After hearing all submissions in connection with the proposed settlement and after a remarkably brief one-day hearing, Judge Homan declared that while the government had mismanaged Native resources on a staggering scale, he believed that the settlement agreement provided at least a measure of certainty to Native individuals and a reasonable exit "from this complicated legal morass."[111] The only major point of contention centered on the attorneys' fees. Homan rejected the efforts of Cobell's attorneys to raise their share of the settlement to $223 million and awarded them $99 million as a "fair and reasonable" amount.

After Homan's ruling, Cobell, who was recuperating from cancer surgery, said that while the settlement was not perfect and that it did not compensate for all that had been lost, she believed that it was a fair and reasonable conclusion to an arduous process that had taken a mighty toll. Sadly, Cobell, who had spearheaded the fight against the federal government for over fourteen years, lost her battle with cancer just four months after the settlement's final approval. She passed away on October 16, 2011. She was sixty-five years old.[112]

Despite the final approval of the settlement and before Cobell's passing, several appeals were filed in August and September 2011 by individual natives, including Carol Eve Good Bear, Kimberly Craven,

Ortencia Ford, Donnelly Villegas, Mary Johns, and Charles Colombo. No funds may be distributed until all such appeals have been resolved. Mary Johns, one of the appellants, said that she had filed her appeal in part because she doubted that the BIA could effectively or efficiently use the $1.9 billion set aside for land consolidation and she was concerned that the federal government would wield too much authority over the consolidated lands.[113] Kimberly Craven contended that the distribution scheme was unfair to the class members "because it bears no relation to the underlying claims and perversely undervalues the claims of the most injured class members while providing windfalls to class members who have suffered little or no injury."[114] By the end of 2012 the appeals had been dismissed or withdrawn, with the appellate courts stressing that the settlement was as fair as possible given the complexity of the case. On December 11, 2012, the district court formally approved the commencement of payments to Historical Accounting Class member and distribution of checks to all living class members began the week of December 17, 2012.[115]

In January 2012 Cobell's legal team, anxious to receive its pay, took the highly unusual step of writing a letter online and via email, listing the addresses and phone numbers of the individuals who had filed appeals to the settlement act. Class members were urged to write the appellants "because . . . payments cannot be made until after the appeals have been resolved [and] no one knows when that will occur."[116] Several knowledgeable individuals said such an action bordered on the unethical, and they expressed grave concerns that the appellants might be harassed as a result. Ted Frank, an attorney for Kimberly Craven, said, "We do not believe that the suggestion for class members to contact appellants is appropriate or productive."[117]

Additionally, in February 2012, federal officials, after holding several consultation meetings with tribal representatives from the Midwest and western states in 2011, released their proposed plan on how to spend the $1.9 billion designated to buy fractionated lands to return to tribal ownership. Interior had identified some 88,638 fractionated land tracts owned by some 227,331 individuals. The draft plan proposed a voluntary buyback and consolidation of fractionated and restricted fee land interests over a ten-year period. With tribal members insisting that they have a direct role in the administration and implementation of the land program, the BIA identified three broad goals: (1) reduce land fractionation in highly fractionated areas; (2) consolidate land in areas of tribal preference—to be determined through formal government-to-government arrangements, like memorandum of understandings; and (3) implement a plan that is time and cost efficient.[118]

The burden then shifted to Fawn Sharp (Quinault), Peterson Zah (Navajo), Stacy Leeds (Cherokee), Tex Hall (Three Affiliated Tribes), and Bob Anderson (Boise Forte Ojibwe)—the members of the National Commission on Indian Trust Administration and Reform—and prominent natives all—to arrive at a comprehensive plan in the next two years to address the ongoing trust issues that have long plagued the federal government and Native peoples.

It is far too early to tell whether the settlement act, assuming it is eventually fully implemented, will actually lead to a fundamental reconciliation between the federal government and the several hundred thousand IIM account holders. As with the ICC, lawyers will secure extremely generous compensation, with the average IIM account holder netting only between one and two thousand dollars, and with the BIA still in charge of overseeing the remaining trust resources and consolidated lands, it is problematic whether this lengthy litigation/legislation will truly culminate in natives believing that genuine justice has been attained.

8. A RESEARCH PROGRAM FOR INDIGENOUS CLAIMS

JAMES SHEEHAN HAS said that "a claim is neither a request nor a demand." It is, in fact, "an appeal to some standard of justice, some sort of right, but it is also to assert a willingness to back up this appeal with some sort of action."[1] For powerful or even semi-powerful international states the form of action can be in the nature of war, or at least the threat of violent action. For most Native nations in North America, by the mid to late 1800s, such recourse was no longer feasible, given the devastating demographic and territorial losses they had sustained. Thus for a majority of these reduced nations, legal, political, and moral arguments became the go-to "form of action" they were required to use as they contested the dispossession or gross reductions of their rights and resources. In some cases, of course, Native peoples employed such nonviolent tactics even while they still possessed the military power to confront their radically altered conditions.[2]

Vine Deloria, Jr., put the issue of claims this way: "The basic idea behind claims is that a politically superior entity can injure a person, group, or smaller political entity without punishment but then in so doing it can cancel the effect of that injury by offering a money payment in compensation."[3] This attitude, clearly evident in the previous chapters, generally does not lead to justice or improved interracial relations. The claims discussed throughout this book represent a much deeper problem than a simple land transaction or accounting error. All Native nations endured profound erosions (sometimes extinctions) of their religions, cultures, languages, territories, and governing capacities in the last several centuries. No negotiated settlement, monetary judgment, or judicial ruling will be effective unless major changes are also made in the manner in which the federal government's laws and policies are applied to Native peoples.[4]

As shown in the previous pages, and particularly in regards to *Cobell*, it has generally been futile for Native nations and individuals to submit claims against the U.S. through the litigation process. This was evident very early to natives and to at least one commissioner of Indian Affairs, Thomas J. Morgan. In his annual report to the secretary of the Interior in 1890 Morgan used these bristling and surprisingly frank words to describe the difficulties natives experienced in the process and explained why the federal government was obligated to do more. A lengthy quote is necessary so that the clarity of Morgan's concerns is manifestly seen:

> In the settlement of every Indian claim against the government there are two great factors, the Indian Office and Congress. The records of all treaties and agreements made with Indians and of all moneys paid to them are kept in the Indian Office, and any attorney for the Indians, prosecuting any claim in their behalf, is necessarily obliged to depend almost entirely upon the records of this office for the presentation of his case. . . . The faithful and intelligent prosecution of this work requires the advice and services of a solicitor, who should be appointed for this purpose by the government. So far as the work of this office is concerned I see little if any necessity why the Indians should be at large expense for employing attorneys to prosecute their claims. . . . The Indians should not be forced to employ attorneys for the transaction of any business that they can transact themselves or which should be transacted for them by their agent or by the Indian Office.
>
> There may be, doubtless are, and will continue to be those cases where it is perfectly proper for an attorney to be employed in the preparation and prosecution of Indian claims. I must confess, however, that I am greatly embarrassed, as the Commissioner charged with the administration of the affairs

> of the Indians, and standing in an important sense for the time being as their legal guardian and as a representative of a wise and just government, when I am appealed to sanction a contract authorizing an attorney to receive from the Indians 25 per centum or more of moneys claimed to be due to them as payment for services rendered in persuading the government, through congressional legislation, executive action, or judicial decision, to perform its clearly recognized duty. I shall continue to withhold my approval from all contracts that are not clearly in the interest of the Indians, and unless a failure to approve would be a disadvantage to them.[5]

Morgan's remarks indicate that he had a level-headed approach to claims that, if responded to, might have alleviated some of the more pressing problems confronting Native peoples. In particular, he properly stressed that the federal government should operate with the utmost good faith, that indigenous claims should be handled swiftly and fairly, and that the U.S. should bear the brunt of costs associated with prosecuting such claims since federal actors and policies were generally the cause of the complaints.

However, developing a research program a century and a quarter later to deal constructively with indigenous claims still appears insurmountable to many people because it has been the fashion for scholars and practicing attorneys not to cooperate with each other except on particular pieces of litigation. Additionally, very little progress has been made in the development of an effective strategy for creating consistency in federal Indian policy and law.[6] Federal Indian law, as an area of study and practice, remains exceptionally complex and will not easily lend itself to full reform.

What follows are specific topics that might be involved in any research program to deal with the persistent problem of Native claims. An adequate program would deal with all of these topics as well as others identified as research unfolded. Because the research would be directed primarily at resolving some of these questions, scholars, attorneys, and policymakers would find that working together would considerably ease the burden on any particular person or organization, since cross-fertilization of ideas would enable everyone to progress much faster on individual topics.

This final chapter raises some of the more obvious and immediate questions about indigenous claims in the hope that readers will be inspired to engage these issues more critically and systematically. Addressing the panoply of claims issues that continue to bedevil Native nations and intergovernmental affairs will be a lengthy process that will take years to address. However, once the ideological framework is developed the research should progress with somewhat greater ease, though the resolution of specific claims will still take a great deal of time. Importantly, what is needed is a collective effort of individuals, organizations, and policymakers devoted to bringing a semblance of order to this complex and diversified field that will enable indigenous parties and their allies to contribute to the task of developing a comprehensive and long-term research program.

If a comprehensive research project is to be developed, historians, political scientists, geographers, linguists, sociologists, archivists, and, of course, legal experts will need to be intimately involved. These scholars will help to refine the categories to be addressed and their research should yield interesting questions and data that could be used in litigation, negotiation, or power-sharing arrangements. The resulting literature would educate Native governments, the federal government, state and local governments, and the general public about claims and how the federal government has frequently violated the standard of common decency in trying to avoid righting the wrongs it has wrought on Native peoples.

Types of Claims

Traditionally, claims have been made in a number of identifiable areas: injuries to persons, property losses, land cessions, treaty provisions, accounting procedures used for tribal and individual funds, and dishonorable dealings, among others. Let us examine a few of these.

Injuries to Persons. During the most active treaty era, 1778–1868, these claims were usually handled through negotiations at the next treaty. There are, however, sufficient congressional reports dealing with personal losses and numerous Indian depredation cases to categorically demonstrate that non-Indians were often compensated for their losses whereas Indians were not. During the twentieth century there were several attempts to provide compensation for the massacres of natives at Sand Creek in Colorado and Wounded Knee in South Dakota, although the U.S. Army generally opposed any compensation, arguing that those horrific events were "battles," not full-blown massacres. Although "it is impossible to objectively quantify the value of injuries inflicted upon Indian people across history, and morally odious to try,"[7] the fact that other ethnic groups who endured the wrath of federal policy have been compensated, for example, the Japanese-American citizens who were unjustly interned in concentration camps during World War II, means that it is possible for such a policy to be implemented for similarly aggrieved descendants of Native injuries. This would require, at a minimum, overturning the 1973 Court of Claims case *Fort Sill Apache Tribe v. United States*,[8] in which descendants of the Chiricahua Apache tribe brought suit for compensation for the loss of their power to hold territory, to live their lives and gather resources, and to govern themselves resulting from their arrest and imprisonment for twenty-seven years in Florida, Alabama, and Oklahoma between 1886 and 1913. In this case, the court ruled that the Indian Claims Commission did not provide for claims for individual Indians, but only for tribes, bands, and groups. As Nell Jessup Newton noted, while European states often include compensation for such personal harms, U.S. law "has not provided any mechanism to compensate Indian tribes for loss of political freedom, the destruction of culture, and other intangible harms."[9]

Minimally, this area would provide vital materials for political use and could become a major part of any movement to secure better compensation for existing claims dealing with other topics.

Property Losses. These claims are also bountiful in the Indian depredations materials, but Native nations have only sometimes been successful in trying to secure compensation for property losses. The Lakota did get a token payment for loss of their horses in 1876, and some Northwest Indians did receive some compensation for losses of critical fishing grounds, such as the various places flooded by the many dams that were constructed in Washington and Oregon. Today, however, Native peoples are still sometimes exploited by oil companies, timber corporations, and other extractive industries that cause considerable damage to reservation lands and renewable and non-renewable resources, whether by collusion, neglect, or outright theft.[10]

Two U.S. Supreme Court cases point out both the difficulty and the opportunity Native nations face in contesting property losses. On March 4, 2003, the High Court handed down two major rulings involving the trust property of two tribal nations. In *United States v. White Mountain Apache Tribe*,[11] the court agreed with Apaches that the historic military post, Fort Apache, which was said to be held by the U.S "in trust" for the tribe, had been allowed to fall into disrepair, which violated the government's trust obligation to "maintain, protect, repair and preserve" the fort for the benefit of the tribe. The tribe's lawsuit, seeking $14 million in damages, was affirmed.

By contrast, in *United States v. Navajo Nation*[12] tribal leaders, who had sought to recover some $600 million in lost coal royalties from their federal trustee, learned that the 1938 Mineral Leasing Act did not control all aspects of coal leasing and therefore did not impose any specific fiduciary duties on the federal government to ensure a royalty rate greater than the federal minimum. More recently, in a 2011 case, *Wolfchild v. United States*,[13] the Court of Federal Claims handed down its eighth decision in a long-pending litigation involving over 20,000 Dakota who are the lineal descendants of the Mdewakanton Sioux. These individuals had maintained their loyalty to the U.S. during the 1862 conflict in Minnesota. The court agreed that the Indians were entitled to over $600,000 derived from the leasing and licensing of lands dating back to the late nineteenth century but rejected other claims on the grounds that the Indian plaintiffs were not a "tribe" under the meaning of that term as defined in the Trade and Intercourse Act and because that act and other land grants acts did not create a trust relationship or a money-mandating duty upon the government.

Additionally, historical property losses should also be considered after carefully examining the impact, activity, and flaws associated with the Native American Graves Protection and Repatriation Act of 1990.[14] That important law had two main purposes: to allow Native nations to recover religious and cultural items that rightfully belonged to them and their citizens and then held in federally funded institutions, and to protect the right of tribal nations to safeguard all human remains and related funerary objects that might be found or excavated on federal or tribal land. An important, if flawed measure, this act does not apply to objects found on non-federal land, including state and locally owned territory. And it does not apply to the graves and related objects of non-recognized indigenous peoples.

An important modification was made in 2010 when the Department of Interior codified a rule that addressed so-called culturally unidentifiable human remains. Prior to this time such remains were retained by the institutions—some 650 universities, colleges, and museum, among others—housing them, despite Native objections, because the law had not clearly specified what was to be done with them. The new regulation states that museums and other organizations must notify tribal nations whose current or ancestral lands once held the remains. The tribes are then entitled to have the remains returned to them to be dealt with as they see fit.[15]

Land Cessions. These claims remain at the forefront of the intergovernmental and interracial relationship between Native nations and the federal government, states, counties, and even municipalities, and they are a persistent burr in the saddle of these different, yet overlapping, polities. With Native peoples having lost title to some 98 percent of their land in the last five centuries, and with burgeoning populations, tribal governments are always looking to expand their generally meager land bases. But they are frequently confronted by non-native governments, corporate actors, and private individuals who remain intent on retaining and even expanding their own land bases.

The ICC's work was theoretically designed to bring justice and finality for Native peoples who had lost lands, had treaty provisions violated, and so on, and, of course, to extinguish title to Indian land that had not been properly or fairly purchased or ceded in the past. And while a number of "awards" were made, including one involving the Western Shoshone Identifiable Group in 1977, the distribution of funds—some $26 million (plus interest, which by 2004 had risen to a settlement fund of over $186 million)—to members of this group was not authorized by Congress until 2004.[16] In fact, as of January 2012, over $100 million had not been distributed to eligible Shoshone citizens.

The more traditional Western Shoshone, considered a dissident faction by Congress and more than ably represented for years by sisters Mary and Carrie Dann,[17] on the other hand, unsuccessfully challenged the Claims Commission decision and the distribution judgment by Congress. They did, however, file a successful petition before the Inter-American Commission on Human Rights (IACHR), which determined in 2002 that the U.S. had "failed to ensure the Danns' right to property under conditions of equality contrary to Article II, XVIII, and XXIII of the American Declaration in connection with their claims to property rights in the Western Shoshone ancestral lands."[18] But the U.S. has largely ignored the IACHR report, while at the same time denying that the commission had jurisdiction to hear the case.

Thus what is needed is a thorough review of the Indian Claims Commission and its successor to determine what exactly the Investigation Division did during its existence. This would require a thorough reexamination and analysis of all the claims brought by petitioning Native communities.[19]

One major land claims involves the desired return of the Paha Sapa, the sacred Black Hills, to the Great Sioux nation, in South Dakota. This long-standing and tragic land battle dates to the 1868 Ft. Laramie Treaty. A raft of literature has been written about this critical case,[20] yet it remains unresolved, despite the Supreme Court ruling in 1980 that the U.S. "illegally took" the Black Hills and its granting an award of some $122 million to the Lakota people. The several bands of Lakota have thus far refused to accept the cash award, and the award amount, with accrued interests, is now over $1 billion.

Since 1971 over a dozen individual settlement acts addressing land and other claims of various Native nations have been enacted into law. But the Supreme Court's 2005 *City of Sherrill* decision,[21] which addressed the taxable status of Indian land located within a tribe's original territory, has cast a pall over other pending land claims cases because the intent of the court appeared designed to limit future land claims litigation between Native nations and local governments. As Justice Ruth Bader Ginsburg put it, if the court recognized the Oneida lands as being "Indian Country," "little would prevent [the tribe] from initiating a new generation of litigation to free the parcels from local zoning or other regulatory controls that protect all landowners in the area."[22] For example, just after *City of Sherrill* was handed down, the Court of Appeals for the Second Circuit dismissed the Cayuga nation's land claims in *Cayuga Indian Nation of New York v. Pataki*.[23] The judges in that case held that the Supreme Court's recent ruling "[had] dramatically altered the legal landscape against which we consider plaintiffs' claims," and the Cayuga were thus barred by equitable doctrines from seeking any remedy for treaty-protected lands that had been taken in violation of the Trade and Intercourse Act.[24] In 2006 the Shinnecock people of New York also had their treaty-based land claim dismissed, following the *City of Sherrill* precedent.[25]

Land cessions continue to generate intense emotions for tribal nations that have lost their court battles in recent years, but especially for the Lakota and the traditional Western Shoshone, who continue to seek a path that may eventually culminate in some explicit recognition of their aboriginal homelands, since these two nations have powerful arguments that, in fact, they never effectively ceded their lands to the U.S. More research on how the alleged transfers took place may help solidify the tribes' positions as they seek land restoration.

Treaty Provisions. These claims have oftentimes been litigated in the Court of Claims (now the Court of Federal Claims). The extensive Sioux litigation of the 1930s and 1940s shows how treaty provisions were frequently interpreted. For the most part it was not possible to fit these claims into a theory of recovery because there was often uncertainty over whether the provision constituted a contract or a tort. Other questions arose as well: How were damages to be measured? Were the treaty provisions always mandatory on the federal government? Seemingly, explicit treaty language would provide Native nations with a firm basis for the rights. But that has only sometimes been the case.

For example, in February 2011, the Court of Federal Claims in *Klamath Tribe Claims Committee v. United States*[26] closely examined an 1864 treaty between the United States and the Klamath[27] in which the tribe ceded about 12 million acres of land while reserving some 800,000 acres and "the exclusive right of taking fish in the streams and lakes." A diversion dam was later built that adversely affected several endangered fish species. The dam was removed in 2008. The Klamath Claims Committee filed suit in 2009, alleging several causes and actions, two of which involved the dam's removal, which, the tribe argued, "effectuated a taking of the Tribes' associated water and fishing rights and constituted a breach of fiduciary duties established by the 1864 Treaty and the 1954 [Termination] Act."[28] But since the Klamath tribe was not a party in this suit, the court determined that it could not rule on the treaty question in the tribe's absence.

In addition, what about cases involving the educational provisions in treaties when tribal nations and individual parents refused to consent to having their children attend government schools yet found them compelled to attend? Do Native governments and their citizens have a claim against the U.S. in this matter? These kinds of claims would also be suitable for negotiated settlements, and they cannot be overlooked when thinking of the scope of claims.

Accounting Procedures. These claims, at least the smaller amounts prior to *Cobell*, were reasonably well handled in the past by most lawyers because they were easiest to prove: an analyst closely examined the financial records, did the required accounting, and submitted a bill for resolution. But accounting, as *Cobell* showed, also means that the gist of the federal trust relationship is deeply implicated, and in that respect these types of cases are vitally important.[29] For instance, the Tohono O'odham people of Arizona brought two separate but overlapping suits against the U.S. in 2009—one in the Court of Federal Claims, the other in the District Court for the District of Columbia—asserting that the federal government had breached its fiduciary duty by engaging in self-dealing and imprudent investment "and failed to provide an accurate accounting of the assets held in trust" for the tribal nation. But in 2011, the U.S. Supreme Court held in *United States v. Tohono O'odham Nation*[30] that the two lawsuits represented basically the same claim, thereby precluding jurisdiction in the Court of Federal Claims. This decision has adversely affected a large number of similar tribal suits.

Dishonorable Dealings. These claims have historically received less priority than land claims, but they are important nonetheless. The Gila River Community of Arizona was one of the first Native peoples to file a claim for breach of fair and honorable dealings, which they did in 1970.[31] They sought compensation from the federal government because of actions that had deprived them of much of their lands and water resources. The tribe essentially claimed that the U.S. actions had "reduced them to wardship with no concomitant benefits."[32] The Court of Claims ruled against the Gila River people, holding that the tribe's claims were moral and were beyond the scope of the Indian Claims Commission act. Although the fair and honorable dealings clause has heretofore not been a very effective clause for Indians to rally behind, so long as the trust doctrine exists it might still be of use.

Miscellaneous Claims. Other possible claims could involve issues such as the following: should the Cherokee, the Navajo, the Ojibwe, and other Native nations be compensated when their tribal names are used for products? What about Hollywood movies, television programs, and video games that exploit indigenous names and cultures? Do Native peoples have claims against those churches that were given tribal lands during the nineteenth century? There are many other kinds of claims and many other defendants than the federal government. Identifying new kinds of claims and writing up a literature justifying these claims would be important in any long-term research program on indigenous claims.

Problems in Claims Litigation

Some of the primary problems in claims litigation in the Court of Claims and before the Indian Claims Commission are discussed below. The lists presented here is not exhaustive, and additional research will no doubt reveal other issues. The area of Indian law is, unfortunately, exceedingly technical, and a concerted effort will have to be made to explain each topic in a manner palatable to as broad an audience as possible.

The Court of Claims

Prejudgment of Issues. Tribal nations had to submit their claims to Congress in order to get permission to go to court, but did this requirement pre-judge the worth of the claim and did the subsequent act of admission narrow the issues that could be raised and the remedies that could be given so rigidly that it precluded any just resolution of the issue? The evidence is overwhelming that the jurisdictional acts were so complicated in language and were so often used as an excuse to deny tribes any recovery, that the entire exercise was unjust and fundamentally failed to resolve claims.

Language of the Jurisdictional Acts. Here we must distinguish between language that would be used in admitting ordinary citizens and corporations to the court and language used to admit Native nations to the court. Were certain doctrines of federal Indian law brought into the Court of Claims through the language in the enabling act that precluded any meaningful recovery? If, for example, a corporation challenges a federal act, it would be judged according to constitutional doctrines. Since the tribes were admitted as plaintiffs, did they stand on the same legal basis or were other more debilitating legal doctrines brought into the court, like the so-called plenary power of Congress?

Application of Contract and Tort Law. Since the courts were able to bring contract and tort law into their decision-making processes, and they often did, how could doctrines in these fields of law be overturned or ignored in favor of federal Indian law? In other words, in contract law there must be a "meeting of the minds," but how could minds meet if congressional plenary powers were being wielded? What was the measure of damages that tribes suffered? How can you transfer the fact of a Native community being able to feed and clothe itself to a money-damages system and deny recovery for the loss of buffalo, deer, timber, water, and other natural resources?

The Creation or Manipulation of Legal Doctrines. How many times in Court of Claims cases, ICC rulings, or eastern Indian land claims did the courts "create" new doctrines or redefine existing ones in order to deny Native peoples any recovery? Doctrines such as plenary power, discovery, aboriginal title, trust, and laches were regularly invoked—then and now—by judges and justices and are only sometimes interpreted in a manner that benefits Native peoples. This propensity to manipulate or create law was evident in the Indian depredations cases and continued through the entire history of claims cases.

This area needs to be carefully analyzed because we are suggesting that the very nature of the way the U.S. tried to resolve indigenous claims was unjust, and in the creation or manipulation of special legal doctrines that had and have no application except to a particular Indian case, we have a clear example of courts making law to suit themselves or the co-equal branches of the federal government they share political power with, and not actually rendering decisions that ensure that justice has been done for particular Native communities. This area may well be the single most important topic that needs to be addressed, and the comparison should be to how other plaintiffs are treated—not to how other Native nations were treated.

Isolation of a Case from Ordinary Case Law. Many Indian cases suggest that the holdings in a specific case do not apply to any other circumstances or situation. For example, we have the situation involving California Native communities where the attorney general of California sued on behalf of the tribes yet the State of California had previously demanded, and successfully so, that the 1851–52 treaties negotiated between a number of California tribal nations and the U.S. should be rejected by the Senate and sealed away for some sixty years before they could be made public.

The isolation of these cases made it possible to deny any cumulative effect of this kind of litigation. That is to say, no common body of law emerged with respect to indigenous claims, so that each tribal nation, in effect, had to start anew as if no prior claims had ever been decided.

The Indian Claims Commission

ICC as a Commission. Numerous articles make it clear that the ICC was supposed to be a commission; it was supposed to act informally, hold hearings, investigate claims on its own initiative, and allow anyone to appear before it who had something to say about a particular claim. This basic fact, that it was to act as a commission and not as a court, overshadows everything else when we examine its history and legacy. Research into this important body must be done with this fact in mind, especially when we consider the adverse effects that transpired when it transformed from commission to court against the wishes of Congress. Congress, of course, also bears some responsibility for not challenging this profound shift in orientation.

Identification of Parties. How can any court tell the plaintiffs who can and cannot appear on their behalf? That is to say, of the available representatives of the tribe, does a court have the authority to choose one segment or faction over another, thereby preempting the other parties? In some cases the legitimate tribal governing body did not authorize a suit nor did it sanction the individuals who represented the tribe. In these cases, how can a suit be considered legally binding and valid? What procedures, in other words, should have been used to identify plaintiffs? This concern circles back to the fact that had the ICC functioned as a commission, such issues would have been thoroughly addressed. But once the ICC began operating as a court it did not raise such questions or permit those kinds of inquiries.

Adoption of Court of Claims Procedures. Why were the procedures of the Court of Claims basically transferred to the ICC? What place did the steps of agreeing upon the date of "taking" and that of "evaluation" occupy in predetermining the outcome of the case? The Black Hills, for example, were appraised as if they were merely cattle country complete with a decent stand of useful timber for building corrals and cabins. Yet the dominant reason for the taking of the Black Hills was gold. In other words, historically everyone knew the value of this vast area, and yet the ICC adopted the pretense, transferred to it from the Court of Claims, that the taking was a simple land transaction which transferred only the mass market value of the land.

What other procedures or attitudes were transferred from the Court of Claims that placed substantial obstacles in the way of any tribal recoveries? Did the transfer of these procedures bring with them the belief that land could not be restored? Finally, the important and understudied subject of how attorneys were chosen to represent tribes must also be closely examined.

Failure to Use Investigative Division. The investigative powers of the ICC were clearly outlined in the statute, yet they were never used. Who bears responsibility for this grievous flaw? Why would the ICC not want to use its investigative powers if the purpose of the ICC was to fully resolve indigenous claims, insure justice, and bring a sense of finality to such matters? What might have been investigated had the ICC fully embraced its stated charge?

ICC Returned Lands. Should the Indian Claims Commission have been allowed to return lands to Native nations? Almost every other commission established to deal with tribal matters had great flexibility when it came to dealing with lands. The Klamath Boundary Commission is a case in point: it was charged with determining the exact boundary of the reservation and issuing a final report. Later on, legislation was introduced to deal with land title and compensation. Why could this procedure not have been followed by the ICC?

Should Indigenous Claims Be Litigated?

There is a fundamental question that must be considered regarding research on claims: should claims be litigated or should they instead be the subject of negotiations? Having a lawyer argue about the facts of a case, the date of taking, the area of occupancy, and the value of lands, among other issues, is not negotiation; it is merely shortcutting the procedural barriers. In such instances, there is very little involvement of the Native plaintiffs. The argument is based on technical strategies and rarely reaches the true substance of the claim. Here we need to address the basic injustice of requiring Native nations to litigate when most of the subjects they wanted resolved should have been handled via negotiation.

Since the United States originally dealt with indigenous nations in a diplomatic manner, through treaties, agreements, covenants, and so on, and is now using the same procedure in water rights, gaming compacts, and Indian child welfare agreements, among others, is not the area of claims litigation an exceedingly expensive and basically fruitless detour from the basic political relationship between the U.S. and Native nations? Some of the strongest arguments dealing with indigenous claims will have to be raised in this area—that litigation cannot, under ordinary circumstances, deal justly with claims that tribal nations have because of the very nature of the claims and because of the nature of litigation. Among the reasons for this are the following.

Litigation Requires a Judicial Balancing of Interests. Claims, in contrast, revolve significantly if not exclusively around the question of what happened in history and what should have happened, given the existing law and conditions of the time. Litigation requires that history be rewritten when the occasion requires. One need only look at the Lakota claims involving the Black Hills to see that courts sometimes take excessive liberties with historical facts in reaching their decisions. If a court can rewrite history in order to accommodate the government, is not the entire process fundamentally flawed? In a claims case affecting non-Indians against the government, the court cannot alter the date and circumstances under which the claim arose. But it has done this in some Indian cases in order to reach a decision.

Stipulations Can Easily Pervert the Litigation Process. When a common fact is agreed upon, two parties can stipulate that it is acceptable and proceed. In Indian cases, however, a great deal of stipulation is done simply to circumvent the tedious and difficult work that would otherwise be necessary. A "taking" date is chosen, and it then becomes an official historical fact—even if it is impossible to verify the date by historical research. Such a choice was one problem in the claim of the dissident Western Shoshones: the alleged date of taking, 1872, was actually a year in which no such thing happened. How can the government base judicial rulings, congressional statutes, and judgment distributions on an invented date, a year when no land was actually "taken?"

Indian Claims Are the Only Claims That Have Offsets. Private non-Indian citizens receive incredible benefits from the federal government, and corporations receive gratuities and tax breaks. When private individuals and corporations initiate lawsuits against the government, nothing is deducted for Social Security, FDIC, and various other subsidies. Why is it, then, that tribal nations were required to pay offsets for services they received when the intent of those services was to destroy Native culture and political status, not to enhance it. A strong moral and legal argument needs to be devised to address this important question. We may well discover that the federal government prefers not to fully compensate Native peoples for the true value of their claims because of the sheer costs involved and because in doing so the U.S. would be admitting the extent of the fraud that has been perpetrated on Native peoples.

Federal Courts Are Not Impartial Institutions. These important institutions are subject to the whims of national politics, public sentiment, and other institutions of governance. Very few federal judges or justices will rule in favor of natives if the decision is going to be very controversial or if it will impact large numbers of non-native Americans, at least without some overwhelming body of evidence that cannot be denied, such as was the case of the fishing tribes in Washington and Oregon in the 1970s. The Wounded Knee cases of that same era reveal even more forcefully how easy it is to deny reasonably sound theories of law.

Since no federal court (or any court for that matter) can ever be completely impartial, it should follow that for something as important as the relationship between Native nations and the United States a more impartial forum should be found or created. Commissions, in theory, are supposed to be just such a forum, which is why the ICC was originally established as such. But as described in the preceding chapters, a variety of factors, including cash-hungry attorneys and pious bureaucrats, conspired to take away that body's "impartial" capability and turn it into a court-like body. International venues such as the Permanent Forum and documents like the United Nations Declaration on the Rights of Indigenous Peoples, adopted in 2007, will hopefully come to play a more prominent role for those Native nations seeking a less hostile environment in which to make their claims cases.

Doctrines of Law. Stare decisis, res judicata, and the doctrine of laches are sometimes used in a manner that close off and terminate legal questions. When used in the claims process, they essentially stymie the possibility of having a continuing relationship between Native nations and the United States. Yet the relationship between these parties continues. But Native peoples have had many of their remedies terminated by claims litigation and in negotiated settlements; they have reduced powers to bargain for subjects of concern whereas and the federal government has an ever increasing set of powers it may draw upon in dealing with them. Strangely, these doctrines of law are rarely invoked on the federal government. For instance, when the federal government promises to never again ask for Indian land cessions, nothing in federal Indian law precludes the U.S. from doing just that. Doctrines, in other words, are sometimes created to circumvent what should have been legal safeguards for the tribes.

Make the Nature of the Relationship between Native Nations and the U.S Consistent? There should be a consistent definition of the actual character of the relationship between tribal nations and the U.S., one that would clearly articulate the rights and responsibilities of both parties and identify what steps can and should be taken to resolve disputes when they arise. The same clarity should also be extended to the tribal-state relationship. History shows that sometimes Native nations are viewed as independent polities, sometimes as domestic entities, sometimes as state-like entities, and sometimes as having an international character. Many of these statuses dates to Chief Justice John Marshall's decisions in the 1820s and 1830s,[33] These are radically different political and legal statuses, but the U.S. has never maintained a consistent definition of what the status of indigenous peoples is nor of what the relationship between the federal or state governments and Native peoples actually is.

Careful definition of the relationship between these parties based on the actual status of the U.S. and Native nations that comports with each party's historical status and evolution would be of real aid in clarifying which institutions and procedures, and at what level—tribal, state, national, or international—are required to resolve particular kinds of problems.

Modern Statutory Settlements

The trend since the 1970s is to use negotiated settlements as a means of resolving longstanding claims, and/or new claims that would be prohibitively expensive in litigation. This is evident in a number of the land claims settlement acts, water rights settlements, and the *Cobell* settlement. Additional literature examining the merits of this process needs to be developed to determine if negotiation, rather than litigation, is always the better mechanism to enhance the distinctive political relationship between the United States and Native nations. Daniel McCool's important study of water rights settlements in 2002, *Native Water: Contemporary Indian Water Settlements and the Second Treaty Era*,[34] confirms only that "water settlements have promised a great deal: certainty, finality, wet water, secure rights to a specific amount of water, federal funding, and peace and harmony brought about by 'good faith' bargaining." He continues, "That is a tall order, yet it is clear that, in some cases, some of these goals have been realized."[35] But he quickly cautions, "What may look like an opportunity, however, may also offer hidden dangers." He hastens to add that when it comes to water, "a new approach to water policy in general" is needed that takes into account how indigenous cosmology describes the relationship between human beings and the land and water we are dependent upon. Such a cautionary tale would also likely hold for land claims, accounting failures, and other claims.

Statutory settlements, as McCool noted, are flawed by the fact that Congress sometimes believes that a settlement is final—primarily because federal lawmakers do not wish to involve themselves in any more Indian problems than necessary. Part of a broader research effort would be to advocate that negotiated settlements are never absolutely final, but rather that they represent important steps in a never-ending adjustment of the continuing relationship between Native nations and the United States. In other words, if something goes awry, there is no need to construct a new set of rules and regulations to correct the problem; neither do the parties need to rush to court. Instead, the parties should agree to meet again and devise a new statement of what is wrong and identify and establish adjustments in the relationship to address the problem.

The Nature of the Research Project

A comprehensive research agenda of the kind outlined in this chapter would require the cooperation of scholars and practicing attorneys and constant work with Native nations, interest groups, and organizations. An organization might be formed to serve as a preliminary vehicle for exploring the details of the research envisioned in the previous pages; it could become a major sponsor or simply a cooperating group. This project would necessarily involve highly creative individuals thinking radical, even heretical, thoughts. Those participating in the project should be willing to work with one another on developing an idea, and also willing to gracefully withdraw in favor of a more capable or more enlightened colleague, if such is the best course. People should accept assignments from the group as well as pursue their own individual research and action projects.

A network of people who would be in regular contact with one other should be developed. An annual conference to discuss research, publication, negotiation, and litigation results should be held. Regional or topical conferences of smaller groups should be encouraged. The network should include some means of exchange of writings and documents on a reasonably confidential basis. The network should be prepared to do very long term writing and research as well as to develop short, immediate position papers that can be used for immediate, specific needs.

There should be a central coordinating official who would keep the network functioning and producing. The work of this individual would be primarily one of keeping lines of communication open, informing network members of research in progress, and being aware of any developments happening outside the group that would affect the group's work.

Most research should be done on an individual basis without large grants and media hoopla; research should be an ongoing part of the intellectual life of both the practicing attorney and the professional academic. Funds should be raised to support the central officer, for conferences, and for occasional consultations between members of the group. More time should be spent doing research than in meetings to discuss research.

Such a long-term project could mature into a productive avenue leading to vital research that would educate all necessary parties in a manner that might ultimately lead to genuine reconciliation between indigenous nations and the federal government and to justice for all indigenous nations and their citizens.

Notes

Preface

1. Lytle, for his part, wrote several chapters, but Deloria's attention had shifted to other topics, and the project was essentially stifled.

2. http://www.indianfarmclass.com. Accessed April 15, 2012.

3. Matthew L. M. Fletcher, "Federal Government Trust Management Settlement with 41 Tribes Announced," http://turtletalk.wordpress.com/2012/04/11/federal-government-trust. Accessed April 16, 2012.

4. "Plenary" has other meanings as well, including exclusive authority and preemptive power, and these meanings are historically and constitutionally appropriate. See David E. Wilkins and Tsianina Lomawaima, *Uneven Ground* (Norman: University of Oklahoma Press, 2001), esp. ch. 3.

5. 522 U.S. 329, 343 (1998).

6. Vine Deloria, Jr., "Laws Founded in Justice and Humanity: Reflections on the Content and Character of Federal Indian Law," *Arizona Law Review* 31, no. 2 (1989): 206.

7. See "Indian Claims," in Lucy Kramer Cohen, ed., *The Legal Conscience: Selected Papers of Felix S. Cohen* (New Haven: Yale University Press, 1960), 265.

8. Vine Deloria, Jr., "Trouble in High Places: Erosion of American Indian Rights to Religious Freedom in the U.S.," in Annette Jaimes, ed., *The State of Native America: Genocide, Colonization, and Resistance* (Boston: South End Press, 1992), 267–90.

9. Ibid., 271.

10. The doctrine of discovery, like the trust doctrine and the doctrine of plenary power, has multiple meanings. See Chief Justice John Marshall's conflicting definitions in *Johnson v. McIntosh* (1823) and *Worcester v. Georgia* (1832). Various commentators have also chimed in on this powerful doctrine, as it continues to form the conflicted basis of indigenous land tenure and how that tenure is understood by the federal lawmakers. See, e.g., Vine Deloria, Jr., *Behind the Trail of Broken Treaties* (Austin: University of Texas Press, 1985); Milner S. Ball, "Constitution, Court, Indian Tribes," *American Bar Foundation Research Journal* 1 (1987): 1–139; David E. Wilkins and Tsianina Lomawaima, *Uneven Ground* (Norman: University of Oklahoma Press, 2001); and Blake Watson, *Buying America from the Indians* (Norman: University of Oklahoma Press, 2012).

11. Deloria, "Trouble in High Places," 275.

12. Derick Fay and Deborah James, eds., *The Rights and Wrongs of Land Restitution: "Restoring What Was Ours"* (New York: Routledge-Cavendish, 2009), xii.

13. Katherine Verdery, as quoted in Fay and James, *Rights and Wrongs of Land Restitution*, xii.

14. Ibid.

One. Native Nations and the Court of Claims

1. Russel Lawrence Barsh, "Indian Land Claims Policy in the United States," *North Dakota Law Review* 58 (1982): 7.

2. Ibid., 7–8.

3. See Charles Royce, comp., *Indian Land Cessions in the United States*, in pt. 2, *1896–1897* (Washington, DC: Government Printing Office, 1899); Vine Deloria, Jr., and Raymond DeMallie, eds., *Documents of American Indian Diplomacy: Treaties, Agreements, and Conventions, 1775–1979*, 2 vols. (Norman: University of Oklahoma Press, 1999); and Stuart Banner, *How the Indians Lost Their Land: Law and Power on the Frontier* (Cambridge: The Belknap Press of Harvard University Press, 2005).

4. Nell Jessup Newton, "Compensation, Reparations, and Restitution: Indian Property Claims in the United States," *Georgia Law Review* (1994): 455.

5. Cohen, "Indian Claims," 269.

6. 21 U.S. 543 (1823).

7. As articulated by the court in *McIntosh*, "discovery" broadly meant that European explorers who had arrived in North America—and the U.S. as successor—gained an "exclusive right to extinguish the Indian titles of occupancy, either by purchase or conquest." This also meant that the "discovering" nation had effectively preempted other European powers' involvement with the Native nations in a particular geographic area. More important, as interpreted by Western policymakers and legal scholars, this doctrine has effectively excluded indigenous peoples from direct participation as national entities in the international arena.

8. 1 Stat. 137.

9. Banner, *How the Indians Lost Their Land*, 135.

10. Ibid., 4.

11. Ibid.

12. Harvey D. Rosenthal, "Indian Claims and the American Conscience: A Brief History of the Indian Claims Commission," in Imre Sutton, ed., *Irredeemable America: The Indians' Estate and Land Claims* (Albuquerque: Native American Studies, 1985), 35.

13. See Heidi K. Stark's study, "Stealing Fire, Scattering Ashes: Anishinaabe Expressions of Sovereignty, Nationhood, and Land Tenure in Treaty Making with the U.S. and Canada, 1785–1923" (Ph.D. diss., University of Minnesota, 2008), for a detailed analysis of this nation's understanding of property and land tenure.

14. Rosenthal, *Their Day in Court: A History of the Indian Claims Commission* (New York: Garland, 1991), 4.

15. Banner, *How the Indians Lost Their Land*, 68.
16. Margaret Hunter Pierce, "The Work of the Indian Claims Commission," *American Bar Association Journal* 63 (1977): 232.
17. Robert W. Barker, "The American Indian, Federal Citizen and State Citizen," *Federal Bar Journal* (Summer 1960): 241.
18. Sandra Danforth, "Repaying Historical Debts, the Indian Claims Commission," *North Dakota Law Review* 49 (Winter 1973): 359.
19. Vine Deloria, Jr., *Behind the Trail of Broken Treaties: An Indian Declaration of Independence* (Austin: University of Texas Press, 1985), 208.
20. Banner, *How the Indians Lost Their Land*, 82–83.
21. 10 Stat. 612.
22. See Larry Skogen, *Indian Depredations Claims, 1796–1920* (Norman: University of Oklahoma Press, 1996), 126.
23. Congressional Globe, 37th Cong., 2nd Sess. (1861).
24. 12 Stat. 765.
25. 11 Stat. 611.
26. 12 Stat. 765, 767.
27. *Standing Bear v. Crook*, 25 F. Cas. 695 (C.C.D. Neb. 1879).
28. Pierce, "Work of the Indian Claims Commission," 227.
29. Barsh, "Indian Land Claims," 10.
30. Rosenthal, *Their Day in Court*, 12.
31. 25 F. Cas. 695 (C.C.D. Neb. 1879).
32. Rosenthal, *Their Day in Court*, 15.
33. Thomas Henry Tibbles, *The Ponca Chiefs: An Account of the Trial of Standing Bear* (Lincoln: University of Nebraska Press, 1972), 134.
34. 21 Stat. 504.
35. Glen A. Wilkinson, "Indian Tribal Claims before the Court of Claims," *Georgetown Law Journal* 55 (December 1966): 513.
36. Ibid., 511.
37. Cong. Rec., 59th Cong., 2nd Sess. (1907), pt. 3: 2145.
38. Cong. Rec., 63rd Cong., 3rd Sess. (1915), pt. 3: 2846.
39. Cong. Rec., 63rd Cong., 3rd Sess. (1915), pt. 4: 3550.
40. Cong. Rec., 66th Cong., 2nd Sess. (1920), pt. 4: 3706.
41. Ibid.
42. 43 Stat. 253.
43. Deloria, *Behind the Trail of Broken Treaties*, 217.
44. Danforth, "Repaying Historical Debts," 362.
45. Michael Lieder and Jake Page, *Wild Justice: The People of Geronimo vs. The United States* (New York: Random House, 1997), 121.
46. Rosenthal, *Their Day in Court*, 19.
47. Lurie, "Indian Claims Commission," 57.
48. 33 Stat. 194.

49. Wilkinson, "Indian Tribal Claims," 511–12.

50. Lewis Meriam, *The Problem of Indian Administration* (Baltimore: Johns Hopkins University Press, 1928), 805–11.

51. 95 Ct. Cl. 642 (1942).

52. 13 Stat. 663.

53. 58 Ct. Cl. 302 (1923).

54. 39 Stat. 47.

55. 63 Ct. Cl. 270 (1927).

56. Ibid., 271.

57. 27 Ct. Cl. 1 (1891).

58. *U.S. v. Old Settlers*, 148 U.S. 427, 428 (1893).

59. Deloria, *Behind the Trail of Broken Treaties*, 218–19.

60. In 1990 Congress via a concurrent resolution did formally acknowledge "deep regret" over the killing of some 350 to 375 men, women, and children. But to date no financial reparations have been provided for the descendants of those slain. See Senate Cong. Res. 153, Cong. Rec., 101st Cong., 3rd Sess. (1990), pt. 1: 138 in Senate Select Committee on Indian Affairs, "Proposed Wounded Knee Park and Memorial," 102nd Cong., 1st Sess. (April 30, 1991), 86–87.

61. Lieder and Page, *Wild Justice*, 56.

62. Ibid.

63. David Getches, Charles Wilkinson, and Robert Williams, Jr., *Federal Indian Law*, 5th ed. (St. Paul: Thompson/West, 2005), 284.

64. Monroe E. Price, *Law and the American Indian* (Indianapolis: Bobbs-Merrill 1973), 496.

65. John R. White, "Barmecide Revisited: The Gratuitous Offset in Indian Claims Cases," *Ethnohistory* 25, no. 2 (Spring 1978): 191.

66. 81 Ct. Cl. 101 (1935).

67. 43 Stat. 21.

68. *Shoshone Tribe v. United States*, 82 Ct. Cl. 23 (1935).

69. 98 Ct. Cl. 583 (1942).

70. Price, *Law and the American Indian*, 495.

71. U.S. Congress, Senate Committee on Indian Affairs, *Hearings on S. 2731 to Create an Indian Claims Commission*, 74th Cong., 1st Sess. (June 10, 1935), 12–13.

72. 49 Stat. 571, 596.

73. White, "Barmecide Revisited," 190.

74. Wilkinson, "Indian Tribal Claims," 517, note 47.

75. Lieder and Page, *Wild Justice*, 57.

76. Price, *Law and the American Indian*, 499.

77. Lieder and Page, *Wild Justice*, 56.

78. Ibid., 58.

Two. The Indian Depredations Acts

1. See, e.g., Raymond D. Austin, *Navajo Courts and Navajo Common Law: A Tradition of Tribal Self-Governance* (Minneapolis: University of Minnesota Press, 2009), and Matthew L. M. Fletcher, *American Indian Tribal Law* (New York: Aspen Publishers, 2011), which describe the historic and contemporary structure and values of the Navajo nation's customary systems and the systems of a variety of indigenous peoples across the country.
2. U.S. House Committee on Indian Affairs, *Claims Arising From Indian Depredations*, 51st Cong., 1st Sess. (1890), H. Rept. 1079, 2–3.
3. *Report of the Attorney General*, 5 Opinion of A.G. (1950), 268.
4. Treaty with the Cherokee, June 26, 1794. 7 Stat. 43.
5. 22 Stat. 804.
6. 26 Stat. 851.
7. 1 Stat. 137.
8. Ibid., 138.
9. 1 Stat. 469.
10. Ibid., 472.
11. Larry C. Skogen, *Indian Depredations Claims, 1796–1920* (Norman: University of Oklahoma Press, 1996), 34–35.
12. *Leighton v. United States and the Ogalalla Band of Indians*, 29 Ct. Cls. 288, 303 (1894).
13. 4 Stat. 743.
14. Skogen, *Indian Depredations Claims*, xv.
15. *Jaeger v. the United States and the Yuma Indians*, 29 Ct. Cl. 278 (1894).
16. 4 Stat. 729.
17. 11 Stat. 401.
18. U.S. House Committee on Indian Affairs, *Claims Arising From Indian Depredations* (1890), 4.
19. 16 Stat. 335, 360 (July 15, 1870).
20. 17 Stat. 165, 190 (May 29, 1892).
21. 23 Stat. 362, 376 (March 3, 1885).
22. U.S. House Committee on Indian Affairs, *Claims Arising from Indian Depredations* (1890), 5.
23. Skogen, *Indian Depredations Claims*, 114.
24. Ibid., 1.
25. Ibid., 3.
26. Ibid.
27. Ibid.
28. Ibid., 5.
29. Ibid., 7–8.
30. 26 Stat. 851.

31. Slogan, *Indian Depredations Claims*, 148.
32. 26 Stat. 851, 853 (1891).
33. 24 Stat. 388.
34. 48 Stat. 984.
35. Skogen, *Indian Depredations Claims*, 207.
36. Ibid., 212.

Three. The Struggle to Create an Indian Claims Commission

1. Quoted by Ernest L. Wilkinson before the Subcommittee of the Committee on the Judiciary on February 14, 1940, on land claims. Wilkinson's testimony is included in the House Committee on Indian Affairs, *Creating an Indian Claims Commission, Hearings on H.R. 1198 and H.R. 1341*, 79th Cong., 1st Sess. (June 1945), 96.

2. See, Vine Deloria, Jr., and Raymond J. DeMallie, comps., *Documents of American Indian Diplomacy: Treaties, Agreements, and Conventions, 1775–1979*, 2 vols. (Norman: University of Oklahoma Press, 1999); and Donald L. Fixico, ed., *Treaties with American Indians: An Encyclopedia of Rights, Conflicts, and Sovereignty*, 3 vols. (Santa Barbara: ABC Clio, 2008).

3. Wilkinson, *Hearings on H.R. 1198 and H.R. 1341*, 103.

4. As quoted in John Vance, "The Congressional Mandate and the Indian Claims Commission," *North Dakota Law Review* 45 (1968–1969): 326–27.

5. As quoted in Lieder and Page, *Wild Justice*, 60.

6. Lewis Meriam, et al., *The Problem of Indian Administration* (Baltimore: Johns Hopkins University Press, 1928), 805.

7. See Thomas E. Leubben, "The United States Indian Claims Commission: A Remedy for Ancient Wrongs, A Source of New Wrongs," in *Redressing Injustices through Mass Claims Processes: Innovative Responses to Unique Challenges*, ed. International Bureau of the Permanent Court of Arbitration (New York: Oxford University Press, 2006), 152–78, for a good overview of the ICC.

8. Senate Subcommittee of the Committee on Indian Affairs, *Hearings on the Survey of Conditions of Indians in the United States, Indian Claims against the Government*, pt. 25. *Hearings on S. Res. 79 and 308*, 70th Cong., and S. Res. 263 and 416, 71st Cong. (1930 and 1931), 13409–10.

9. Ibid., 13409–10.
10. Ibid., 13411.
11. Ibid.
12. Ibid., 13414.
13. Ibid.
14. Ibid., 13552.
15. Ibid., 13417.
16. Ibid.

17. Ibid., 13521.
18. Ibid., 13494.
19. Ibid., 13474.
20. Ibid., 13522.
21. Ibid., 13520.
22. Ibid., 13626–27.
23. Ibid., 13671–13677 for a copy of the bill.
24. As quoted in H. D. Rosenthal, *Their Day in Court: A History of the Indian Claims Commission* (New York: Garland Publishing, 1990), 53.
25. 48 Stat. 984. And see Vine Deloria, Jr., *The Indian Reorganization Act: Congresses and Bills* (Norman: University of Oklahoma Press, 2002), and Elmer R. Rusco, A *Fateful Time: The Background and Legislative History of the Indian Reorganization Act* (Reno: University of Nevada Press, 2000) for good treatments of this important law.
26. Rusco, *Fateful Time*, 270.
27. Kenneth R. Philp, *John Collier's Crusade for Indian Reform, 1920–1954* (Tucson: University of Arizona Press, 1977), 94.
28. Cong. Rec., 71st Cong., 2nd Sess. (December 21, 1929), pt. 1: 1051–53.
29. Ibid.
30. Ibid.
31. U.S. House Committee on Indian Affairs, *Creating an Indian Claims Commission, Hearings on H.R.* 7837, 74th Cong., 1st Sess. (1935), 4.
32. Rosenthal, *Their Day in Court*, 61.
33. Ibid., 9.
34. Ibid., 17.
35. Ibid., 19.
36. Ibid., 18.
37. Ibid., 17.
38. Lieder and Page, *Wild Justice*, 56–58.
39. Ibid., 21.
40. U.S. House Committee on Indian Affairs, *To Create an Indian Claims Commission on H.R. 1198 and H.R. 1341*, 79th Cong., 1st Sess. (1945), 19.
41. Ibid., 24.
42. Ibid., 32.
43. Ibid., 46.
44. Ibid., 47.
45. Ibid., 75.
46. Ibid., 43.
47. Ibid., 44.
48. Ibid., 69.
49. See the following studies of Cohen's life and work that emphasize his prominent role in the development of federal Indian law: David E. Wilkins, ed., *On the*

Drafting of Tribal Constitutions (Norman: University of Oklahoma Press, 2006), and Dalia Tsuk Mitchell, *Architect of Justice: Felix S. Cohen and the Founding of American Legal Pluralism* (Ithaca: Cornell University Press, 2007).

50. U.S. House Committee on Indian Affairs, *To Create an Indian Claims Commission* (1945), 132.

51. Rosenthal, *Their Day in Court*, 82.

52. Ibid., 103.

53. Ibid., 103.

54. Ibid., 106.

55. Ibid.

56. Ibid., 81.

57. Ibid., 88.

58. Ibid., 16.

59. Ibid., 149.

60. Ibid., 150.

61. Ibid., 156.

62. Ibid., 152.

63. Ibid., 114.

64. Ibid.

65. Senate Committee on Indian Affairs, *To Create an Indian Claims Commission, Hearings on H.R. 4497*, 79th Cong., 2nd Sess. (1946), 25.

66. Ibid., 16.

67. Ibid., 18.

68. Ibid., 60.

69. Rosenthal, *Their Day in Court*, 82. Importantly, "earlier versions of the bill limited attorney fees to a maximum of ten percent of recovery and barred any government employee from aiding the claimant while in office and for two years after they left their official position." Ibid., 77.

70. Ibid., 19.

71. Ibid.

72. Ibid., 36.

73. Ibid., 23.

74. Cong. Rec., 79th Cong., 2nd Sess. (1946), 92, 5314.

75. Lieder and Page, *Wild Justice*, 64.

76. 66 Stat. 1049.

77. U.S. President, *Public Papers of the President of the United States. Harry S. Truman*. 1946 (Washington, DC: Government Printing Office, 1962), 414.

78. Russel L. Barsh, "Indian Land Claims Policy in the United States," *North Dakota Law Review* 58 (1982): 14.

79. Senate Committee on Indian Affairs, "To Create an Indian Claims Commission" (1946), 15.

80. Barsh, "Indian Land Claims," 11.

81. As quoted in Barsh, "Indian Land Claims," 15.

82. 60 Stat. 812.

83. 60 Stat. 939.

84. Rosenthal, *Their Day in Court,* 93–94.

Four. The Indian Claims Commission: From Hope to Reality

1. Lieder and Page, *Wild Justice*, 64.

2. P. G. McHugh, *Aboriginal Societies and the Common Law: A History of Sovereignty, Status, and Self-Determination* (New York: Oxford University Press, 2004), 553.

3. Sandra Danforth, "Repaying Historical Debts, the Indian Claims Commission," *North Dakota Law Review* 49 (Winter 1973): 373–75.

4. Nancy O. Lurie, "Epilogue," in Imre Sutton, ed., *Irredeemable America: The Indians' Estate and Land Claims* (Albuquerque: Native American Studies), 369.

5. Rosenthal, *Their Day in Court,* 144.

6. Ibid., 144–46.

7. 25 U.S. Code, Sections 81–84.

8. Leubben, "United States Indian Claims Commission," 166.

9. Vine Deloria, Jr., *Behind the Trail of Broken Treaties: An Indian Declaration of Independence,* reprint ed. (Austin: University of Texas Press, 1985), 226.

10. Vine Deloria, Jr., "Reflections on the Black Hills Claim," *Wicazo Sa Review* 4, no. 1 (Spring 1988): 35.

11. Leubben, "United States Indian Claims Commission," 152.

12. Ibid.

13. Sandra Danforth, "Repaying Historical Debts, the Indian Claims Commission," *North Dakota Law Review* 49 (Winter 1973): 390–391.

14. Leubben, "United States Indian Claims Commission," 164.

15. David Wishart, as quoted in P. G. McHugh, *Aboriginal Societies and the Common Law*, 554.

16. Deloria, *Behind the Trail of Broken Treaties*, 224.

17. Danforth, "Repaying Historical Debts," 373.

18. Indian Claims Commission, *Final Report* (1978), 7.

19. Leubben, "The United States Indian Claims Commission," 162–63, and see Petra T. Shattuck and Jill Norgren, *Partial Justice: Federal Indian Law in a Liberal Constitutional System* (Providence, RI: Berg Publishers, 1993), 146–48.

20. As quoted in Danforth, "Repaying Historical Debts," 374.

21. Michael Coyle, "ADR Processes and Indigenous Rights: A Comparative Analysis of Australia, Canada, and New Zealand," in Benjamin J. Richardson, Shin Imo, and Kent McNeil, eds., *Indigenous Rights and the Law: Comparative and Cultural Perspectives* (Portland, OR: Hart Publishers, 2009), 380.

22. *Western (Old Settler) Cherokee Indians v. U.S.*, 1 Ind. Cl. Comm. 20 (1948).

23. *Western (Old Settler) Cherokee Indians v. U.S.*, 116 Ct. Cl. 665 (1950).

24. Rosenthal, *Their Day in Court*, 143–44.

25. Ibid., 115.

26. Indian Claims Commission, *Final Report*, 5.

27. Shattuck and Norgren, *Partial Justice*, 147.

28. Barsh, "Indian Land Claims," 16.

29. 2 Ind. Cl. Comm. 355 (1953).

30. 131 Ct. Cl. 593 (1955).

31. 348 U.S. 272 (1955).

32. Nell Jessup Newton has written the most articulate analysis of this important case, "At the Whim of the Sovereign: Aboriginal Title Reconsidered," *Hastings Law Journal* 31 (1980): 1215–85.

33. 348 U.S. 272, 290–91.

34. Lurie, "Indian Claims Commission" (1957), 64–65.

35. David E. Wilkins, *American Indian Sovereignty and the U.S. Supreme Court: The Masking of Justice* (Austin: University of Texas Press, 1997), 185.

36. Rosenthal, *Their Day in Court*, 123.

37. Indian Claims Commission, *Final Report*, 12.

38. Rosenthal, *Their Day in Court*, 150–51.

39. Ibid., 151.

40. Berlin B. Chapman, *Otoe and Missouria: A Study of Indian Removal and the Legal Aftermath* (New York: Times Journal Publishers, 1965), 261.

41. Ibid.

42. Ibid., 263.

43. 70 Stat. 624.

44. Indian Claims Commission, *Final Report*, 13.

45. Lieder and Page, *Wild Justice*, 160.

46. Ibid., 14.

47. Ibid.

48. 81 Stat. 11.

49. It is interesting that Blue, a member of a non-federally recognized tribal nation, was the one native appointed to the commission. State-recognized and non-federally-recognized Native peoples were denied the right to file claims before the ICC. See the following studies to learn more about the interesting history of the Lumbee people: Adolph Dial and David Eliades, *The Only Land I Know: A History of the Lumbee Indians* (San Francisco: Indian Historian Press, 1975); Gerald Sider, *Lumbee Indian Histories: Lumbee and Tuscarora People in North Carolina* (Chapel Hill: University of North Carolina Press, 2003); and Malinda Maynor Lowery, *Lumbee Indians in the Jim Crow South: Race, Identity, and the Making of a Nation* (Chapel Hill: University of North Carolina Press, 2010).

50. Rosenthal, *Their Day in Court*, 222.

51. Indian Claims Commission, *Final Report*, 18.

52. 86 Stat. 114.

53. Rosenthal, *Their Day in Court*, 233.

54. 105 Ct. Cl. 658 (1946).

55. *The Creek Nation v. United States*, 97 Ct. Cl. 591.

56. Ralph A. Barney, "Legal Problems Peculiar to Indian Claims Litigation," *Ethnohistory* 2 (Fall 1955): 316.

57. Nancy O. Lurie, "The Indian Claims Commission," *Annals of the American Academy of Political and Social Science* 311 (May 1957): 63.

58. Saliha Belmessous, ed., *Native Claims: Indigenous Law against Empire, 1500–1920* (New York, Oxford University Press, 2012):12.

59. *Sac and Fox Tribes v. United States*, 161 Ct. Cl. 189, 201 (1963).

60. *Tee Hit Ton Indians v. United States*, 128 Ct. Cl. 82 (1954). This ruling, as discussed earlier in the chapter, was affirmed by the Supreme Court the following year.

61. *Otoe and Missouria Tribe v.United States*, 131 Ct. Cl. 593 (1955).

62. U.S. House Committee on Indian Affairs, *To Create an Indian Claims Commission, Hearings on H.R. 7837*, 74th Cong., 1st Sess. (1935), 6.

63. Nancy O. Lurie, "The Indian Claims Commission," *Annals of the American Academy of Political and Social Science* 436 (May 1978): 107.

64. *Gila River Pima-Maricopa Indian Community v. United States*, 20 Ind. Cl. Comm. 131 (1968).

65. Ibid., 427 F.2d 1194, 1196 (1970).

66. Ibid., 1201.

67. Ibid., 1200.

68. Danforth, "Repaying Historical Debts," 390.

69. Leubben, "U.S. Indian Claims Commission," 176.

Five. The Indian Claims Commission: Its Politics and Operations

1. Shattuck and Norgren, *Partial Justice*, 148–50.

2. John T. Vance, "The Congressional Mandate and the Indian Claims Commission," *North Dakota Law Review* 45 (1968/1969): 333.

3. Vance, "Congressional Mandate," 325.

4. Alfred L. Kroeber, "Nature of the Land-Holding Group," *Ethnohistory* 2, no. 4 (Fall 1955): 313.

5. Lieder and Page, *Wild Justice*, 270.

6. Lurie, "Indian Claims Commission," 60.

7. Ibid., 61.

8. See Lieder and Page, *Wild Justice*, 120–24, for a good overview of this complex situation.

9. See Omer C. Stewart, "Kroeber and the Indian Claims Commission Cases," *Kroeber Anthropological Society Papers* 25 (Fall 1961): 181–90, for a good analysis of

the ICC case, and also *Indians of California v. United States* (98 Ct. Cls. 583, 1942), which examines the unique dimensions of the California situation.

10. *Thompson ex rel. Indians of California v. United States*, 1 Ind. Cl. Comm. 358 (1950).

11. *Thompson ex rel. Indians of California v. United States*, 122 Ct. Cl. 348, 360 (1952).

12. Ibid.

13. *Mole Lake Band v. United States*, 126 Ct. Cl. 596 (1953).

14. *Ottawa Tribe of Indians v. United States*, 2 Ind. Cl. Comm. 461 (1953).

15. Ibid., 467–68.

16. *McGhee v. United States*, 122 Ct. Cl. 380, 391 (1952).

17. U.S. Indian Claims Commission, *Final Report*, 10.

18. Ibid.

19. See, Heidi K. Stark, "Stealing Fire, Scattering Ashes: Anishinaabe Expressions of Sovereignty, Nationhood, and Land Tenure in Treaty Making with the United States and Canada, 1785–1923" (Ph.D diss., University of Minnesota, 2008), who has written extensively about land tenure among the Anishinaabe; and McMillen, *Making Indian Law*, chapter 6 for a good analysis of the differing conceptions of land tenure.

20. See McMillen, *Making Indian Law*, xv and 173–76, where it is persuasively argued that the ICC process and the Supreme Court's 1941 decision *U.S. v. Santa Fe Pacific Railroad Co.* effectively created a new field of study, ethnohistory.

21. Leubben, "U.S. Indian Claims Commission," 167.

22. Thomas Le Duc, "The Work of the Indian Claims Commission under the Act of 1946," *Pacific Historical Review* 26 (February 1957): 9.

23. Ibid., 10.

24. 317 U.S. 369 (1943).

25. 131 Ct. Cl. 593 (1955).

26. Lurie, "Indian Claims Commission," 103.

27. *Sioux Tribe of Indians v. U.S.*, 146 F. Supp. 229 (1956).

28. Leubben, "U.S. Indian Claims Commission," 167.

29. *Crow Indians v. U.S.*, 151 Ct. Cl. 284 (1960).

30. *Kaw Tribe v. U.S.*, 1 Ind. Cl. Comm. 608 (1951).

31. *Red Lake, Pembina, and White Earth Bands v. U.S.*, 6 Ind. Cl. Comm. 247 (1958).

32. *Indians of California v. U.S.*, 8 Ind. Cl. Comm. 1 (1959).

33. *Miami Tribe of Oklahoma v. U.S.*, 175 F. Supp. 926 (1959).

34. Sandra C. Danforth, "Repaying Historical Debts: The Indian Claims Commission," *North Dakota Law Review* 49 (1972/1973): 397.

35. 97 F. Supp. 381 (1951).

36. Leubben, "U.S. Indian Claims Commission," 145.

37. Danforth, "Repaying Historical Debts," 39.

38. Ibid.

39. See Rosenthal, *Their Day in Court*, 191–92, and Lieder and Page, *Wild Justice*, 145–46.

40. As quoted in Lurie, "Indian Claims Commission," 103.

41. Ibid.

42. Shattuck and Norgren, *Partial Justice*, 153.

43. Cohen, *Handbook of Federal Indian Law*, 2005 ed., 454–55.

44. U.S. Indian Claims Commission, *Final Report*, 7.

45. Robert W. Barker, "The Indian Claims Commission—The Conscience of the Nation in Its Dealings with the Original American," *Federal Bar Journal* 20 (Summer 1960): 243.

46. 1 Ind. Cl. Comm., 43 (1948), reversed 119 Ct. Cl. 592 (1951).

47. 119 Ct. Cl. 592, 602–3.

48. Ibid., 613–14.

49. U.S. Indian Claims Commission, *Final Report*, 6.

50. Lieder and Page, *Wild Justice*, 270.

51. Donald C. Gormley, "The Role of the Expert Witness," *Ethnohistory* 2 (Autumn 1955): 330.

52. Helen H. Tanner, "An Expert Witness View of the ICC," in Daniel M. Cobb and Loretta Fowler, eds. *Beyond Red Power: American Indian Politics and Activism since 1900* (Santa Fe: School for Advanced Research, 2007), 183.

53. Lurie, "Indian Claims Commission," 60.

54. Rosenthal, "Indian Claims and the American Conscience," 48.

55. Gormley, "Role of the Expert Witness," 329.

56. Rosenthal, *Their Day in Court*, 124.

57. Tanner, "Expert Witness View," 183.

58. See Lurie's "Epilogue" (1985), 363–82, which contains a good discussion of the documentary evidentiary problems that confronted Native peoples in their quest for justice.

59. 177 Ct. Cl. 184, 202 (1966).

60. *Yakima Tribe v. United States*, 158 Ct. Cl. 672 (1972).

61. Ibid., 692.

62. *Pueblo de Zia v. U.S.*, 165 Ct. Cl. 501, 505 (1964).

63. Ibid.

64. Danforth, "Repaying Historical Debts," 374–75.

65. Ibid., 375.

66. Ibid., 374, note 47.

67. See, Lurie, "Epilogue," 363–82; Shattuck and Norgren, *Partial Justice*, 147–48; and Lieder and Page, *Wild Justice*, 88–89.

68. Vance, "Congressional Mandate," 335–36.

69. Lieder and Page, *Wild Justice*, 89.

70. U.S. Indian Claims Commission, *Final Report*, 17.

71. Lieder and Page, *Wild Justice*, 162.

72. Rosenthal, *Their Day in Court*, 231.

73. Robert W. Barker, "The Indian Claims Commission—The Conscience of the Nation in Its Dealings with the Original American," *Federal Bar Journal* 20 (Summer 1960): 245.

74. U.S. Indian Claims Commission, *Final Report*, 15.

75. Vance, "Congressional Mandate," 334, note 37.

76. Danforth, "Repaying Historical Debts," 386–87.

77. 8 Ind. Cl. Comm. 392, 414–15 (1960).

78. Michelle Smith and Janet C. Neuman, "Keeping Indian Claims Commission Decisions in Their Place: Assessing the Preclusive Effect of ICC Decisions in Litigation Over Off-Reservation Treaty Fishing Rights," *University of Hawaii Law Review* 31 (Summer 2009): 482.

79. See, e.g., Jeffrey Ostler, *The Lakotas and the Black Hills: The Struggle for Sacred Ground* (New York: Viking, 2010), 173–76.

80. Vine Deloria, Jr., *Behind the Trail of Broken Treaties: An Indian Declaration of Independence* (Austin: University of Texas Press, 1985), 227–28.

81. McMillen, *Making Indian Law*, provides a detailed analysis of not only this important Supreme Court ruling but also the critical role ethnohistorians played in the litigation and throughout the ICC era.

82. Ibid., 173.

83. U.S. Indian Claims Commission, *Final Report*, 21.

84. Leubbens, "U.S. Indian Claims Commission," 177–78.

Six. The Resurgence of Eastern Natives

1. 528 F. 2d 370 (1975).

2. Richard S. Jones, "Indians: Land Claims by Eastern Tribes," Congressional Research Service, Issue Brief IB 77040 (Washington, D.C.: Government Printing Office, 1977; updated in 1982). And see George P. Generas, Jr., and Karen Gantt, "This Land Is Your Land, This Land Is My Land: Indian Land Claims," *Journal of Land, Resources, and Environmental Law* 28, no. 1 (2008): 1–18.

3. Christopher Vecsey, "Introduction: The Issues Underlying Iroquois Land Claims," in Christopher Vecsey and William A. Starna, eds., *Iroquois Land Claims* (Syracuse: Syracuse University Press, 1988), 3.

4. Jack Campisi, "The Trade and Intercourse Acts: Land Claims on the Eastern Seaboard," in Imre Sutton, ed., *Irredeemable America: The Indians' Estate and Land Claims* (Albuquerque; University of New Mexico Press, 1985), 344.

5. 92 Stat. 813.

6. Jones, "Indians: Land Claims by Eastern Tribes" (1982), 1–2.

7. See Karim M. Tiro, "Claims Arising: The Oneida Nation of Wisconsin and the Indian Claims Commission, 1951–1982," *American Indian Law Review* 32 (2007–2008): 509–24.

8. 414 U.S. 661 (1974). This case is also known simply as *Oneida I.*

9. 470 U.S. 226 (1985). This case is known as *Oneida II.*

10. 544 U.S. 197 (2005).

11. See, Amy Borgman, "Stamping Out the Embers of Tribal Sovereignty: *City of Sherrill v. Oneida Indian Nation* and Its Aftermath," *Great Plains National Resources Journal* 10 (2006): 59–72, and Jennifer R. Sunderlin, "One Nation, Indivisible: American 'Indian Country' in the Wake of *City of Sherrill v. Oneida Indian Nation,*" *Albany Law Review* 70 (2006–2007): 1563–87.

12. The Aroostook band of Micmacs was not part of the 1980 settlement since they were not recognized at the time. They would receive federal recognition in 1991, while simultaneously agreeing to the extinguishment of their aboriginal title to lands in Maine (105 Stat. 1143). See Nicole Friederichs, "A Reason to Revisit Maine's Indian Claims Settlement Acts: The United Nation's Declaration on the Rights of Indigenous Peoples," *American Indian Law Review* 35 (2010–2011): 497–526.

13. Jones, "Indians: Land Claims by Eastern Tribes" (1982), 2.

14. 1 Stat. 137.

15. Jack Campisi, "The Trade and Intercourse Acts: Land Claims on the Eastern Seaboard," in Imre Sutton, ed., *Irredeemable America: The Indians' Estate and Land Claims* (Albuquerque: University of New Mexico Press, 1985), 338.

16. Vine Deloria, Jr., and Raymond DeMallie, eds., *Documents of American Indian Diplomacy: Treaties, Agreements, and Conventions, 1775–1979,* vol. 2 (Norman: University of Oklahoma Press 1999), 1091–92.

17. Campisi, "Trade and Intercourse Acts, 342.

18. Francis J. O'Toole and Thomas N. Tureen, "State Power and the Passamaquoddy Tribe: A Gross National Hypocrisy?" *Maine Law Review* 23 (1971): 38.

19. *Passamaquoddy Tribe v. Morton,* 388 F. Supp. 649, 653 (1975).

20. Ibid., 660.

21. *Joint Tribal Council of the Passamaquoddy Tribe v. Morton,* 528 F. 2d 370, 377, note 7 (1975).

22. Jones, "Indians: Land Claims by Eastern Tribes" (1982), 4.

23. U.S. Senate Select Committee on Indian Affairs, *Authorizing Funds for the Settlement of Indian Claims in the State of Maine,* 96th Cong., 2d Sess. (1980), S. Rep. 96–957, 13.

24. Reynold Nebel, Jr., "Resolution of Eastern Indian Land Claims: A Proposal for Negotiated Settlement," *American University Law Review* 27 (1977/1978): 699.

25. Ibid., 696, note 10.

26. Austin Scott, "President Chooses Georgia Justice as Indian Negotiator," *Washington Post,* March 12, 1977, p. 3.

27. Richard C. Ehlke, "Indian Claims under the Nonintercourse Act," Congressional Research Service, 78–47A (Washington, D.C.: Government Printing Office, 1978), 13–14.

28. Ibid., 14.

29. U.S. Senate Select Committee on Indian Affairs, *Authorizing Funds for the Settlement of Indian Claims*, 13–14.

30. 599 F. 2d 1061 (1979).

31. 404 A.2d 551 (1979).

32. U.S. Senate Select Committee on Indian Affairs, *Proposed Settlement of Maine Indian Land Claims: Hearings on S. 2829*, 96th Cong., 2d Sess. (1980), 378.

33. Ibid., 379.

34. U.S. House Committee on Interior and Insular Affairs, *Settlement of Indian Land Claims in the State of Maine: Hearings on H.R. 7919*, 96th Cong., 2d Sess. (1980), 264–65.

35. Alexander Tallchief, "Money vs. Sovereignty: An Analysis of the Maine Settlement," *American Indian Journal* (May 1980): 20.

36. Ibid., 21.

37. 94 Stat. 1785.

38. Granville Ganter, "Sovereign Municipalities? Twenty Years after the Maine Indian Claims Settlement Act of 1980," in Bruce E. Johansen, ed., *Enduring Legacies: Native American Treaties and Contemporary Controversies* (Westport, Conn.: Praeger, 2004), 30.

39. Ibid., 32.

40. 75 F. 3d 784 (1996).

41. Sharon Kiley Mack, "High-Stakes Bingo Coming Soon to Down East," *Bangor Daily News*, May 19, 2010, http://www.bangordailynews.com/detail/143958.html.

42. Campisi, "Trade and Intercourse Acts," 347.

43. Nicole Friederichs, "A Reason to Revisit Maine's Indian Claims Settlement Acts: The United Nations Declaration on the Rights of Indigenous Peoples," *American Indian Law Review* 35 (2010/2011): 525.

44. Ibid., 497.

Seven. The *Cobell* Trust Fund Litigation and Settlement Plan

1. This subtitle is borrowed from an excellent article by Julia Witty in *Mother Jones* 30, no. 5 (September/October 2005) that provided a fairly comprehensive treatment of the *Cobell* litigation to that point.

2. 124 Stat. 3064.

3. Justin Guilder, "Focus on *Cobell v. Salazar*," *Federal Lawyer* (March/April 2010): 31.

4. *Cobell v. Babbitt*, 30 F. Supp. 2d 24, 39 (D.D.C. 1998).

5. 30 U.S. 1 (1831).

6. 485 U.S. 439 (1988).

7. 131 S. Ct. 2313 (2011).

8. Ibid., 2319.
9. Ibid.
10. Ibid., 2324.
11. 463 U.S. 206 (1983).
12. 316 U.S. 286 (1942).
13. 131 S. Ct. 2313, 2327–28.
14. Ibid., 2330.
15. See Vine Deloria, Jr., and Raymond DeMallie's outstanding volumes on indigenous-state diplomacy: *Documents of American Indian Diplomacy: Treaties, Agreements, and Conventions, 1775–1979*, 2 vols. (Norman: University of Oklahoma Press, 1999). One of their major arguments, contrary to what is often maintained, is that treaty-making did not end in 1871 but that the process has continued unabated—the diplomatic products have simply been renamed—from treaties, to agreements, to negotiated settlements.
16. U.S. Congress, House, " 'Misplaced Trust': The Bureau of Indian Affairs: Mismanagement of the Indian Trust Fund," House Report 102–499, 102d Cong., 2d Sess. (Washington, D.C.: Government Printing Office, 1992), 6.
17. 7 Stat. 381.
18. 1 Stat. 131.
19. 4 Stat. 729.
20. Francis P. Prucha, *American Indian Policy: The Indian Trade and Intercourse Acts, 1790–1834* (Lincoln: University of Nebraska Press, 1962): 57–58.
21. As quoted in Lawrence F. Schmeckebier, *The Office of Indian Affairs: Its History, Activities and Organization* Service Monograph of the U.S. Government, no. 48 (Baltimore: Institute for Government Research, 1927), 27.
22. 4 Stat. 564.
23. 4 Stat. 735.
24. 9 Stat. 395.
25. Felix S. Cohen, *Handbook of Federal Indian Law*, reprint ed. (Albuquerque: University of New Mexico Press, 1972), 76.
26. U.S. Congress, House, "Abstracted Indian Trust Bonds," House Report No. 78, 36th Cong., 2d Sess. (Feb. 12, 1861), 20.
27. See, N. Bruce Duthu, *American Indians and the Law* (New York: Viking Books, 2008), 168.
28. 36 Stat. 855.
29. 40 Stat. 561.
30. 52 Stat. 1037.
31. Ibid.
32. Bureau of Municipal Research, "Report to the Joint Commission of the Congress . . ." (1915), 1.
33. Ibid., 1–2.
34. Ibid., 2.

35. Ibid., 32.

36. Ibid.

37. 40 Stat. 561, 591.

38. U.S. Congress, House, "Misplaced Trust" (1992), 6.

39. 52 Stat. 1037.

40. See, e.g., Lawrence C. Kelly's *John Collier and the Origins of Indian Policy Reform* (Albuquerque: University of New Mexico Press, 1983) for good treatment of Collier life and policy goals.

41. 48 Stat. 984.

42. See Emily Greenwald, *Reconfiguring the Reservation: The Nez Perce, Jicarilla Apaches and the Dawes Act* (Albuquerque: University of New Mexico Press, 2002), 34.

43. Armen H. Merjian, "An Unbroken Chain of Injustice" (2010/2011), 619.

44. U.S. Congress, House, "Misplaced Trust" (1992), 2.

45. Ibid., 17.

46. Ibid.

47. Ibid.

48. Ibid., 1.

49. 108 Stat. 4239.

50. Ibid., 4240.

51. Ibid., 4244.

52. Tim Kenworthy, "Native Americans Could Win $10B in Century-Old Dispute," *USA Today*, February 14, 2002, 1a.

26. U.S. Congress, House, "Abstracted Indian Trust Bonds," House Report No. 78, 36th Cong., 2d Sess. (Feb. 12, 1861), 20.

54. Ibid.

55. Julia Whitty, "Accounting Coup," *Mother Jones* 30, no. 5 (2005): 56.

56. Old Person, former chairman of the Blackfeet Nation, was removed by order on March 5, 2003.

57. Mildred Kleghorn died two years later and was replaced by her daughter, Penny Cleghorn.

58. *Cobell v. Kempthorne*, No. 05–5269. The government had unsuccessfully tried to remove Lamberth earlier, claiming that he had received information outside the adversarial process.

59. Ibid., 33.

60. Merjian, "Unbroken Chain of Injustice," 643.

61. 30 F. Supp. 2d 24 (1998).

62. Ibid., 28.

63. Ibid., 29.

64. Merjian, "Unbroken Chain of Injustice," 621.

65. 30 F. Supp. 2d 24, 29 (1998).

66. Ibid., 45.

67. 91 F. Supp. 2d 1 (1999).

68. Ibid., 6.

69. *Cobell v. Norton*, 240 F. 3d 1081 (2001).

70. Ibid., 1081.

71. M. Maureen Murphy, "The Indian Trust Fund Litigation: An Overview of *Cobell v. Kempthorne*" (Congressional Research Report, August 2008), 4.

72. *Cobell v. Norton*, 226 F. Supp. 1 (2002). In fall 2002, the government made its first push to have Lamberth removed from the case, asking him to recuse himself and to disqualify the special monitor. Lamberth rejected the government's call on both counts.

73. *Cobell v. Norton*, 334 F. 3d 1128 (2003).

74. U.S. Congress, House, Oversight Hearing Before the Committee on Resources, "Status of the Indian Trust Fund Lawsuit." *Cobell v. Norton*, 109th Cong., 1st Sess. (Feb. 16, 2005), 10.

75. *Cobell v. Norton*, 283 F. Supp. 2d 66,212 (2003).

76. Merjian, "Unbroken Chain," 639.

77. 118 Stat. 2809 and 119 Stat. 499.

78. *Cobell v. Norton*, 392 F. 3d 461 (2004).

79. *Cobell v. Norton*, 337 F. Supp. 2d 298 (2005).

80. *Cobell v. Norton*, 4289 F. 3d 1073, 1077 (2005).

81. Ibid., 1077.

82. Merjian, "Unbroken Chain," 641.

83. *Cobell v. Kempthorne*, 455 F. 3d 317 (2006).

84. *Cobell v. Norton*, 229 F. R. D. 5 (D.D.C. 2005).

85. *Cobell v. Kempthorne*, 455 F. 3d 317, 326–28 (2006).

86. Ibid.

87. Ibid., 329.

88. Ibid., 335.

89. Ibid.

90. M. Maureen Murphy, "Indian Trust Fund Litigation: Legislation to Resolve Accounting Claims in *Cobell v. Norton* (Congressional Research Report, RS 22343, March 8, 2007), 4–5.

91. *New York Times*, "Fixing an Old Injustice," August 4, 2005.

92. Murphy, "Indian Trust Fund Litigation" (2007), 6.

93. Merjian, "Unbroken Chain," 646.

94. *Cobell v. Kempthorne*, 532 F. Supp. 2d 37 (2008).

95. Merjian, "Unbroken Chain," 650.

96. *Cobell v. Kempthorne*, 569 F. Supp. 2d 223 (2008).

97. Ibid., 231.

98. Ibid., 240.

99. Ibid., 251.

100. 573 F. 3d 808 (2009).

101. Ibid., 813.

102. 124 Stat. 3064.

103. Ibid.

104. Justin Guilder, "Focus on *Cobell v. Salazar*," *Federal Lawyer* 57 (March/April 2010): 32–33.

105. But see Jered T. Davidson, "This Land Is Your Land, This Land Is My Land? Why the *Cobell* Settlement Will Not Resolve Indian Land Fractionation," *American Indian Law Review* 35 (September 2011): 575–619.

106. "Salazar Names Indian Trust Administration and Reform Panel" (November 30, 2011), http://www.indianz.com/News/2011/003911.asp.

107. *Cobell v. Salazar*, No. 1:96 CV01285 (Dec. 10, 2010), 9. Joint Motion for Preliminary Approval of Settlement.

108. Ibid. (Dec. 14, 2010), 3. Plaintiffs' Petition for Class Counsel's Fees, Expenses and Costs through Settlement.

109. Rob Capriccioso, "*Cobell* Lawyers Reprimanded for Money Requests," *This Week from Indian Country Today* (February 23, 2011): 1.

110. Ibid.

111. *Cobell v. Salazar*, No. 1:96 CV01285 (July 27, 2011), 2. Order Granting Final Approval to Settlement.

112. Rob Capriccioso, "Warrior Woman Walks On," *This Week from Indian Country Today* 1, no. 40 (November 2, 2011): 24–25.

113. Rob Capriccioso, "The Scarlet Letter," *This Week from Indian Country Today* 2, no. 5 (February 15, 2012): 20–21.

114. *Craven v. Salazar*, 2012 U.S. App. Lexis 10230 (May 22, 2012), 6.

115. "Indian Trust Settlement," http://indiantrust.com/index.

116. *Craven v. Salazar*, 2012 U.S. App. Lexis 10230 (May 22, 2012), 21.

117. Ibid.

118. U.S. Department of Interior, "Cobell Land Consolidation Program Draft Plan" (February 2012), 30–31. www.doi.gov/cobell.

Eight. A Research Program for Indigenous Claims

1. James Sheehan, "The Problem of Sovereignty in European History," *American Historical Review* 111, no. 1 (February 2006): 3.

2. Saliha Belmessous, "Introduction: The Problem of Indigenous Claim Making in Colonial History," in Saliha Belmessous, ed., *Native Claims: Indigenous Law Against Empire: 1500–1920* (New York: Oxford University Press, 2012), 3.

3. "Reflections on the Black Hills Claim," *Wicazo Sa Review* 4, no. 1 (Spring 1988): 34.

4. Ibid., 37.

5. U.S. House, Annual Report of the Commissioner of Indian Affairs, House Executive Document No. 1, 51st Cong., 2d Sess. (Washington, D.C.: Government Printing Office, 1890), lxxxi.

6. One important exception to this broad reality is the Tribal Supreme Court Project, which is part of the Tribal Sovereignty Protection Initiative established in 2001 by the National Congress of American Indians in partnership with the Native American Rights Fund. The aim of this initiative is to help coordinate and improve strategy on court cases that might impact all Native nations. It now consists of a working group of over 200 attorneys and academics who specialize in federal Indian law (http://www.narf.org/cases/supctproj.html).

7. William A. Bradford, "Beyond Reparations: An American Indian Theory of Justice," *Ohio State Law Journal* 66 (2005): 83.

8. 477 F. 2d 1360 (Ct. Cl. 1973).

9. Nell Jessup Newton, "Compensation, Reparations, & Restitution: Indian Property Claims in the United States," *Georgia Law Review* 28 (1994): 458.

10. See, e.g., Richmond L. Clow and Imre Sutton, eds., *Trusteeship in Change: Toward Tribal Autonomy in Resource Management* (Boulder: University Press of Colorado, 2001); and Judith V. Royster and Michael C. Blumm, *Native American Natural Resources Law: Cases and Materials*, 2d ed. (Durham, N.C.: Carolina Academic Press, 2008).

11. 537 U.S. 465 (2003).

12. 537 U.S. 488 (2003).

13. 2011 WL 3438414 (Fed. Cl., August 5, 2011).

14. 104 Stat. 3048 (1990).

15. Sudhin Thanawala, "Tribes Recovering Ancestral Remains," *Washington Post*, January 8, 2012, http://www.washingtonpost.com/politics/tribes-receiving-ancestral.

16. 118 Stat. 805 (2004).

17. See Leubben, "U.S. Indian Claims Commission," 169–75.

18. http://www.cidh.oas.org/annual/rep/2002eng/USA.11140.htm.

19. Vine Deloria, Jr., "The Western Shoshone," *American Indian Journal* 2, no. 1 (January 1976): 20.

20. See, e.g., Vine Deloria, Jr., "Reflections on the Black Hills Claim," *Wicazo Sa Review* 4, no. 1 (Spring 1988): 33–38; Nell Jessup Newton, "Indian Claims in the Courts of the Conqueror," *American University Law Review* 41 (1992): 753–854; and John P. LaVelle, "Rescuing *Paha Sapa*: Achieving Environmental Justice Restoring the Great Grasslands and Returning the Sacred Black Hills to the Great Sioux Nation," *Great Plains National Resources Journal* 5, nos. 1 & 2 (Spring/Summer 2001): 40–101.

21. *City of Sherrill v. Oneida Indian Nation*, 544 U.S. 197 (2005).

22. Ibid., 220.

23. 413 F. 3d 266 (2005).

24. Ibid., and see Wenona T. Singel and Matthew L. M. Fletcher, "Power, Authority, and Tribal Property," *University of Tulsa Law Review* 41, no. 1 (Fall 2005) for good analysis of these cases.

25. *The Shinnecock Indian Nation v. The State of New York*, No. 05-CV-2887, 2000 U.S. Dist. Lexis 87516 (November 28, 2006). And see Indian Law Resource Center, "Draft Principles of Law Relating to Native Lands and National Resources," Native

Land Law Project (Little Canada: MN.: Indian Land Tenure Foundation, 2010), 67–68.

26. 97 Fed. Cl. 203 (2011).

27. 16 Stat. 707.

28. 97 Fed. Cl. 203, 209 (2011).

29. See, e.g., Kevin Gover, "An Indian Trust for the Twenty-First Century," *Natural Resources Journal* 46, no. 2 (Spring 2006): 317–74, and Curtis G. Berkey, "Rethinking the Role of the Federal Trust Responsibility in Protecting Indian Land and Resources," *Denver University Law Review* 83, no. 4 (2006): 1069–81.

30. 131 S. Ct. 1723.

31. *Gila River Pima-Maricopa Indian Community v. United States*, 427 F. 2d 1194 (Ct. Cl. 1970).

32. Quoted in Newton, "Indian Claims in the Courts of the Conqueror," 778.

33. See *Johnson v. McIntosh*, 21 U.S. 543 (1823); *Cherokee Nation v. Georgia*, 30 U.S. 1 (1831); *Worcester v. Georgia*, 31 U.S. 515 (1832); and *Mitchel v. United States*, 34 U.S. 711 (1835).

34. Daniel McCool, *Native Water: Contemporary Indian Water Settlements and the Second Treaty Era* (Tucson: University of Arizona Press, 2002.

35. Ibid., 191.

Bibliography

Barker, Robert W. "The American Indian, Federal Citizen and State Citizen." *Federal Bar Journal* 20 (Summer 1960): 211–41.

Barsh, Russel L. "Indian Land Claims Policy in the United States." *North Dakota Law Review* 58, no. 1 (1982): 7–82.

Belmessous, Saliha, ed. *Native Claims: Indigenous Law against Empire, 1500–1920.* New York: Oxford University Press, 2012.

——. "Introduction: The Problem of Indigenous Claim Making in Colonial History." In Saliha Belmessous, ed., *Native Claims: Indigenous Law against Empire, 1500–1920.* New York: Oxford University Press, 2012, 3–18.

Berkey, Curtis. "Rethinking the Role of the Federal Trust Responsibility in Protecting Indian Land and Resources." *Denver University Law Review* 83, no. 4 (2006): 1069–81.

Blancke, Brian. " 'We'll Never Give in to the Indians': Opposition to Restitution in New York State." In Derick Fay and Deborah James, eds., *The Rights and Wrongs of Land Restitution: 'Restoring What Was Ours.'* New York: Routledge-Cavendish, 2009, 235–59.

Borgman, Amy. "Stamping Out the Embers of Tribal Sovereignty: *City of Sherrill v. Oneida Indian Nation and Its Aftermath*." *Great Plains Natural Resources Journal* 10, no. 1 (Spring 2006): 59–72.

Bradford, William. "Beyond Reparations: An American Indian Theory of Justice." *Ohio State Law Journal* 66 (2005): 1–104.

——. " 'With a Very Great Blame on Our Hearts': Reparations, Reconciliation, and an American Indian Plea for Peace with Justice." *American Indian Law Review* 27 (2002–2003): 1–175.

Brodeur, Paul. "Annals of Law: Restitution." *New Yorker* (October 17, 1982): 76–155.

——. *Restitution: The Land Claims of the Mashpee, Passamaquoddy, and Penobscot Indians of New England.* Boston: Northeastern University Press, 1985.

Bureau of Municipal Research. "Report on the Business and Accounting Methods Employed in the Administration of the Office of Indian Affairs." Prepared for the Joint Commission of the Congress of the U.S. to Investigate Indian Affairs Relative to Business and Accounting Methods Employed in the Administration of the Office of Indian Affairs." 63rd Cong., 3d Sess. Washington, DC: Government Printing Office, 1915.

Campisi, Jack. *The Mashpee Indians.* Syracuse: Syracuse University Press, 1991.

——. "The Trade and Intercourse Acts: Land Claims on the Eastern Seaboard." In Imre Sutton, ed., *Irredeemable America: The Indians' Estate and Land Claims.* Albuquerque: University of New Mexico Press, 1985, 337–62.

Capriccioso, Rob. "*Cobell* Concludes with the Rich Getting Richer." *Indian Country Today* (June 27, 2011). http://indiancountrytodaymedianetwork.com/2011/06/cobell-conclude.

——. "*Cobell* Lawyers Reprimanded for Money Requests." *Indian Country Today* (February 23, 2011). http://www.indiancountrytodaymedianetwork.com/2011/02/cobell-lawyers.

——. "Judge Grants *Cobell* Settlement Final Approval." *Indian Country Today* (June 21, 2011). http://www-indiancountrytodaymedianetwork.com/2011/06/judge-grants.

——. "The Scarlet Letter." *Indian Country Today* (February 15, 2012): 20–21.

Carlson, Leonard A. "What Was It Worth? Economic and Historical Aspects of Determining Awards in Indian Land Claims Cases." In Imre Sutton, ed., *Irredeemable America: The Indians' Estate and Land Claims*. Albuquerque: University of New Mexico Press, 1985, 87–109.

Clemmer, Richard O. "Land Rights, Claims, and Western Shoshones: The Ideology of Loss and the Bureaucracy of Enforcement." *PoLAR: Political and Legal Anthropology Review* 32, no. 2 (November 2009): 279–311.

Clinton, Robert N., and Margaret J. Hotopp. "Judicial Enforcement of the Federal Restraints on Alienation of Indian Land: The Origins of the Eastern Land Claims." *Maine Law Review* 31, no. 1 (1979).

Clow, Richmond L., and Imre Sutton, eds. *Trusteeship in Change: Toward Tribal Autonomy in Resource Management*. Boulder: University Press of Colorado, 2001.

Cohen, Felix S., comp. *Cohen's Handbook of Federal Indian Law*. 2005 ed. Edited by Nell Jessup Newton. Newark, NJ: LexisNexis, 2005.

——, comp. *Handbook of Federal Indian Law*, reprint ed. Albuquerque: University of New Mexico Press, 1972.

——. "Indian Claims." In Lucy Kramer Cohen, ed., *The Legal Conscience: Selected Papers of Felix S. Cohen*. New Haven: Yale University Press, 1960, 264–72.

Coulter, Robert T., and Steven M. Tullberg. "Indian Land Rights." In Sandra L. Cadwalader and Vine Deloria, Jr., eds., *The Aggressions of Civilization: Federal Indian Policy Since the 1880s*. Philadelphia: Temple University Press, 1984, 185–213.

Coyle, Michael. "ADR Processes and Indigenous Rights: A Comparative Analysis of Australia, Canada and New Zealand." In Benjamin J. Richardson, Shin Imai and Kent McNeil, eds. *Indigenous Peoples and the Law: Comparative and Critical Perspectives*. Portland, OR: Hart Publishing, 2009, 371–99.

Danforth, Sandra. "Repaying Historical Debts, the Indian Claims Commission." *North Dakota Law Review* 49 (Winter 1973): 359–403.

Davidson, Jered T. "This Land Is Your Land, This Land Is My Land? Why the *Cobell* Settlement Will Not Resolve Indian Land Fractionation." *American Indian Law Review* 35 (September 2010–2011): 575–619.

Deloria, Vine, Jr. *Behind the Trail of Broken Treaties: An Indian Declaration of Independence*. Austin: University of Texas Press, 1985.

———. "Laws Founded in Justice and Humanity: Reflections on the Content and Character of Federal Indian Law." *Arizona Law Review* 31, no. 2 (1989): 203–223.

———. "Reflections on the Black Hills Claim." *Wicazo Sa Review* 4, no. 1 (Spring1988): 33–38.

———. "The Western Shoshones." *American Indian Journal* 2, no. 1 (January 1976): 16–20.

Deloria, Vine, Jr., and Raymond J. DeMallie, comps. *Documents of American Indian Diplomacy: Treaties, Agreements, and Conventions, 1775–1979*. 2 vols. Norman: University of Oklahoma Press, 1999.

Dwyer, William E., Jr. "Land Claims under the Indian Non-Intercourse Act: 25 U.S.C. 177." *Boston College Environmental Law Review* (December 1978): 259–92.

Economist. "A Long Overdue Scalping." Vol. 362, no. 8265 (March 23, 2002): 33.

Ehlke, Richard C. "Indian Claims under the Non-Intercourse Act." Congressional Research Service, 78–47 A. Washington, DC: Government Printing Office, 1978.

Fay, Derick, and Deborah James. " 'Restoring What Was Ours': An Introduction." In Derick Fay and Deborah James, eds., *The Rights and Wrongs of Land Restitution: "Restoring What Was Ours."* New York: Routledge-Cavendish, 2009, 2–23.

———, eds. *The Rights and Wrongs of Land Restitution: "Restoring What Was Ours."* New York: Routledge-Cavendish, 2009.

Files, John. "Appeals Panel Removes Judge Presiding over Indian Lawsuit." *New York Times*, July 12, 2006. http://www.nytimes.com/2006/07/12/washington/12indian.html.

———. "One Banker's Fight for a Half-Million Indians." *New York Times*, April 20, 2004. http://www.nytimes.com/2004/04/20/politics/20INDI.htm.

———. "U.S. Is Ordered to Tell Indians before Selling Trust Property." *New York Times*, October 4, 2004. http://www.nytimes.com/2004/10/04/politics/04trusts.html.

Friederichs, Nicole. "A Reason to Revisit Maine's Indian Claims Settlement Acts: The United Nations Declaration on the Rights of Indigenous Peoples." *American Indian Law Review* 35 (2010/2011).

Ganter, Granville, "Sovereign Municipalities? Twenty Years after the Maine Indian Claims Settlement Act of 1980." In Bruce E. Johansen, ed., *Enduring Legacies: Native American Treaties and Contemporary Controversies*. Westport, CT: Praeger, 2004, 25–43.

Garvey, Todd. "The Indian Trust Fund Litigation: An Overview of *Cobell v. Salazar*." Congressional Research Service Report. RL 34628 (January 3, 2011).

Generas, George P. Jr., and Karen Gantt. "This Land Is Your Land, This Land Is My Land: Indian Land Claims." *Journal of Land, Resources, and Environmental Law* 28, no. 1(2008): 1–18.

Gormley, Donald C. "The Role of the Expert Witness." *Ethnohistory* 2 (Autumn 1955): 326–46.

Gover, Kevin. "An Indian Trust for the Twenty-First Century." *Natural Resources Journal* 46, no. 2 (Spring 2006): 317–74.

Guilder, Justin. "Focus on: *Cobell v. Salazar*." *Federal Lawyer* (March/April 2010): 31–34.

Harmon, Alexandra. *Rich Indians: Native People and the Problem of Wealth in American History*. Chapel Hill: University of North Carolina Press, 2010.

Harper, Keith. "*Cobell v. Norton*" *Human Rights* 33, no. 2 (Spring 2006): 5–6.

Indian Law Resource Center. *Native Land Law Project: Draft General Principles of Law Relating to Native Lands and Natural Resources*, gen. ed. Little Canada, MN: Indian Land Tenure Foundation, February 2010.

Jones, Richard S. "American Indian Policy: Background, Nature, History, Current Issues, Future Trends." Congressional Research Report, 87–227. Washington, DC: Government Printing Office, 1987.

———. "Indians: Land Claims by Eastern Tribes." Congressional Research Service, Issue Brief Number IB77040. Washington, DC: Government Printing Office, 1982.

Kenworthy, Tom. "Native Americans Could Win $10b in Century-Old Dispute." *USA Today* (February 14, 2002).

Kickingbird, Kirke, and Karen Ducheneaux. *One Hundred Million Acres*. New York: MacMillan, 1973.

Kim, Yule. "The Indian Trust Fund Litigation: An Overview of *Cobell v. Salazar*." Congressional Research Service Report for Congress. RL 34628 (March 2, 2010).

Kinney, J. P. A *Continent Lost, a Civilization Won: Indian Land Tenure in America*. Baltimore: Johns Hopkins University Press, 1937.

LaVelle, John. "Rescuing *Paha Sapa*: Achieving Environmental Justice by Restoring the Great Grasslands and Returning the Sacred Black Hills to the Great Sioux Nation." *Great Plains Natural Resources Journal* 5, nos. 1 & 2 (Spring/Summer 2001): 40–101.

Lazarus, Edward. *Black Hills/White Justice: The Sioux Nation versus the United States, 1775 to the Present*. New York: Harper Collins, 1991.

Le Duc, Thomas. "The Work of the Indian Claims Commission under the Act of 1946." *Pacific Historical Review* 26 (February 1957): 1–16.

Lieder, Michael, and Jake Page. *Wild Justice: The People of Geronimo vs. the United States*. New York: Random House, 1997.

Locklear, Arlinda F. "The Oneida Land Claims: A Legal Overview." In Christopher Vescey and William A. Starna, eds., *Iroquois Land Claims*. Syracuse: Syracuse University Press, 1988, 141–53.

Luebben, Thomas E. "The United States Indian Claims Commission: A Remedy for Ancient Wrongs, a Source of New Wrongs." In International Bureau of the Permanent Court of Arbitration, ed., *Redressing Injustices Through Mass Claims Processes: Innovative Responses to Unique Challenges*. New York: Oxford University Press, 2006, 151–78.

Lurie, Nancy O. "Epilogue." In Imre Sutton, ed., *Irredeemable America: The Indians' Estate and Land Claims*. Albuquerque: University of New Mexico Press, 1985, 363–82.

———. "The Indian Claims Commission Act." *Annals of the American Academy of Political and Social Science* 311 (May 1957): 56–70.

———. "The Indian Claims Commission," *Annals of the American Academy of Political and Social Science* 436 (1978): 97–110.

Mack, Sharon Kiley. "High-Stakes Bingo Coming Soon to Down East." *Bangor Daily News*, May 19, 2010. http://www.bangordailynews.com/detail/143958.html.

McHugh, P. G. *Aboriginal Societies and the Common Law: A History of Sovereignty, Status, and Self-Determination*. New York: Oxford University Press, 2004.

———. *Aboriginal Title: The Modern Jurisprudence of Tribal Land Rights*. New York: Oxford University Press, 2011.

McSloy, Stephen Paul. "Revisiting the 'Courts of the Conqueror:' American Indian Claims against the United States." *Federal Bar News & Journal* 41 (September 1994): 552–60.

Meriam, Lewis. *The Problem of Indian Administration*. Baltimore: Johns Hopkins University Press, 1928.

Merjian, Armen H. "An Unbroken Chain of Injustice: The Dawes Act, Native American Trusts, and *Cobell v. Salazar*." *Gonzaga Law Review* 46, no. 3 (2010/2011): 609–59.

Mohawk, John. "The Iroquois Land Claims: A Legacy of Fraud, Politics, and Dispossession," In Bruce E. Johansen, ed., *Enduring Legacies: Native American Treaties and Contemporary Controversies*. Westport, CT: Praeger, 2004, 80–93.

Murphy, M. Maureen. "The Indian Trust Fund Litigation: An Overview of *Cobell v. Kempthorne*." Congressional Research Service Report for Congress. RL 34628 (August 20, 2008).

———. "Indian Trust Fund Litigation: Legislation to Resolve Accounting Claims in *Cobell v. Norton*. Congressional Research Service Report for Congress. RS 22343 (March 8, 2007).

Nebel, Reynold, Jr. "Resolution of Eastern Indian Land Claims: A Proposal for Negotiated Settlement." *American University Law Review* 27 (1977–1978): 695–731.

Newton, Nell Jessup. "At the Whim of the Sovereign: Aboriginal Title Reconsidered." *Hastings Law Journal* 31, no. 6 (July 1980): 1215–1285.

———. "Compensation, Reparations, and Restitution: Indian Property Claims in the United States." *Georgia Law Review* 28 (1994): 453–80.

———. "Federal Power over Indians: Its Sources, Scope, and Limitations." *University of Pennsylvania Law Review* 132 (1984): 195–288.

———. "Indian Claims in the Courts of the Conqueror." *American University Law Review* 41 (1992): 753–854.

———. "Indian Claims for Reparations, Compensation, and Restitution in the United States Legal System." In Roy L. Brooks, ed., *When Sorry Isn't Enough: The Controversy over Apologies and Reparations for Human Injustice*. New York: New York University Press, 1999, 61–269.

New York Times. "Congress Shortchanges the Indians." Opinion. March 16, 2010. http://www.nytimes.com/2010/03/16/opinion/16tue4.html.

———. "Fixing an Old Injustice." Opinion. August 4, 2005. http://www.nytimes.com/2005/08/04/opinion/04thu2.html.

———. "Judge Approves $3.4 Billion in Indian Royalties Settlement." Opinion. June 21, 2011.

———. "Redeeming a Historic Trust." Opinion. April 30, 2001. http://www.nytimes.com/2001/04/30/opinion/redeeming-a-historic-trust. Accessed 7/27/2011.

———. "Settling Indian Trusts." Opinion. December 15, 2009. http://www.nytimes.com/2009/12/15/opinion/15tue3.html.

———. "The Verdict: It's Broken." Opinion. February 1, 2008. http://www.nytimes.com/2008/02/01opinion/01fri2.html.

Olivero, Melanie B. "Northeastern Indians Make a Bid for Recognition." *American Indian Law Review* 5, no. 12 (December 1979): 23–25.

Ostler, Jeffrey. *The Lakota and the Black Hills: The Struggle for Sacred Ground*. New York: Viking, 2010.

O'Toole, Francis J., and Thomas N. Tureen. "State Power and the Passamaquoddy Tribe: A Gross National Hypocrisy?" *Maine Law Review* 23, no. 1 (1971): 1–39.

Powers, Patricia. "Mismanaged Indian Trust is a Scandal." *National Catholic Reporter* (September 30, 2005).

Price, Monroe E. *Law and the American Indian: Readings, Notes and Cases*. Indianapolis: Bobbs-Merrill, 1973.

Rosenthal, Harvey D. "Indian Claims and the American Conscience: A Brief History of the Indian Claims Commission." In Imre Sutton, ed., *Irredeemable America: The Indians' Estate and Land Claims*. Albuquerque: University of New Mexico Press, 1985, 35–70.

———. *Their Day in Court: A History of the Indian Claims Commission*. New York: Garland, 1990.

Royce, C. C., comp. *Indian Land Cessions in the United States*. Eighteenth Annual Report of the Bureau of American Ethnography. Pt. 2. Washington, DC: Government Printing Office, 1899.

Savage, Charlie. "U.S. Will Settle Indian Lawsuit for $3.4 Billion." *New York Times*, December 9, 2009. http://www.nytimes.com/2009/12/09/us/09tribes.html.

Scott, Austin. "President Chooses Georgia Justice as Indian Negotiator." *Washington Post*, March 12, 1977, p. 3.

Sheehan, James. "The Problem of Sovereignty in European History." *American Historical Review* 111, no. 1 (February 2006): 1–15.

Singel, Wenona T., and Matthew L. M. Fletcher. "Power, Authority, and Tribal Property." *Tulsa Law Review* 41, no. 1 (Fall 2005): 21–50.

Singer, Joseph William. "Well Settled? The Increasing Weight of History in American Indian Land Claims." *Georgia Law Review* 28 (1994): 481–532.

Skogen, Larry. *Indian Depredations Claims, 1796–1920*. Norman: University of Oklahoma Press, 1996.

Smith, Michelle, and Janet C. Neuman. "Keeping Indian Claims Commission Decisions in Their Place: Assessing the Preclusive Effect of ICC Decisions in Litigation Over Off-Reservation Treaty Fishing Rights." *University of Hawaii Law Review* 31 (Summer 2009): 475–506.

Southall, Ashley. "Senate Approves Payment of Black Farmers' Claims." *New York Times*, November 19, 2010. http://www.nytimes.com/2010/11/20/us/politics/20farm.html.

Sunderlin, Jennifer R. "One Nation, Indivisible: American 'Indian Country' in the Wake of *City of Sherrill v. Oneida Indian Nation*." *Albany Law Review* 70, no. 4 (2007): 1563–87.

Sutton, Imre. *American Indian Territoriality: An Online Research Guide*. Edition of October 17, 2003.

———. *Indian Land Tenure: Bibliographical Essays and a Guide to the Literature*. New York: Clearwater Press, 1975.

———, ed. "The Continuing Saga of Indian Land Claims." *American Indian Culture and Research Journal* 24, no. 1 (2000): 129–98.

———, ed. *Irredeemable America: The Indians' Estate and Land Claims*. Albuquerque: University of New Mexico Press, 1985.

Swimmer, Ross O. "Separating Fact from Fiction." *Human Rights* 33, no. 2 (Spring 2006): 7–8.

"Symposium on Indian Law: The Eastern Indian Land Claims." *Maine Law Review* 31, no.1 (November 1979).

Tallchief, Alexander. "Money v. Sovereignty: An Analysis of the Maine Settlement." *American Indian Journal of the Institute for the Development of Indian Law* 6, no. 5 (May 1980): 19–22.

Tanner, Helen Hornbeck. "In the Arena: An Expert Witness View of the Indian Claims Commission." In Daniel M. Cobb and Loretta Fowler, eds., *Beyond Red Power: American Indian Politics and Activism since 1900*. Santa Fe: School for Advanced Research, 2007, 178–200.

Tibbles, Thomas Henry. *The Ponca Chiefs: An Account of the Trial of Standing Bear*. Lincoln: University of Nebraska Press, 1972.

Tiro, Karim M. "Claims Arising: The Oneida Nation of Wisconsin and the Indian Claims Commission, 1951–1982." *American Indian Law Review* 32 (2007–2008): 509–24.

Tittemore, Brian D. "The Dann Litigation and International Human Rights Law: The Proceedings and Decision of the Inter-American Commission on Human Rights." *American Indian Law Review* 31 (2006–2007): 593–617.

U.S. Government, House. " '*Misplaced Trust': The BIA's Mismanagement of the Indian Trust Fund*." H. Report 102–499. 102nd Cong., 2d Sess. Washington, DC: Government Printing Office, 1992.

———. *Proposed Settlement of Indian Land Claims in the State of Maine*. Hearings on H.R. 7919. 96th Cong., 2nd Sess., August 25, 1980. Washington, DC: Government Printing Office, 1980.

U.S. Government. Indian Claims Commission. *Final Report*. Washington, DC: Government Printing Office, 1978.

U.S. Government. Senate. *Final Report and Legislative Recommendations: A Report of the Special Committee on Investigations of the Select Committee on Indian Affairs*. S. Report 101–216. 101st Cong., 1st Sess. Washington, DC: Government Printing Office, 1989.

———. *Indian Trust Fund Litigation*. Hearing Before the Committee on Indian Affairs. 110th Cong., 1st Sess., March 29, 2007. Washington, DC: Government Printing Office, 2007.

———. *Indian Trust Fund Oversight*. Hearing Before the Select Committee on Indian Affairs. 99th Cong., 2nd Sess., Sept. 23, 1986. Washington, DC: Government Printing Office, 1987.

———. *Proposed Settlement of Maine Indian Land Claims*. Hearing Before the Select Committee on Indian Affairs on S. 2829. 96th Cong., 2nd Sess., July 1 and 2, 1980. Vols. 1–2. Washington, DC: Government Printing Office, 1980.

———. Senate. Report No. 96–957. *Authorizing Funds for the Settlement of Indian Claims in the State of Maine*. 96th Cong., 2nd Sess., on S. 2829, September 17, 1980. Washington, DC: Government Printing Office, 1980.

Vance, John T. "The Congressional Mandate and the Indian Claims Commission." *North Dakota Law Review* 45 (Spring 1969): 325–36.

Vescey, Christopher. "Introduction." In Christopher Vescey and William A. Starna, eds., *Iroquois Land Claims*. Syracuse: Syracuse University Press, 1988, 3–16.

Volman, Tim. "A Survey of Eastern Land Claims: 1970–1979," *Maine Law Review* 31, no.1 (1979).

Walke, Roger. "Major Indian Issues in the 108th Congress," Congressional Research Service Report for Congress. RS 21670 (July 15, 2004).

Weekly Documents Compiled by the President. "Statement on the Approval of the Settlement in the *Cobell* Class-Action Lawsuit on Indian Trust Management" (June 20, 2011) DCPD201100459.

——. "Statement on the Settlement of the *Cobell* Class Action Lawsuit on Indian Trust Management" (December 8, 2009) DCPD 200900977.

White, John R. "Barmecide Revisited: The Gratuitous Offset in Indian Claims Cases." *Ethnohistory* 25, no. 2 (Spring 1978): 179–92.

Wiesenthall, Maxwell. "Longley Backs Plan to Settle Indian Land Claims in Maine." *Washington Post*, October 24, 1978, p. 2.

Wilkinson, Glen A. "Indian Tribal Claims before the Court of Claims." *Georgetown Law Journal* 55 (December 1966): 511–28.

Witty, Julia, "Accounting Coup." *Mother Jones* 30, no. 5 (September/October 2005): 56–86.

Index

Pages with tables are indicated by *t*.